MUSIC THERAPY IN THE TREATMENT OF ADULTS WITH MENTAL DISORDERS

MUSIC THERAPY IN THE TREATMENT OF ADULTS WITH MENTAL DISORDERS

Theoretical Bases and Clinical Interventions

Edited by Robert F. Unkefer

SCHIRMER BOOKS
A Division of Macmillan, Inc.
New York

Collier Macmillan Canada
Toronto

Maxwell Macmillan International
New York   Oxford   Singapore   Sydney

Schirmer Books
A Division of Macmillan, Inc.
866 Third Avenue, New York, N.Y. 10022

Collier Macmillan Canada, Inc.
1200 Eglinton Avenue East, Suite 200
Don Mills, Ontario M3C 3N1

Library of Congress Catalog Card Number: 89-10203

Printed in the United States of America

printing number

1   2   3   4   5   6   7   8   9   10

Library of Congress Cataloging-in-Publication Data

Music therapy in the treatment of adults with mental disorders:
   theoretical bases and clinical interventions / edited by Robert F. Unkefer.
     p. cm.
  ISBN 0-02-873032-1
  1. Music therapy   2. Mental illness—Treatment.   I. Unkefer, Robert F.
ML3920.M899   1990
616.89'1654—dc20   89-10203
                                                              CIP
                                                              MN

CONTENTS

PREFACE

This manual represents the culmination of a project that was initiated during the 1985 spring meeting of the Michigan Music Therapists. A challenging speaker from a "sister" activity therapy discipline focused on the need for more precise reporting to identify exact clinical practices in all of the activity therapy specialities, and particularly in those that use the fine and performing arts as the media for the therapist/client relationship.

In a small group meeting that followed, the participants expressed very strong support for a series of clinical manuals that would include both theory and practice of music therapy with special populations; completed research to support both the theory and practice would be reported. Several uses of the series of manuals were suggested: (1) a base for reference by legislators and members of licensing and accrediting agencies; (2) a reference for administrators of health insurance organizations; (3) a reference manual for music therapy clinical training; (4) a reference for study for the certification examination; (5) an introductory textbook. Overall, the expressed hope was for a series of documents that would serve to breed desirable consistency in music therapy education and clinical practices. It was also projected that the manuals would have to arise from a grass-roots effort. A number of participants expressed enthusiasm for the project and agreed to participate in an initial planning meeting to be held June 1985.

At the initial planning session there were ten participants. Several very capable educators and clinicians hoped to participate, but were not able to clear their schedules to be present at the planning and discussion meetings.

It was decided that the project should be initiated with a manual for music therapy in psychiatric treatment. Modern music therapy "grew up" in psychiatry stemming from efforts largely in Veterans Administration Psychiatric Units following the end of World War II. *Music in Therapy*, edited by Gaston (1968), included a section on Adult Psychiatric Disorders, which loosely linked music therapy theory and practice through the publication of psychiatric case vignettes. That volume was also the result of a group effort. Lathom and Eagle (1984) edited a very important series of manuals that detail music therapy practice with children. No recent comprehensive publication has been focused on music therapy in psychiatry for adults.

After a long period of separatism between those therapists supporting the behaviorist movement and those labeled "traditionalists," there now seems to be a recognition of similar knowledge, training, and practice that will allow publication of a core of information useful to all practicing music therapists.

By the third planning meeting six of the ten original participants had retained enough enthusiasm and commitment to continue the project. These six were within a travel distance of 70 miles and free enough in their schedules to meet often for critical discussion. Each had known the five other participants both personally and professionally for at least five years. Even so, the initial meetings served to build respect for each others' points of view, and provided opportunity for the members to learn that they, indeed, had a common understanding and common points of reference. Among the six members of the central group the years of experience as teachers and therapists add to a total in excess of 90.

The six members of the group, in alphabetical order, are Becki Houghton, Mary Scovel, Roger Smeltekop, Michael Thaut, Robert Unkefer, and Brian Wilson. Kate Gfeller was drafted to write three theoretical chapters.

The Diagnostic and Statistical Manual of Mental Disorders, Third Edition (DSM-III), published by the American Psychiatric Association, was used as the basic reference source for terminology and diagnostic labels. The third edition (DSM-III-R) (1987) became available during the final preparation of this manuscript; the references have been updated to conform with the new edition.

Part One of this book contains five chapters detailing a theoretical position of music therapy. Part Two includes five chapters describing factors impacting on levels of music therapy interventions. Part Three is a taxonomy of music therapy techniques with carefully detailed descriptions of specific techniques and interventions. Part Four is an outline for adult mental disorders in the form of a table that lists diagnostic categories with related clinical features, characteristic behaviors, needs, and music therapy interventions.

Although the idea for this manual began with the members during a meeting of the Michigan Music Therapists, the responsibility for the viewpoints and practices described herein rests with the six members of the central writers' group. Their thanks are expressed to spouses and members of their immediate families, and to their various employers for support and understanding during the many hours of meeting and writing.

ACKNOWLEDGMENTS

The authors wish to express their thanks to a number of colleagues who were asked to read and comment on major portions of the manuscript. Many of their suggestions were incorporated into the final text.

Darlene Brooks—DePaul Northshore Hospital, Covington, Louisiana
Anthony Decuir—Loyola University, New Orleans, Louisiana
James Dziwak—Iowa City, Iowa
Alice C. Gibbons—University of Kansas, Lawrence, Kansas
Frances Goldberg—Langley Porter Institute, San Francisco, California
Nancy Lloyd—University of Wisconsin, Oshkosh, Wisconsin
Christina Lucia—Chicago, Illinois
Cheryl Maranto—Temple University, Philadelphia, Pennsylvania

Michael G. McGuire—Eastern Michigan University, Ypsilanti, Michigan
Belinda S. Murray—Veteran's Administration Medical Center, Battle Creek, Michigan
Marilyn Sandness—University of Dayton, Dayton, Ohio
Richard Scalenge—Joint Commission on Accreditation of Health Care Organizations, Chicago, Illinois
Marjorie Thom—Veterans Administration Medical Center, Battle Creek, Michigan

Special thanks is paid to Virginia Unkefer, who read and edited a large portion of the text, and to Pamela Spray, for her many hours of extra effort in transcribing the original transcript to a word processor.

Robert F. Unkefer
East Lansing, Michigan

CONTRIBUTORS

Kate E. Gfeller, Ph.D., RMT-BC (guest author), is assistant professor of music at the University of Iowa, Iowa City, Iowa

Becki A. Houghton, B.M., RMT-BC, is senior mental health therapist at Clinton County Day Treatment, St. Johns, Michigan

Mary A. Scovel, M.M., RMT-BC, is assisant professor of music at Western Michigan University, Kalamazoo, Michigan

Roger A. Smeltekop, M.M., RMT-BC, is associate professor of music at Michigan State University, E. Lansing, Michigan.

Michael H. Thaut, Ph.D., RMT-BC, is assistant professor of music at Colorado State University, Boulder, Colorado

Robert F. Unkefer, M.M., RMT-BC, is professor emeritis of music at Michigan State University, E. Lansing, Michigan

Brian L. Wilson, M.M., RMT-BC, is professor of music at Western Michigan University, Kalamazoo, Michigan

MUSIC THERAPY IN THE TREATMENT OF ADULTS WITH MENTAL DISORDERS

PART ONE

PSYCHOMUSICAL FOUNDATIONS OF MUSIC THERAPY

Part One of this volume contains five chapters that detail the theoretical foundation for music therapy practice. The authors supply research data to support the theoretical framework.

During the past four decades, music therapists have moved through several periods in which their practice has shifted from one theoretical model to another or through periods of over-emphasis to periods of de-emphasis of music. Some therapists believe that music activity is no different, no better or worse, than any other kind of activity. It is hoped that the five chapters comprising Part One will help the reader understand the unique qualities of music stimuli.

Chapter 1 examines the neuropsychological processes in music perception. Music is proven to be a unique stimulus that can be used to modify affect.

Chapter 2 presents an appraisal of clinical and research data on the influence of music stimuli on physiological responses in the human organism.

Music as communication is examined in Chapter 3. This chapter includes a section on the relationship of music to speech and specific information concerning the use of music in conjunction with other forms of communication.

Chapter 4 explores music's function as a therapeutic agent from a historical perspective and from within the cultural context of preliterate and industrialized societies.

Chapter 5 identifies the function of aesthetic stimuli in the therapeutic process. Aesthetic stimuli have therapeutic potential in terms of focus, perception, cognition, and affect.

Chapter 1

Neuropsychological Processes in Music Perception and Their Relevance in Music Therapy

Michael H. Thaut

This chapter appraises clinical and research data directed toward an analysis of music stimulus properties, their neuropsychological processing mechanism, their influence on perceptual and affective behavior processes, and their specific applications in therapy. Among other scientific insights, evidence from neurophysiology, psychobiology, and empirical aesthetics is of paramount importance for this inquiry about music in therapy.

The core question asked in this chapter is: how can music stimuli evoke and influence thinking and feeling processes in a meaningful and predictable way in order to change abnormal behavior in desired directions? The answer is found in five steps:

1. by reviewing and appraising relevant theories of emotion and arousal in music;
2. by surveying neurobiological information relevant to music processing;
3. by appraising the relevance of music-evoked responses for therapy processes;
4. by presenting an integrative model of stimulus processing and clinical applications;
5. by illustrating the proposed model through clinical examples.

The main thesis of this discourse shall be that music, based on its unique stimulus properties and differential-processing in the central nervous system (CNS), evokes meaningful affective responses that can be used to modify affect in clinical situations whereby affect modification is considered an essential component of behavioral learning and change.

AFFECT AND AROUSAL IN MUSIC

Theories of Emotion and Arousal in Music

What is the nature of our experience when we listen to or produce musical sounds? What thoughts and/or feelings are evoked through music perception?

3

Is the perceptual process exhausted in assigning meaning to the structure and form of sound patterns or does the quality of the music-evoked experience bear influence on nonmusical behavior as well? How do the physical attributes of the music stimulus influence our thinking and feeling in the perceptual process? Why is music such a pervasive sensory stimulus in our environment, giving us immediate sensations of reward and pleasure? Why has music often been called, from philosophical points of view, closest to the experience and expression of human emotion? Perhaps because music is of essentially nonverbal quality and, unlike many other aesthetic media, its patterns evolve in time, just as the content and form of our thoughts and feelings evolve in time?

In order to understand the influence of music on behavior it is necessary to develop at least a working hypothesis of what types of psychological and physiological responses are evoked through the perception of music stimuli. Furthermore, the relationship between these responses and behavior change, focused on in therapy, needs to be investigated. However, a meaningful answer to both of these investigations must rely first on an understanding of how meaning is perceived in music, i.e., what cognitive and affective processes are elicited in the perceptual process. Stimulus properties as well as determinants and variables in the perceptual process of the music recipient need to be identified and analyzed. Without this first step it would be impossible to initiate a predictable, measurable, and goal-directed process of behavioral change, using music as the catalyst for change.

In order to justify the use of music in therapy we have to develop a view of stimulus-processing where the perception of stimulus properties is not an end in itself but leads to responses that can be meaningful determinants of nonmusical behavior as well. Three theories are reviewed here to help in a conceptual development of the influence of music on behavior: Meyer's (1956) theory of emotion and meaning in music; Mandler's (1984) cognitive theory of emotion; Berlyne's (1971) theory of emotion, arousal, and reward in aesthetic perception.

Meyer develops the view that meaning and emotion in music perception arise through the perception of patterns within the stimulus itself, i.e., the formal and structural components of a musical piece. He bases his theory on Dewey's (1934) conflict theory of emotion and McCurdy's (1925) theory that a tendency of an organism to respond needs to be blocked in order to arouse affect. Meyer transfers the tenets of these theories into music perception by postulating that listeners develop expectancy schemes when following musical patterns. A carefully crafted interruption of the expectation—followed by a period of suspension and resolution in the composition—will evoke an affective experience in the recipient. Obviously, conscious attention to the stimulus as well as familiarity with formal properties of a musical style are necessary for a response pattern as postulated by Meyer.

Important to note is that in Meyer's view, meaning and emotion in music are a result of perceiving the musical structures and the carefully planned manipulations thereof. He further contends that the genesis of emotional experience in music is not different from emotional experiences in daily life, with two exceptions: (1) musical tension-resolution patterns, leading to emotional responses, are usually satisfactory and pleasing, and (2) are offered within the same stimulus modality. In daily life, tension in one area often needs to be compensated for with a pleasant release in a different area. Meyer acknowledges the existence of designated mood experiences, imagery, and memories in music perception, which can also cause emotional responses. However, since these responses are learned through association and not through perception of the stimulus patterns themselves, Meyer considers these responses of only secondary importance. Meyer's view leads us to consider that the perceptual focus on the music itself induces emotional responses in a manner similar to nonmusical events, however, with certain qualities that are actually desirable in certain therapy situations, by offering pleasant resolutions. Meyer's view also leads us to consider the question of whether music perception in therapy settings, and the resultant emotional response, follows his proposed model, or whether there is any reason to emphasize only, e.g., the associative response type. There are no data that give us reason to believe that clients in therapy do not receive their primary emotional response to music from perceiving intrinsic musical patterns. Therefore, we have to consider the relevance of music-induced mood states, based on stimulus patterns, for nonmusical behavior in therapy, i.e., behavioral change and learning.

Mandler's theory (1984) resembles Meyer's account in basic outline. Mandler develops a comprehensive view of the genesis of emotional experience in general, with special consideration to the biologically adaptive value of emotional reactions. An emotional reaction is preceded by biological arousal of the autonomic nervous system. Arousal is caused by an interruption of expectancy or anticipation patterns that are based on perceptual-motor schemata. These schemata are created through the modus operandi of human cognition, in order to predict and plan for upcoming events. Thus for Mandler, human cognition unfolds in the continuous interplay between prediction and sensory confirmation. When something unexpected happens, arousal is triggered as an alerting signal to search for an interpretation of the interruption. In the interplay between arousal and interpretation an emotional experience of a particular quality is produced. Arousal might alert the human organism to a potentially life-threatening situation, or it might indicate the imminent arrival of a very pleasurable event. The cognitive interpretation of the arousal-triggering circumstances will define the quality of the emotional experience.

Mandler's theory can be applied to music stimuli when we look at the considerable evidence that emotional reactions to music involve strong arousal of the autonomic nervous system (ANS), and also accept Meyer's account of how the process of interruption-suspension-resolution in perceiving musical structures induces emotional responses. For Mandler, emotion or affect is strictly post-cognitive, and that view is consistent with prevalent views in cognitive psychology (Lazarus, 1984). However, contesting views present rapidly accumulating evidence for the existence of sequences of fast-acting arousal reactions that contain affective qualities by leading to immediate action before cognitive analysis can take place (Zajonc, 1984). Both theories may be actually correct, if we assume cognition and affect as two partially independent systems that can mutually influence each other (Rachman, 1984). Relevant to our inquiry into music perception, both Meyer and Mandler connect the process of assigning meaning with physiological arousal states, the interpretation of which results in an affective experience of a particular quality.

Berlyne's (1971) theory of emotion, arousal, and reward in aesthetic perception has similarities with the previous views in its emphasis on the role of arousal in music perception. Berlyne, however, expands and specifies the role and quality of arousal and its relationship to stimulus properties and corresponding affective response qualities. Berlyne views arousal not only as an alerting signal indicating an interruption in physiological homeostasis or cognitive prediction patterns. He proposes that the main process underlying healthy CNS functioning is to seek out sensory input. For example, moderate increases in arousal, decreases from extremely high arousal, or temporary increases followed by immediate decreases are perceived by an individual as pleasurable and rewarding. Changes in arousal, a measure of the state of alertness, wakefulness, excitement, stimulation, or readiness, are reflected in four psychophysiological response types:

1. central responses (EEG, evoked potential, etc.);
2. motor responses (motor neural activity, bodily movement, etc.);
3. sensory changes (change in sensitivity of sense organs and sensory pathways);
4. autonomic responses (Galvanic Skin Response GSR, heart rate, respiration, etc.).

It is believed, from a neurobiological view, that physiological arousal states are mediated by brain structures in the thalamic, hypothalamic, and brain stem areas.

In agreement with Meyer and Mandler, Berlyne contends that arousal states are the physiological accompaniment of emotional states, and thus differentiate the latter from so-called nonemotional states. Berlyne has shown in great detail that art works, including music stimuli, contain stimulus patterns that have specific arousal-influencing potential, and thus can induce affective experiences. A determination of music's arousal potential and influence on affective responses in regard to clinical populations is dependent on identifying and analyzing these stimulus patterns or stimulus properties and their corresponding property-specific responses in therapy settings. Three classes of stimulus properties have been studied extensively (Berlyne, 1971; Mc-Mullen, 1980). They are presented here as they pertain to music stimuli:

1. *Psychophysical properties,* including the perception of intensity, tempo, color/wave form, rate of change (distribution of energy). These properties are considered to constitute the experience of *activation* (energy, excitement, stimulation) through the perceived stimulus object.

2. *Collative properties,* including the perception of structural elements in the composition. These properties are considered to constitute the experience of *novelty, surprise, order, clarity,* and their respective opposites, through the perceived stimulus object.

3. *Ecological properties,* including the perception of elements in music that have acquired learned associations with extramusical events and experiences. These properties are considered to constitute the experience of *associations* (e.g., designated moods, connotations, memories, private images) through the perceived stimulus object.

Research, measuring various aspects of listeners' responses to music stimuli, has commonly substantiated similar dimensions of response (McMullen, 1977, 1980; Crozier, 1973; Hedden, 1971). The perception of emotional experiences in music as a function of musical structures has also been demonstrated and analyzed in experimental studies by Nielzen and Cesarec (1981, 1982), Gardner, Silverman, Denes, Semenza, and Rosenstiel (1977), Wedin (1972), and Vitz (1966). The main findings in these studies support three basic arguments: (1) that music is an efficient signal in transferring emotional messages; (2) that factor analysis of musical structures and elements does correlate with subjective emotional experiences, even when musically untrained listeners are used; (3) that communication of emotional meaning in music remains unmodified by single personality traits but seems to be affected by complex interactions of personality traits with gender, age, mood, and musical selection.

Classification of Emotional States

In the preceding section theories were presented that gave an account of how emotion and meaning are perceived in music. Central to all theories is the concept of the arousal-inducing potential of music, which leads to affective experiences. Primarily, the perception of patterns within the stimulus, i.e., the psychophysical and collative attributes, and, secondarily, extramusical learned associations with the actual stimulus, induces arousal reactions and affective responses. In Berlyne's model these responses are property specific and may be subsumed under the terms activation/energy, novelty/surprise/order/clarity, and associations. Perceptual focus on specific attributes of the stimulus may thus facilitate affective responses within particular qualities.

However, how can these evoked affective responses be related and made relevant for the challenge of behavior modification in therapy setting, where we often deal with emotional states characterized by fear, anger, anxiety, dysphoric mood, and lack of motivation? Central to all reviewed models of meaning in music is the affective response based on the perception of stimulus patterns. There appear to be no generic sound patterns to translate fear, anger, or happiness in the semantic sense of spoken language, except in a stimulus-response connection through learned associations.

How then can the music-evoked feeling process be classified, interpreted, and made relevant for behavior in therapy other than music-oriented behavior? Three steps are suggested to develop a meaningful link between music-evoked affective responses and behavioral learning and change in therapy:

1. select a framework for the classification of emotional states;
2. demonstrate the relationship between arousal/affective responses and evaluation thereof regarding reward value, motivation, incentive value, and attractiveness for the human organism;
3. establish the importance of modified affect for behavior modification.

A discussion of the last step has to be deferred to the last segment of this chapter; the first two steps are delineated here.

Ordinary language contains innumerable words to describe emotional states. Attempts have been made in the psychological literature to find verbal classification systems for all possible shades of emotional experience. Two basic approaches have emerged in this respect. The first approach lists categories of different emotions or affective states. Most noticeable attempts at those categories are found in the works of McDougall (1908), Watson (1924), and Plutchik (1962). Since music-evoked affective experiences, as suggested earlier, refer only in specific instances to referential verbal classifications of affect, this approach seems of limited value to our discussion.

A second approach, based on Wundt's (1974) dimensional classification of affective states, offers a better understanding of the relationship between music and affective experiences that are relevant for nonmusical behavior as well. Within the framework of this approach, all emotional states, regardless of attempts to define them semantically, are located within a continuum of independent dimensions or qualities. A survey of the pertinent literature (McMullen, 1980; Berlyne, 1971) reveals that all systems within the dimensional approach have two dimensions in common: *direction,* referring to the dimension of pleasantness vs. unpleasantness; and *intensity,* referring to the level of activation through the perceived stimulus object.

Following this dimensional viewpoint, every music-evoked affective experience can be classified and understood as an emotional state with a quality of direction and intensity that is common to all emotional experiences. We therefore can disregard the apparent dichotomy between nonreferential music-evoked affective responses and referential verbal definitions of emotional states evoked in daily life.

Arousal, Affect, and Reward

We still need to establish the influence of music-evoked affective states, i.e., an experience that is pleasurable and sustained with appropriate intensity, for nonmusical behavior processes. In this respect, Berlyne's theory on the connection among arousal, affect, and reward in aesthetic perception is of considerable importance. His contention is that aesthetic stimuli, depending on their arousal potential, are evaluated by the human organism in respect to their hedonic value. Hedonic value refers to the experience of intrinsic reward, incentive value, motivation, attractiveness, and positive feedback when perceiving the stimulus in question. The reward value is the end product of the arousal-inducing stimulus properties and determines the quality of the affective experience as well as its function in influencing behavior processes. The human organism is motivated to pursue behavior and stimulation that is associated with strong reward experiences.

Berlyne relates reward experiences to the function of the brain reward system, because centers in the brain controlling hedonic processes and the centers controlling the fluctuations of arousal overlap to a large extent in the limbic system (Olds & Olds, 1965; Olds, 1962). Since these same centers play a major part in processing of music stimuli, it is reasonable to assume that music stimuli may have influence on those aspects of human behavior which are related to the function of those brain areas, i.e., emotionality, motivation, mood, alertness, etc. It is therefore suggested that through music-induced changes in arousal level, the following changes may occur: changes in alertness, level of activation, emotional responses, perception of reward, pleasure, positive feedback, and level of motivation. Different lines of research seem to support this notion, by measuring the reward potential of music in behavior modification (Madsen, Greer, & Madsen, 1975), psychophysiological responses to music stimuli (Clynes, 1978; Peretti & Swenson, 1974; Shatin, 1957; Stevens, 1971), mood/emotional responses to music (Pike, 1972; Schoen, 1927; Orton, 1953; Eagle, 1973; Panzarella, 1977), and the effect of music on anxiety/relaxation states (Biller, Olsen, & Breen, 1974; Jellison, 1975; Greenberg & Fisher, 1972).

In our discussion about the therapeutic value of music stimuli for behavior change we have presented models that give plausible accounts of how emotional experiences are perceived in music. All models center around the concept of physiological arousal and its relationship to affective responses. Further, we have presented properties within the stimulus and their specific arousal-inducing qualities that center around the perception of patterns within the stimulus as well as extrinsic associative experiences. Each stimulus property has a set of corresponding psychological experiences that contribute to the specific quality of the affective experience evoked by the music stimulus.

The affective experience, within a dimensional framework of direction and intensity, is then evaluated regarding its reward for the human organism. The reward value determines the function and relevance of the stimulus-evoked experience as determinant for behavioral change and learning. Before assigning specific therapeutic function to the link between stimulus-specific evoked experience and behavioral change in therapy, we will need to undertake two more excursions to understand better the unique effectiveness of music stimuli in the therapeutic process. We will start with some brief remarks about music and perception and then present, in more detail, findings on CNS processes relevant for music processing in therapy settings.

Music and Perception

The following five steps propose that music exploits stimulus properties that facilitate perception by effectively controlling exploration, attention, motivation, and reinforcement.

First, it has been shown previously that music stimuli entail arousal-influencing properties that can influence the state of readiness to perceive. Second, exploratory behavior (i.e., seeking out new perceptual experiences) can be promoted by music stimuli, since the behavior of perceptual curiosity is connected to and driven by the experience of reward through arousal reduction or arousal increment (Berlyne & Borsa, 1968). Third, processes of selective attention and abstraction can be achieved by conveying stimulus information in a particular (musical) sensory modality that results in inhibition of information reception from stimuli in other modalities (Hernandez-Peon, 1961; Marteniuk, 1976). Within the structural domain, music stimuli are ordered according to the principles of grouping of stimulus patterns (e.g., melodic or rhythmic patterns). Using musical presentation to facilitate grouping or chunking of extramusical information is of relevance for perception, retention, and recall in learning processes (Gfeller, 1983). Fourth, psychological and physiological research points to the fact that perceptual process can have emotional accompaniments that may lead to the perception-enhancing experiences of pleasure, reward, and positive feedback. As discussed previously, music stimuli may aid in promoting positive emotional experiences via their arousal-influencing potential (Berlyne, 1971). Last, music may function in the form of a mediating response, adding distinctive stimulation to an external stimulus situation and thus facilitating discrimination learning. Music can take different forms of mediating response, for example, eliciting motor, imitative, or empathetic responses, which provide vital information for apprehension and comprehension of the stimulus situation in question.

The influence of music stimuli on perceptual processes can be used effectively in areas of therapy or education where efficient perceptual behavior is essential to improved functioning, e.g., in special education settings, in working with populations with perceptual deficits (memory deficiencies, attentional problems), or in therapy situations designed to reinforce behavioral learning.

MUSIC STIMULI AND CENTRAL NERVOUS SYSTEM PROCESSING

Neural Information Processing and Music

Little is known from neurobiological research about the differential neurological processing of music stimuli and its relationship to the influence of music on behavior. The information compiled in this section, however, may help to formulate research questions that may become essential to music therapy practice. This inquiry is guided by two assumptions: (1) that one of the most unusual characteristics of music stimuli is the relative ease with which they feed into the affective system and evoke emotional experiences, and (2) that music offers an effective means of modifying affective states (Goldstein, 1980; Rachman, 1981; Sutherland, Newman, & Rachman, 1982). Therefore, we will concentrate on CNS processes that are considered to play a role in affective behavior.

Roederer (1974) hypothesizes about the neural processes underlying music perception. He bases his theory on Poliakov's (1972) classification of levels and stages of nervous system function. Three evolutionary distinct stages still represented in the human nervous system work together as a system: a fixed and genetically controlled input-output system on the spinal-chord level, delivering preprogrammed responses to given stimuli; an input-analysis/regulation-output system, adaptable to environmental stimuli, on the brainstem and phylogenetically older level of the brain, providing the biologically best-fitted response in form of conditioned reflexes; and an input-analysis/regulation-synthesis/control-output system on the cerebral cortex level that delivers complex responses of higher nervous activity, e.g., by determining and remembering causal relationships in the surrounding physical world, and forming anticipatory perceptual-motor schemata to guide one's own behavior. On this last level, Roederer draws similarities with music perception. Attending to music stimuli involves the activation of mechanisms to predict the structural flow of a given music composition. Unexpected events require increased neural activity to identify the message. Roederer, in this context, uses the term "minimum effort" to denote neural operations in which the brain tries to use the most possible information from previous experiences to anticipate the identification process of new incoming information. In the process of applying additional neural effort for the memory search to compare an unexpected musical passage to previously stored knowledge of musical patterns, Roederer postulates the evolution of musical "tension-resolution" sensations. Roederer's account of neural processes in music perception resembles Meyer's (1956) and Mandler's (1983) theories of emotion in which interruptions of anticipatory schemata (in the stimulus) trigger emotional arousal. The proposed neural processes, however, lack experimental evidence specifically in regard to music perception.

Motivation and Emotion

As therapists, we often discuss the importance of one's own motivation for behavioral learning and change. However, we use the term "motivation" most frequently on an intuitive level without actually probing into the nature and mechanics of motivational behavior. In the neurological literature, Iversen and Fray (1982) and Simonov (1986) have described motivation as a behavioral state in which activity is directed toward satisfying needs. Motivation is described physiologically as a nonspecific increase in arousal in which the specificity of the motivational behavior is directed by the internal and external stimuli producing the arousal about which the organism has to learn or has learned previously. Animal studies cited by Simonov have shown that electrical stimulation of areas of the lateral hypothalamus in rats leads to predictable behavior sequences depending on the strength of the electrical current. Weak stimulation leads to generalized seeking activity without reference to the goal objects present, e.g., food or water. An increase in stimulatory intensity leads to goal-directed activity satisfying actualized needs—the animal is motivated to eat. An even greater increase in current leads to self-stimulating behavior—the rat pushes a lever that activates continuous electrical stimulation of the hypothalamus. The hypothalamus is considered part of brain structures constituting the brain reward system, delivering sensations of emotionally positive reward. The brain reward system will be discussed in more detail later in this chapter.

Simonov conceptualizes the observed behavior sequences as an organization of behavior within a need-motivation-emotion chain based on a gradually expanding involvement of the neural apparatus. Since the same brain structures that are linked to emotional behavior in psychophysiological research, i.e., limbic forebrain and homeostatic centers of the hypothalamus and brain stem, are implicated in the previously mentioned studies, it seems plausible to assume a relationship between motivational and emotional states. Iversen and Fray have suggested considering motivation and emotion as similar states differentiated along an intensity continuum. They also assign a functional role to forebrain dopamin pathways and their biochemical processes as an influence on motivational and emotional states. Motivational behavior is thus seen as behavior characterized by arousal increase, and organized within a model of affective behavior toward maximizing a positive (or minimizing a negative) emotional state. This viewpoint can be linked quite logically to our previous discussion of affect, arousal, and the experience of reward through affective/arousal responses within the dimensions of direction and intensity.

What has been said in the preceding paragraphs is certainly difficult to integrate at this point with music processing in a therapy approach, because not even a conceptual model exists on the influence of music on motivation. However, based on our previous discussion, we may have reason to extend models of music-evoked affective responses to motivational behavior. Given the appropriate context and information to determine the specificity of the motivational behavior in a therapy setting, we then may be able to provide, through music perception, rewarding arousal states that will be actualized as motivated behavior to maximize emotionally satisfying, rewarding, and plea-surable experiences. Considering the lack of empirical data, however, we can only propose a speculative rationale here.

Music Stimuli and Hemispheric Processing

The hemispheric differentiation of the brain has given rise to the notion of two distinct ways of information processing: the sequential and the simulta-neous modes. The right-brain hemisphere is more apt to perceive holistic, spatial synthetic relations. This capacity plays a major role in the perception of music, since this process relies strongly on the spatial and temporal inte-gration of information to determine the holistic quality of the music stimulus. In more structural, analytical tasks the left hemisphere, superior in sequential verbal processing, comes into play in music perception. Both modes coexist and cooperate in processing music stimuli (Springer & Deutsch, 1985). Gates and Bradshaw (1977) have suggested that the left hemisphere may take a greater role when sequential and analytic aspects of music are important, while the right hemisphere may be superior when the sound gestalt or emotional qualities are emphasized.

However, some functions such as singing (without verbal associations), perception of tonal patterns, timbre, loudness, harmonic structures, hum-ming, and other nonverbal sounds are considered dominant in the right hemisphere (Zatorre, 1984). The implications of these two processing modes for the music therapist are manifold: music stimuli may provide alternate or supportive ways of presenting extramusical information relevant to learning or therapy processes of individuals with perceptual disturbances (Litchman, 1977; Gfeller, 1983); music stimuli may provide skill transfer between the brain hemispheres in brain lesions, e.g., using melodic intonation therapy for patients with left-brain damage (Broca's aphasia) or rhythm-based speech-pacing technique for patients with right-brain damage (Cohen, in press); music stimuli may provide an accessible alternative means of expression for individuals with neurological impairments, e.g., autistic disturbances or le-sions to the left hemisphere (Applebaum, Egel, Koegel, & Imhoff, 1979; Thaut, 1987).

In addition to the specific contributions to music processing, the right brain also seems dominant in processing and elaborating certain aspects of emotional content in sensory input. Lamendella (1977) proposed that the right hemisphere processes input, generated by the limbic brain structures, in such a way that it retains its immediateness and rich affective value. Sperry and Gazzaniga (1967) suggest the distinction between conceptual awareness of a sensory stimulus, mediated in the left hemisphere, and representation of its emotional significance in the right hemisphere. In a more recent study, Bear (1983) proposes asymmetric corticolimbic sensory connections as the basis for hemispheric specialization in various emotional functions. The asymmetric volumetric enlargement of the left hemispheric parietotemporal junction, i.e., the angular gyrus region, is suggested to function as a nonlimbic intersensory learning system, responsible for stimulus generalization, crossmodal associations, and language development. Through the insertion of additional layers of interneuronal circuitry, the sensory and limbic conditions are further separated on this side, resulting in a loss of emotional response immediacy in the left hemisphere (Galaburda, Sanides, & Geschwind, 1978; Geschwind, 1965). However, through projections of this side into the left hemispheric ventral limbic structures, specific affective responses, such as affective investment of words, verbal concepts, or love of intellectual reflection, may be mediated (Bear, 1983). Many well-established clinical observations and research findings documenting behavioral changes, especially in temporal lobe epilepsy, are consistent with these views (Bear & Fedio, 1977; Bear & Schenk, 1981).

In the right-brain hemisphere, two separate sensory-limbic pathways, the ventral temporalfrontal and the dorsal parietofrontal, are considered mediators of enhanced unimodal affective associations and investments in ongoing sensory events, leading to more rapid alteration in mood and arousal, and deeper emotive-impulsive experiences (Ungerleider & Mishkin, 1982). For example, the decoding of emotional signals in melodic intonation or facial expression might be a function of the right ventral system because of its suggested independent connections between each cortical sensory system and the limbic system (Heilman, Schwartz, & Watson, 1978). The greater efficiency of the right hemisphere in retaining auditory patterns of melodies might be also based on invoking the same right ventral corticolimbic connections, since the hippocampus and amygdala, which are crucial for memory and affective responses, are also ventral limbic structures (Bever & Chiarello, 1974).

A conclusive connection between the overlapping functions of the right hemisphere in mediating emotional responses and also mediating aspects of music perception has not been established in the research literature. Certainly, the current state of neurophysiology and psychobiology, with respect to brain functions and human behavior, does not permit definite answers. Current and past literature on music, brain, and behavior has often assigned unitary function to the process nature of different parts of the brain, and thus has at times presented popular, but unfounded, interpretations. An appraisal of the presented evidence, therefore, can only lead to cautious hypotheses which may serve heuristic function for further investigations.

Several attributes of music stimuli are processed dominantly in the right-brain hemisphere. We may hypothesize, then, that the processing of these stimulus properties engages the right hemispheric sensorylimbic connections that are superior in mediating strong affective responses within the auditory modality. The right ventral temporofrontal connection may facilitate the decoding of unimodal affective signals in musical structures, whereas the parietofrontal dorsal connection may provide a more general emotional response of arousal and attention to music signals. A more intellectual reflection or crossmodal association of music stimuli, still capable of arousing affective investment, may be a function of the left hemispheric projections into the left ventral limbic structures. Depending on the strategy of decoding and memorizing the stimulus, a shift in hemispheric dominance may take place (Bever & Chiarello, 1974).

Thus it is suggested that there is a neurological basis for the influence of music stimuli on multiple emotional functions, based on hemispheric-specific processing that results in increased functional connectivity between neocortex and limbic structures. The effect on emotional functioning may be particularly relevant when using music stimuli with individuals suffering from mood disturbances, affective disorders, and anxiety conditions.

It is further suggested that different types of affective experience may be induced through music stimulation. The neurological evidence points to the distinction among states of emotionally appropriate arousal and attention, more immediate emotional experiences leading to mood/feeling changes, and affective concomitants of associative or more cognitive-based experiences. Perception, focus, and decoding/memorization strategies employed by the music listener will determine which affective function will be involved by the music stimulus. Thus, when appropriately implemented, music constitutes a powerful facilitator for learning processes, involving emotional perception and communication.

The music therapist is faced with the task of deciding which type of emotional experience supports the desired therapeutic goals. Based on this decision, a music-based therapy activity should be selected that facilitates appropriate perception, focus, and decoding/memorization strategies for the client in therapy settings, emphasizing rewarding, motivating, feelingful experiences, mood change, control of emotional stability, and reduction of anxiety/stress response.

Neural Substrates of Emotion: Limbic System and Brain Reward

The observation that the perception of music leads to strong emotional experiences is an indication that the limbic system is engaged in processing music stimuli (Roederer, 1975; Goldstein, 1980; Hodges, 1980). Specific contributions of the various limbic structures to music processing have not yet been researched systematically and have to be decided from circumstantial evidence relating responses to music to similar response types without music, and from what is known about limbic involvement in those responses. The advent of new brain-imaging techniques, i.e., the study of local cerebral metabolic and blood-flow responses to sensory stimuli through positron emission tomograph (Mazziota & Phelps, 1983) and through magnetic resonance-imaging (Oldendorff, 1983; Norman & Brant-Zawadski, 1983), will make possible the study of corticolimbic functions under the influence of music stimulation. The latter technique, since it is totally noninvasive and allows the scanning of fine cross sections of deeper brain structures, will probably replace previous techniques for most future brain studies.

The major theoretical landmark implicating the limbic brain in emotional and motivational behavior was Papez' study "A proposed mechanism for emotion" (1937). Although somewhat oversimplified, his theory of a loop providing for interaction among neocortex, limbic structures, and diencephalon, considered to be the anatomical substrate of emotional experience, has provided the impetus for a great deal of research into the structure and function of the limbic system. This research has established the special status of the limbic structures as an information-processing system with a wide range of functional responsibilities, including major roles in emotion, arousal, attention, habituation, social behavior, learning, and behavior (MacLean, 1973; Pribram, 1967; Lamendella, 1977; Nolte, 1981). Although no consensus exists on the total list of limbic structures, all authors would include hippocampus and amygdala, whereas hypothalamus, pituitary, and thalamic regions are included by most. Before entering a more detailed subjective description, it needs to be emphasized that sensory information is mediated by the limbic structures before it enters the neocortex, but reciprocal projections also exist, thereby changing the manner in which cortically directed information is processed and relayed by the limbic brain, and thus clearly documenting the existence of complex corticolimbic interactions (Nauta & Feirtag, 1979). For example, auditory information that has reached the auditory cortex is neurally processed through a sequence of neocortical association areas and then projected into the limbic structures of hippocampus and amygdala.

The most clearly documented role of the hippocampus has to do with learning and memory. The most prominent supplier of afferent input into the hippocampal formation is the adjacent entorhinal cortex, located also in the temporal lobe. Through these cortical connections, the hippocampal structures have access to virtually all types of sensory information.

The amygdala is considered an influence on drive-related behavior patterns and subjective feeling experiences. The afferents and efferents of the amygdala are rather complex. Most input is received from the orbital, anterior temporal, and anterior cingulate cortices, the olfactory nerve bulb, and, to a lesser extent, from the hypothalamus.

Both hippocampus and amygdala project most prominently to the hypothalamus, a structure regulating many of the autonomic physiological arousal and homeostatic responses that accompany affective reactions. The hypothalamus is therefore often called the output system of the limbic structures. With respect to auditory processing, Nauta and Domesick (1982) report evidence that within the neural circuitry of subcortical limbic connections, the parabrachial projections to the ventromedial hypothalamic nucleus originate from cells that are located far enough laterally to lie within the lateral lemniscus of the auditory pathway, and thus may convey auditory information to the hypothalamus.

The function of the thalamus is often described as the main relay station of sensory input to the neocortex, and thus involved in most corticolimbic interactions. Lamendella (1977) and Pribram and Kruger (1954) have proposed that the limbic system, ensuring the most beneficial response for the self-preservation of the organism, dispenses sensations of reward, punishment, pleasure, and pain, and thus guides the learning of behavior by the maximum expectancy of reward. The brain structures implicated by these authors are the posterior cingulate juxtallocortex, the anterior temporal cortex, and the hippocampus. Again, with regard to auditory processing, it may be worth noting that stimulation of the parahippocampal gyri often leads to complex auditory associations (Guyton, 1986). These structures receive input about internal physiological states and sensory information about the external world, placing them in a good position to assess positive and negative feedback values of external conditions in response to human behavior. Emotionality, possibly based on hippocampal memory function and amygdala-mediated feeling experiences, may emerge in the context of punishment and reward, dispensed by these brain structures during the actual course of behavior. Pribram (1967) has characterized this process of emotional response as an expression of the relationship between perception and action. It needs to be added here that this process of emotional response can be stimulated in man by internally evoked images (Roederer, 1975).

Sunshine and Mishkin (1975) have shown the existence of a visuolimbic pathway serving to connect the association reward function to visual signals. Based on the previous discussion on hemisphere-specific sensori-limbic connections, we may hypothesize the existence of an auditory-limbic pathway involved in linking reward function to auditory signals.

The limbic brain structures are also implicated in brain reward function from a biochemical view. Olds and Milner (1954) discovered that electric stimulation of certain brain areas caused self-stimulating behavior aimed at sustaining this type of stimulation at a high rate and intensity. The most reactive areas in what is now commonly called the brain reward system center around the medial forebrain bundle, the principal longitudinal fiber pathway in the limbic brain. Direct stimulation of these areas, in experimental treatments for certain psychiatric disorders, has led to diffuse but definite feelings of well-being and pleasantness (Nolte, 1981). The involvement of biochemical substances, such as the catecholamines, dopamin and norepinephrine, and the endogenous opiate neuropeptides of the endorphin and enkephalin group, have been associated with the function of the brain reward system. Since mood-altering drugs such as d-amphetamines or chlorpromazine block the action of the catecholamines and also interfere with self-stimulation, there would seem to be a relationship between brain reward system and mood.

Recent research has extended the boundaries of the brain reward system in man deep into the neocortex and brain stem, thus rendering all types of instinctive or highly intellectual activity subject to the influence of biochemical changes. All areas of the brain reward system have pathways, however, through the limbic medial forebrain bundle that connects through the hypothalamus, thus asserting the influence of limbic functions on all levels of brain activity. Especially implicated by recent brain reward studies in the support of self-stimulating behavior is the entorhinal cortex, where fibers, as discussed earlier, project to the hippocampal structures involved in memory, learning, and emotional behavior (Routtenberg, 1978).

In this context, recent suggestions from neurological research regarding the relationship between the presence of certain neurotransmitter classes and neurohormones during synaptic change and the role of synaptic change in learning may hold considerable importance for future music therapy research (Kety, 1982). The suggestions are that monoamines and neurohormones, released during various emotional states, broadcast over fields of cortical synapses where they facilitate and effect persistent changes in synaptic conductivity. Persistent alteration of synaptic behavior is also an essential feature of learning. Thus, Kety proposes that affective experiences, accompanying, e.g., cognitive learning, could influence learning and memory at the chemical synapse because they are biologically mediated by the same neurotransmitter activation.

Biochemical changes in the limbic structures of the brain reward system in response to music-evoked emotional peak experiences have been investigated by Goldstein (1980). The endorphin antagonist naloxone was used in a double blind study to block self-reported "thrill" experiences to preferred music stimuli. All participants in the study reported emotional peak experiences, accompanied by physiological reactions. Those experiences were significantly attenuated in 3 out of every 10 participants who agreed to receive naloxone injections, in up to 19 independent trials. The results of the study suggest three implications: (1) music is a powerful stimulus, reported as such by most participants in the study and described as more so than other sensory modalities, for evoking rewarding emotional peak experiences; (2) these emotional experiences are accompanied by physical arousal experiences; (3) the statistically significant parts of the data can be interpreted as indicators of neuropeptide reactivity during music-evoked emotional peak experiences. In light of the presented overview of limbic system functions, the brain reward system, and biochemical reactivity, it may come as no surprise that Goldstein implicates these brain structures and their functions as underlying the responses in his study. He proposes specifically the amygdala as a site mediating these emotional peak experiences possibly caused by music-induced endorphin release.

In order for more definite interpretations to be made, much more needs to be known about general brain neurophysiology and applications to music. However, an understanding of the briefly reviewed CNS processes and their functional influence on human behavior is prerequisite to an understanding of the influence of music on behavior in therapy. The music therapist bases the validity of his practice on the assumption that music stimuli can evoke thoughts, feelings, and overt behaviors that are functional to the goals of behavioral change in therapy. The music therapist's curiosity, therefore, cannot be satisfied merely by studying how the brain processes music without reference to the behavioral implications of music processing. The indication, based on the pronounced physiological and affective components of music processing, that specific neurological processes are involved in music perception should lead to a careful investigation of the role of those CNS processes involved in (1) memory, learning, and emotionality, and (2) biochemical changes in the brain reward system affecting mood, motivation, and personality.

With due caution we may then propose that music stimuli have a biologically meaningful effect on human behavior by engaging specific brain functions involved in memory, learning, and multiple motivational and emotional states. The well-documented clinical observations that music elicits powerful mood changes, activates healthy thinking processes, and helps to establish reality contact with withdrawn, brain-damaged, and mentally confused clients need to be linked to progress in neurobiological research in order to move toward better treatment specificity in music therapy.

MUSIC STIMULI IN THERAPY

Music, Affect Modification, and Behavioral Change

The information delineated thus far allows music stimuli to be assigned a more specific function in music therapy processes concerned with the cognitive, affective, and perceptual functioning of clinical populations. The above-outlined principles provide an objective basis for a model depicting music stimulus properties employed in the therapy process, by engaging the client in an active thinking and feeling process directed toward achieving therapeutic goals. The relationship between music stimuli and the affective components of behavior processes (which have been discussed in great detail in the previous sections) has received particular attention for therapy based on recent clinical and research views emphasizing the importance of affective behavior in determining both general behavior patterns and the process of behavior change (Rachman, 1980, 1981; Watts, 1983). Strosahl and Linehan

(1986) state that there is a pressing need for the development and validation of procedures assessing the various dimensions of emotional behavior. They have suggested a conceptual distinction between the two components of affective behavior—internal emotional experiences and emotional communication—that may be required for effective psychosocial functioning. In this context, music therapy, as a powerful tool impacting on affective behavior processes, offers a specialized set of clinical techniques aimed at restoring and strengthening an individual's ability to organize emotional experience internally as well as to conduct emotional communication verbally and nonverbally. In this author's experience a five-stage sequence of emotional behavior in therapy has been shown to be useful for applying music therapy techniques and activities to emotional processing. Music therapy techniques and activities are used to (1) facilitate the experience of emotion; (2) facilitate the identification of emotion; (3) facilitate the expression of emotion; (4) facilitate the understanding of emotional communication of others; and (5) facilitate the synthesis, control, and modulation of one's own emotional behavior.

It has been suggested that the capacity of an individual to interpret emotional communications of others, identify and/or modulate internal emotional experience, and communicate that experience to others nonverbally, is one of the most important determinants of healthy ego function and social integration (Scherer & Ekman, 1984; Kemper, 1978; Zajonc, 1984). By developing a clear understanding of the neuropsychological processes and effects of music stimulus properties that underlie the influence of music on behavior, music therapy becomes an important and efficient treatment modality in which clinically significant emotional deficits are targeted for behavioral interventions. Lang (1970) suggests a three-system analysis of emotion consisting of subjective, behavioral, and physiological behavior components. This system could provide the music therapist with an applicable conceptual understanding of how to target and select for assessment the most abnormally functioning components in a client's behavior.

In the previous two sections of this chapter, information has been gathered and appraised to provide understanding of the unique properties of music stimuli feeding into the affective system and evoking responses that are meaningful for the human experience and expression.

In a last step, it remains to be shown that affective states and modifications thereof can have specific relevance in therapy processes. Rachman (1980) documents this relevance in a detailed survey of studies that show the effectiveness of emotional processing as prerequisite for behavioral change. Lang (1977) and Wolpe (1978) point out that a critical requirement in behavior modification through imagery and emotional processing is that at least partial components of the emotional state, subjected to change in therapy, be present in the imagery process. Their behaviorally based research centers around clinical syndromes such as obsessions, fear, phobias, anxiety states, and grief reactions.

Rachman (1981, 1984) discusses the relationship between cognitive and affective behaviors and their relevance in therapy processes. He goes into great detail as to how the cognitive therapy approach, although quite prevalent in current psychotherapy, often fails to produce significant behavior change. Behaviors in which mood/emotional components are evident are often especially resistant to purely insight-oriented techniques. A similar point has been made by Bandura (1977), who discusses the relative weakness of verbal persuasion as a means to influence behavior.

Many examples exist for cognitive operations altering affective reactions (Beck, 1976; Meichenbaum, 1977). However, based on the premise that affective and cognitive processes are partially independent and mutually influential of each other, Rachman proposes within a clinical paradigm the necessity to establish more and direct therapy procedures for affect modification to facilitate behavior modification. Affect modification is thus seen as prerequisite for certain types of behavior modification. Bandura stated that although change is mediated by cognitive processes, cognitive events are induced and altered most readily by success experiences through performance.

Sutherland et al. (1982) compared a verbal- and a music-based mood-induction procedure in a study comparing the influence of mood state on the ability to remove intrusive, unwanted cognitions. Unwanted thoughts, e.g., in form of distressing obsessions, are prevalent in many psychiatric conditions and seem to be functionally related to fluctuations of mood states (Rachman & Hodgson, 1980). Not surprisingly, then, the results of the Sutherland study show that intrusive, unpleasant thoughts were harder to remove in an induced sad state than in a happy state. However, the music-based mood-induction procedure showed superior results compared to the verbal-based method in altering and sustaining mood states. Consequently, in the music-induced happy condition, unwanted cognitions were removed more efficiently.

Sutherland, in interpreting the relationship between mood state and removing ability, suggests that in a dysphoric mood it is more difficult to replace a negative thought with a more pleasant thought. Teasdale and Taylor (1981) have argued from their research findings that in depressed mood the accessibility of negative information is increased. Consequently, Sutherland proposes a sequential approach for therapy in which existing mood states are the primary focus before specific distressing thoughts and behaviors are considered. The effectiveness of music to alter existing mood/emotional states in psychiatric imprisoned clients, measured via self-report scales, has also been shown by Thaut (in press).

The preceding discussion is of great importance for music therapy because it points out directions in which the music-evoked affective response, capable of modifying affect, becomes relevant as an integral part of therapy processes directed toward behavior modification. The presented data actually allow two conceptual directions for applications of music in, e.g., psychiatric music therapy: (1) that music may evoke specific affective responses through specific associations, which are related to the behavior subjected to intervention; (2) that music may evoke unspecific pleasant emotional/mood change, through perception of psychological/collative properties, which in turn facilitate changes in various thinking and feeling states and overt behavior. The relationship between affect modification and behavior modification, which has received renewed attention in the behavioral and therapy literature, implicates a search for efficient therapy techniques to access and modify affective behavior. Not surprisingly, Rachman (1981) has pointed to music as an effective means to be fed into the affective system for therapy purposes. The understanding and appraisal of this function of music constitutes the last link within a model that relates stimulus properties and neuropsychological processing in music to modification of thinking, feeling, and behavior in therapy.

An Integrative Model of Music in Therapy

Before the presentation of a treatment specific model of stimulus properties, evoked affective responses, and affect modification, four points of practical relevance need to be mentioned.

1. The evoked response can occur in the context of various musical settings, using receptive, listening-based, or expressive, performance-based presentations.

2. In the actual therapy process, treatment specificity of music stimulus properties unfolds in the context of human resources, influenced by each client's individual mental set and social/cultural background. The music therapist thus has to know the client's taste and preference in, and familiarity with, musical styles as well as each client's current level of functioning and arousal needs. Different types of music contain a different arousal potential in direction and intensity for each client, within the framework of current needs, preference, distinct stimulus properties, and associated responses. The music therapist needs to determine which type of music stimulus contains the appropriate psychophysical, collative, and ecological properties to achieve the desired experiences and responses. Thus the music therapist must assess idiosyncratic response patterns to provide meaningful stimuli and facilitate meaningful responses.

3. The music therapist has to develop a therapeutic environment where a meaningful experience through music can occur. That includes appropriate session structure, guidance through activities, trusting rapport and interaction, and mediating focus and meaningful perception through, e.g., instructions, appropriate media, or preparatory exercises.

4. The music therapist needs to evaluate, with the client, the evoked responses in regard to personal well-being and level of functioning and translate this into behavioral objectives for the client. However,

the treatment-specific music experience has to occur first and remains the catalyst for meaningful experiences/responses in the therapy setting.

The following model depicts the variables of music stimulus properties, CNS processing, evoked client responses, and clinical goals, as they relate to each other in the therapy process. The model identifies the three properties of music stimuli that, based on differential CNS processing and mediated perceptual responses, each evoke arousal/affective responses within the specific experiential qualities of activation/energy, novelty/surprise/clarity, and extramusical associations. The character of these experiences determines their emotional, evaluative value for the client in terms of reward, motivation, pleasure, positive feedback, tension relief, and insight. The outcome of this evaluative process determines the consequences of the music therapy experience in terms of perceived benefit, neurological change, and translation of the evoked affect modification into behavioral goals. (See Figure 1–1.)

Psychophysical Properties—Experience in Activation

The positive influence of the psychophysical attributes of music stimuli on activation behavior, energy level, excitement, and stimulation is particularly valuable in providing an immediate reward experience or in reducing anxiety states for the client. The influence performs its function by stimulating residual, healthy, positive feelings and behaviors, and providing motivation for behavior change, in supportive or short-term therapy settings (e.g., when working with schizophrenic patients who function on an apathetic or withdrawn level or respond actively to internal stimulation). Research data previously presented have shown positive, diffuse feelings of well-being in psychiatric disorders through stimulation of brain reward centers. Clinical data suggest that mentally ill patients may respond positively to music stimuli in regard to increased motor activity, increased verbalization, and positive mood change. The influence of music stimuli on level of arousal and its effect on the automatic, central nervous, motor, and sensory systems may account for that change. Conversely, a de-arousal or moderated arousal in states of hyperactivity, anxiety, and tension may be induced through selection of music with the appropriate psychophysical attributes. The experience of excitement, energy, and stimulation through music listening or music performing will also provide a rewarding, pleasurable, and reality-based experience of self. An activation experience through music will provide clients (e.g., multiply handicapped children, who are prevented from achieving in other sensory or motor areas) with a valuable, predictable, and biologically meaningful compensatory stimulus experience.

Collative Properties—Experience in Structure

The structural experience in music is central to several therapeutic goals in music therapy. Clinical data suggest that music stimuli often evoke functional

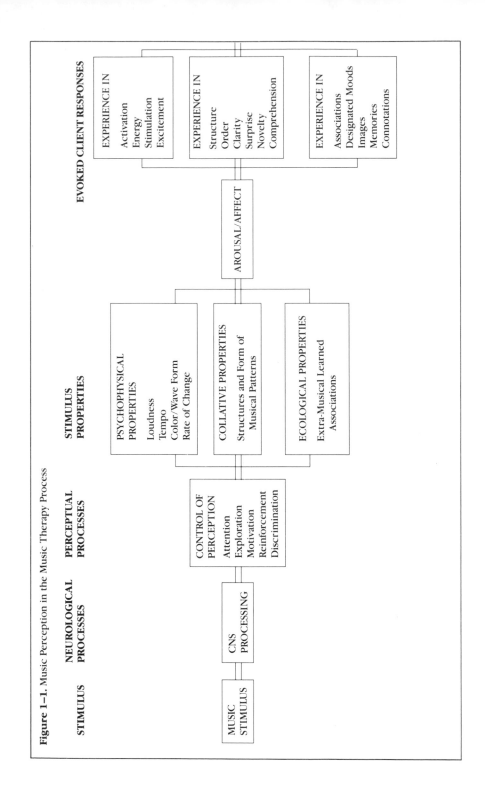

Figure 1–1. Music Perception in the Music Therapy Process

STIMULUS	NEUROLOGICAL PROCESSES	PERCEPTUAL PROCESSES	STIMULUS PROPERTIES	EVOKED CLIENT RESPONSES

MUSIC STIMULUS

CNS PROCESSING

CONTROL OF PERCEPTION

Attention
Exploration
Motivation
Reinforcement
Discrimination

PSYCHOPHYSICAL PROPERTIES

Loudness
Tempo
Color/Wave Form
Rate of Change

COLLATIVE PROPERTIES

Structures and Form of Musical Patterns

ECOLOGICAL PROPERTIES

Extra-Musical Learned Associations

AROUSAL/AFFECT

EXPERIENCE IN

Activation
Energy
Stimulation
Excitement

EXPERIENCE IN

Structure
Order
Clarity
Surprise
Novelty
Comprehension

EXPERIENCE IN

Associations
Designated Moods
Images
Memories
Connotations

Figure 1-1. (*Continued*)

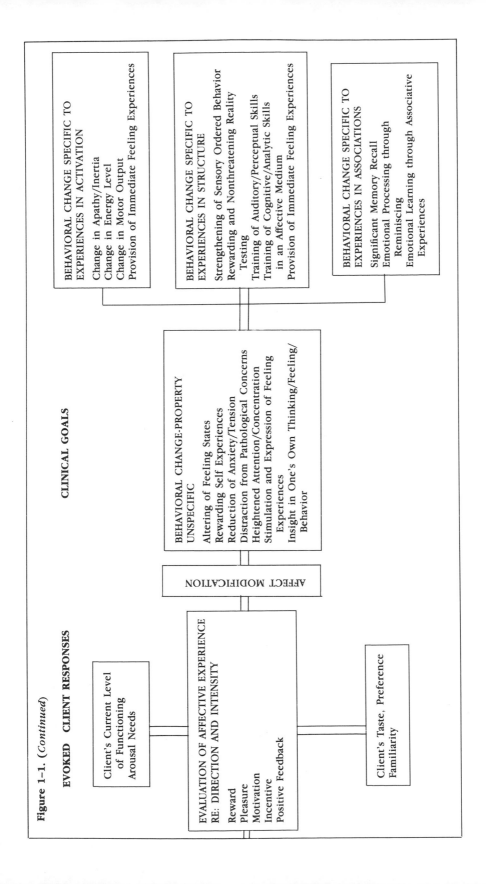

perceptual responses in individuals who are affected by various perceptual problems, e.g., autism, brain injuries, mental disorders (DeLong, 1978; Tanguay, 1976). The perception of rewarding and time-ordered music elements remains functional, based on the neurological principles of music processing, and thus can be used to develop and facilitate reality perception (Gaston & Eagle, 1970). It is a frequent clinical observation that severely mentally ill patients who are not accessible or do not respond appropriately to verbal approaches will respond with functional behavior in music-based therapy exercises.

Furthermore, the cognitive and affective areas of functional behavior in terms of mental organization are stimulated through the experiences with musical structures. This experience does not have to be a highly trained analytical response to music. Based on the principles of neural processing (minimal effort principle and principle of sequential and simultaneous mental processing), each client will be able to generate meaningful perception of music stimuli if the stimuli are selected according to his/her idiosyncratic response pattern. The experience of order, clarity, comprehension, and tension relief in musical structures, through guided listening, playing instruments, and subsequent verbalizing, will help the client to order his behavior in regard to perceiving and responding cognitively and affectively to meaningful sensory stimulation.

A third aspect of the structural experience is the emotional/feeling response that unfolds in the perceptual processing of musical events described by simplicity/complexity, novelty/familiarity, clarity/ambiguity, and tension/resolution, and their hedonic value for the client in terms of reward, pleasantness, positive feedback, and tension relief. This aspect of the structural experience can be used to provide a directed feeling experience, aimed at altering feeling states and promoting stress and anxiety reduction. For example, musical events that build and resolve structural, "musical" tension in a predictable, pleasurable manner, by evoking appropriate arousal or de-arousal in the client according to his/her needs, will constitute a powerful relaxation and anxiety-combating tool.

Ecological Properties—Experience in Associations

The associative experience is not embodied in the content of the music but consists of designated mood or connotative experiences, memories, and private images that have acquired a learned association with the music stimulus. The client responds to an internal psychological event and not to anything that can be heard in the actual music stimulus. The occurrence of associative experiences, therefore, is difficult for the music therapist to control or predict because it constitutes a very idiosyncratic response, shaped and stimulated by the client's past experiences or sometimes by very spontaneous private associations. The music therapist often makes the mistake of emphasizing exclusively this aspect of the music experience as relevant for overt behavioral, thinking, and feeling responses in therapy. Mentally ill clients may benefit more from affective change in their daily functioning through music-evoked experiences in structure and activation than from often introspective, associative thinking and feeling processes. A reality-based "here and now" feeling experience, through structure and activation in music, may support the "sealing over" process in schizophrenic clients or stimulate concrete, immediate, positive experience of self or healthy interaction. For different reasons, physically or sensory disabled children may find more reward and motivation in experiences of structure and activation, through playing instruments or singing therapy, than in music experiences emphasizing associations.

However, associative responses are a well-documented part of the response to music stimuli. They often reflect primary affective processes through, for instance, recall of significant life experiences, because music stimuli evoke affective concomitants in associative experiences even if the primary associated content does not emphasize feelingful behavior. Music stimuli help to interpret the evoked experience in terms of emotional value for the client (Zwerling, 1979). This process may facilitate awareness and recognition of significant feelings in life experiences. Thus awareness of suppressed feelings, recall of significant memories, designated mood experiences, and stress reduction through imagery are main therapeutic goals based on associative experiences in music.

CONCLUSION

The foregoing discussion has emphasized the treatment specificity of music stimuli in order to provide a systematic model for the use of music in therapy focusing on cognitive, affective, and perceptual aspects in the area of healthy psychological functioning in human personality. Both the discussion and model are intended to integrate an objective neurological basis for the effect of music stimuli, and their respective stimulus properties and associated responses, with the subjective variables of perceptual and evaluative music processing, in order to arrive at a predictable, analyzable, and measurable treatment result.

REFERENCES

Applebaum, E., Egel, A., Koegel, R., & Imhoff, B. (1979). Measuring musical abilities of autistic children. *Journal of Autism and Developmental Disorders, 9,* 279–285.

Bandura, A. (1977). *Social learning theory.* Englewood Cliffs, NJ: Prentice-Hall.

Bear, D. M. (1983) Hemispheric specialization and the neurology of emotion. *Archives of Neurology, 40,* 195–202.

Bear, D. M., & Fedio, P. (1977). Quantitative analysis of interictal behavior in temporal lobe epilepsy. *Archives of Neurology, 34,* 454–467.

Bear, D. M., & Schenk, L. (1981). Increased autonomic responses to neutral and emotional stimuli in patients with temporal lobe epilepsy. *American Journal of Psychiatry, 138,* 843–845.

Beck, A. (1976). *Cognitive therapy.* New York: International Universities Press.

Berlyne, D. E. (1971). *Aesthetics and psychobiology.* New York: Appleton-Century-Crofts.

Berlyne, D. E., & Borsa, D. M. (1968). Uncertainty and the orientation reaction. *Perception and Psychophysics, 3,* 77–79.

Berscheid, E. (1983). Emotion. In H. H. Kelley (Ed.), *Close relationships* (pp. 110–168). San Francisco: Freeman.

Bever, T. G., & Chiarello, R. J. (1974). Cerebral dominance in musicians and non-musicians. *Science, 199,* 852–856.

Biller, J. D., Olsen, P. J., & Breen, T. (1974). The effect of "happy" versus "sad" music and participation on anxiety. *Journal of Music Therapy, 11,* 68–72.

Clynes, M. (1978). *Sentics: The touch of emotions.* New York: Anchor Books.

Cohen, N. (1988). The use of superimposed rhythm to decrease the rate of speech in brain-damaged adolescent. *Journal of Music Therapy, 25,* 85–93.

Crozier, J. B. (1973). *Verbal and exploratory responses to sound sequences of varying complexity.* Unpublished doctoral dissertation, University of Toronto.

Delong, G. R. (1978). A neuropsychological interpretation of infantile autism. In M. Rutler and E. Schopler (Eds.), *Autism: A reappraisal of concepts and treatment* (pp. 207–218). New York: Plenum Press.

Eagle, C. T. (1973). Effects on existing mood and order of presentation of vocal and instrumental music on rated mood responses to that music [Review by K. H. Mueller]. *Council for Research in Music Education, 32,* 55–59.

Galaburda, A. M., Sanides, R., & Geschwind, N. (1978). Human brain: Cytoarchitectonic left-right asymmetries in the temporal speech region. *Archives of Neurology, 35,* 812–817.

Gardner, H., Silverman, J., Denes, G., Semenza, C., & Rosenstiel, A. V., (1977). Sensitivity to musical denotation and connotation in organic patients, *Cortex, 13,* 242–256.

Gaston, E. T., & Eagle, C. T., (1970). The function of music in LSD therapy for alcoholic patients. *Journal of Music Therapy, 7,* 3–19.

Gates, A., & Bradshaw, J. (1977). The role of the cerebral hemispheres in music. *Brain and Language, 4,* 403–431.

Geschwind, N. (1965). Disconnexion syndromes in animals and man. *Brain, 88,* 237–294.

Gfeller, K. (1983). Musical mnemonics as an aid to retention with normal and learning disabled students. *Journal of Music Therapy, 20,* 179–189.

Goldstein, A. (1980). Thrills in response to music and other stimuli. *Physiological Psychology, 8,* 126–129.

Greenberg, R. P., & Fisher, S. (1972). Some differential effects of music on projective and structured psychological tests. *Psychological Reports, 28,* 817–820.

Guyton, A. C. (1986). *Textbook of medical physiology.* Philadelphia: W. B. Saunders.

Hedden, S. K. (1971). *A multivariate investigation of reaction profiles in music listeners and their relationship with various autochthonous and experiental characteristics.* Unpublished doctoral dissertation, University of Kansas.

Heilman, K. M., Schwartz, H. D., & Watson, R. T. (1978). Hypoarousal in patients with the neglect syndrome and emotional indifference. *Neurology, 88,* 229–232.

Hernandez-Peon, R. (1961). The efferent control of afferent signals entering the central nervous system. *Annals of New York Academy of Science, 89,* 866–882.

Hodges, D. A. (Ed.) (1980). *Handbook of music psychology.* Lawrence, KS: National Association for Music Therapy.

Iversen, S., & Fray, P. (1982). Brain catecholamines in relation to affect. In A. L. Beckman (Ed.), *The neural basis of behavior* (pp. 229–272). New York: Spectrum.

Kemper, T. (1978). *A social interaction theory of emotions.* New York: Wiley.

Kety, S. (1982). The evolution of concepts of memory: An overview. In A. L. Beckman (Ed.), *The neural basis of behavior.* New York: Spectrum.

Lamendella, J. T. (1977). The limbic system in human communication. In H. Whitaker and H. Whitaker (Eds.), *Studies in neurolinguistics, Vol. 3* (pp. 157–222). New York: Academic Press.

Lang, P. (1970). Stimulus control, response control and the desensitization of fear. In D. Levis (Ed.), *Learning approaches to therapeutic behavior* (pp. 266–281). Chicago: Aldine Press.

Lang, P. (1977). Imagery in therapy. *Behavior Therapy, 8,* 862–886.

Lazarus, R. (1984). Thoughts on the relations between emotion and cognition. In K. Scherer and P. Ekman (Eds.), *Approaches to emotion* (pp. 247–258). Hillsdale, NJ: Lawrence Erlbaum.

Litchman, M. D. (1977). The use of music in establishing a learning environment for language instruction with autistic children. (Doctoral dissertation, State University of New York at Buffalo, 1976). *Dissertation Abstracts International, 37,* 4992 A. (University microfilms, No. 77-3557).

MacLean, P. D. (1973). *A triune concept of the brain and behavior.* Toronto: Toronto University Press.

Madsen, C. K., Greer, R. D., and Madsen, C. K. (Eds.) (1975). *Research in music behavior: Modifying music behavior in the classroom.* New York: Teachers College Press.

Mandler, G. (1984). *Mind and body.* New York: Norton.

Marteniuk, R. G. (1976). *Information processing in motor skills.* New York: Holt, Rinehart & Winston.

Mazziotta, J. C., & Phelps, M. E. (1983). Human neuropsychological imaging. Studies of local brain metabolism and blood flow: strategies and results. *Archives of Neurology, 40,* 767.

McDougall, W. (1908). *An introduction to social psychology.* London: Methuen.

McLaughlin, T. (1970). *Music and communication.* London: Faber and Faber.

McMullen, P. (1980). Music as perceived stimulus object and affective responses: an alternative theoretical framework. In D. A. Hodges (Ed.), *Handbook of music psychology* (pp. 183–193). Lawrence, KS: National Association for Music Therapy.

McMullen, P. (1977, March). *Descriptive models of verbal responses to musical stimuli.* Paper presented at Music Educators National Conference, North Central—Southwestern Division Convention, Kansas City, Missouri.

Meichenbaum, D. (1977). *Cognitive behavior modification.* New York: Plenum.

Meyer, L. (1956). *Emotion and meaning in music.* Chicago: University of Chicago Press.

Nauta, W., & Domesick, V. (1982). Neural associations of the limbic system. In A. L. Beckman (Ed.), *The neural basis of behavior* (pp. 175–206). New York: Spectrum.

Nauta, W., & Feirtag, M. (1979). The organization of the brain. *Scientific American, 241,* 88–111.

Nielzen, S., & Cesarec, Z. (1982). Emotional experience of music as a function of musical structure. *Psychology of Music, 10,* 7–17.

Nielzen, S., & Cesarec, Z. (1981). On the perception of emotional meaning in music. *Psychology of Music, 9,* 17–31.

Norman, D., & Brant-Zawadski, M. (1983). Nuclear magnetic resonance in the diagnosis of CNS disorders. *Archives of Neurology, 40,* 7–68.

Nolte, D. (1981). *The human brain. An introduction to its functional anatomy.* St. Louis: C. V. Mosby.

Noy, P. (1967). The psychodynamic meaning of music—part II. *Journal of Music Therapy, 4,* 7–23.

Oldendorff, W. H. (1983). Principles of imaging structure by nuclear magnetic resonance. *Archives of Neurology, 40,* 767.

Olds, J. (1962). Hypothalamic substrates of reward. *Physiological Review, 42,* 554–604.

Olds, J., & Milner, P. (1954). Positive reinforcement produced by electrical stimulation of septal area and other regions of rat brain. *Journal of Comparative Physiology, 47,* 419–427.

Orton, N. R. (1953). *Application of the iso-moodic principle in the use of music with psychotic and normal subjects.* Unpublished master's thesis, University of Kansas.

Panzarella, R. (1977). *The phenomenology of peak experiences in response to music and visual art and some personality correlates.* Unpublished doctoral dissertation, City University of New York.

Papez, J. W. (1937). A proposed mechanism of emotion. *Archives of Neurology and Psychiatry, 38,* 725–743.

Peretti, P. O., & Swenson, K. (1974). Effects of music on anxiety as determined by physiological skin responses. *Journal of Research in Music Education, 22,* 278–283.

Pike, A. (1972). A phenomenological analysis of emotional experience in music. *Journal of Research in Music Education, 20,* 262–267.

Plutchik, R. (1962). *The emotions: Facts, theories and a new model.* New York: Random House.

Poliakov, G. (1972). *Neuron structure of the brain.* Cambridge, MA: Harvard University Press.

Pribram, K. H. (1967). Emotion: Steps towards a neuropsychological theory. In D. C. Glass (Eds.), *Neurophysiology and emotion,* New York: Rockefeller University Press.

Pribram, K. H., & Kruger, L. (1954). Functions of the "olfactory brain." *Annals of the New York Academy of Sciences, 58,* 109–138.

Rachman, S. (1984). A reassessment of the "primacy of affect." *Cognitive Therapy and Research, 8,* 579–584.

Rachman, S. (1980). Emotional processing. *Behavior Research and Therapy, 18,* 51–60.

Rachman, S. (1981). The primacy of affect: Some theoretical implications. *Behavior Research and Therapy, 19,* 279–290.

Rachman, S., & Hodgson, R., (1980). *Obsessions and compulsions.* Englewood Cliffs, NJ: Prentice-Hall.

Roederer, J. (1974). The psychophysics of musical perception. *Music Educators Journal, 60,* 20–30.

Roederer, J. (1975). *Introduction to the physics and psychophysics of music.* New York: Springer.

Routtenberg, A. (1978). The reward system of the brain. *Scientific American, 239,* 154–164.

Scherer, K., & Ekman, P. (Eds.), (1984). *Approaches to emotion.* Hillsdale, NJ: Lawrence Erlebaum.

Schoen, M. (Ed.) (1927). *The effect of music.* New York: Harcourt Brace.

Shatin, L. (1957). The influence of rhythmic drum beat stimuli upon the pulse rate and general activity of long-term schizophrenics. *Journal of Mental Science, 103,* 172–188.

Simonov, P. V. (1986). *The emotional brain.* New York: Plenum.

Sperry, R. W., & Gazzaniga, M. S. (1967). Language following surgical disconnection of the hemispheres. In C. H. Millikan and F. L. Darley (Eds.), *Brain mechanisms underlying speech and language.* New York: Grune & Stratton.

Springer, S. P., & Deutsch, G. (1985). *Left brain, right brain.* New York: Freeman and Company.

Stevens, E. A. (1971). Some effects of tempo changes on stereotyped rocking movement of low-level mentally related subjects. *American Journal of Mental Deficiency, 76,* 76–81.

Strosahl, K., & Linehan, M. (1986). Basic issues in behavioral assessment. In A. Ciminero, K. Calhoun, & H. Adams (Eds.), *Handbook of behavioral assessment* (2nd ed.) (pp. 12–46). New York: Wiley.

Sunshine, J., & Mishkin, M. (1975). A visual-limbic pathway serving visual associative functions in rhesus monkeys. *Federal Proceedings, 34,* 440.

Sutherland, G., Newman, B., & Rachman, S. (1982). Experimental investigations of the relations between mood and intrusive, unwanted cognitions. *British Journal of Medical Psychology, 55,* 127–138.

Tanguay, P. (1976). Clinical and electrophysiological research. In E. R. Ritvo (Ed.), *Autism: Diagnosis, current research and management* (pp. 75–84). New York: Spectrum.

Teasdale, J., & Taylor, R. (1981). Induced mood and accessibility of memories: An effect of mood state or of induction procedure? *British Journal of Clinical Psychology, 20,* 39–48.

Thaut, M. H. (in press). The influence of music therapy interventions on self-rated changes in relaxation, affect, and thought in psychiatric prisoner-patients. *Journal of Music Therapy.*

Thaut, M. H. (1987). Visual versus auditory (musical) stimulus preferences in autistic children. *Journal of Autism and Developmental Disorders, 17,* 425–432.

Ungerleider, L. G., & Mishkin, M. (1982). Two cortical visual systems. In D. J. Ingle, R. Mansfield, and M. A. Goodale (Eds.), *The analysis of visual behavior* (pp. 549–586). Cambridge, MA: MIT Press.

Vitz, P. C. (1966). Affect as a function of stimulus variation. *Journal of Experimental Psychology, 71,* 74–79.

Watson, J. B. (1924). *Behaviorism.* New York: W. W. Norton.

Watts, R. (1983). Affective cognition: A sequel to Zajonc and Rachman. *Behavior Research and Therapy, 21,* 89–90.

Wedin, L. (1972). A multidimensional study of perceptual-emotional qualities in music. *Scandinavian Journal of Psychology, 13,* 241–257.

Wolberg, L. R. (1977). *The technique of psychotherapy.* New York: Grune & Stratton.

Wolpe, J. (1978). Self-efficacy theory and psychotherapeutic change. *Advances in Behavior Research and Therapy, 1,* 231–236.

Wundt, G. (1874). *Grundzuege der physiolgischen Psychologie.* Leipzig: Engelmann.

Zajonc, R. B. (1984). On primacy of affect. In K. Scherer & P. Ekman (Eds.), *Approaches to emotion.* Hillsdale, NJ: Lawrence Erlbaum.

Zatorre, R. (1984). Musical perception and cerebral function: A critical review. *Music Perception, 2,* 196–221.

Zwerling, I. (1979). The creative arts therapies as "real therapies." *Hospital and Community Psychiatry, 30,* 841–844.

Chapter 2

Physiological and Motor Responses to Music Stimuli

Michael H. Thaut

This chapter will provide an appraisal of clinical and research data regarding the influence of music stimuli on physiological responses in the human organism. Two areas of responses will be discussed: (1) changes of autonomic and central nervous functions, and how they are related to affective arousal and anxiety/relaxation responses, and (2) skeleto-motor responses and how they are related to processes in motor rehabilitation. The goal of this chapter is to validate music therapy interventions in these areas in regard to specific music stimulus properties and their application in clinical techniques.

CENTRAL AND AUTONOMIC NERVOUS SYSTEM EFFECTS

Responses of the autonomic and central nervous systems to music stimuli have been researched and documented through experimental work for more than 100 years. Weld (1912) and Diserens (1923) offer excellent reviews of the research body before 1920, and Dainow (1977) and Hodges (1980) provide both exhaustive and concise surveys of related studies after 1920. The most commonly investigated physiological parameters were heart rate, pulse rate, blood pressure, respiration, skin responses, brain waves, and muscular responses. All studies have quite clearly supported the notion that music stimuli influences physiological response. However, very few clear directions have emerged in the response pattern. Increases or decreases of autonomic effects (e.g., heart rate and skin response) have been found in response to the same types of music stimuli. For example, the relative effects of sedative versus stimulative music, a frequently used differentiation, have produced variable physiological responses (Gaston, 1951).

Hodges (1980), in his review of the literature from 1920 to the present, found seven studies stating that stimulative music tends to increase heart rate or pulse rate, while sedative music tends to decrease these rates. He found two studies stating that either type of music can cause heart rate changes. Hodges also discovered three studies supporting the notion that both types of music will increase heart and pulse rate. Finally, he found six studies in which no changes were caused by any music stimulus. Hodges offers three reasons for the inconsistent results: (1) the definition of stimuli was too broad; (2) the measurements were unreliable and the research designs too varied; and (3) the testing situation itself contained confounding variables.

In a classic experiment, Ax (1953) could differentiate between two distinct physiological patterns in his subjects by exposing the subjects to stimulus situations described as "anger" and "fear." Schachter (1957) was able to replicate these results, but he later found that similar autonomic effects could arise within quite variable psychological experiences. Ultimately, he questioned the existence of physiological distinctions among various emotional states (Schachter, 1964). Lacey and Lacey (1970), in light of the fact that since Ax's experiment (1957) no other unique physiological response had been found for emotional experiences, suggested the concept of individual "response specificity" or "response stereotype." This means that each individual has his own biological response pattern to a given stimulus. He responds in an idiosyncratic manner that shows a consistent relationship among stimulus characteristics, physiological response, and psychological experience. This notion stands in opposition to the search for intersubject response stereotypes. Harrer and Harrer (1978), in reporting research that was supportive of individual response stereotypes, delineated several variables that might determine intrasubject response patterns: (1) lability and stability of the individual's autonomic regulatory processes (influenced by constitution, age, sex, mode of life, physiological fitness, state of health, and temporary fatigue); (2) emotional reactivity of the individual; and (3) individual attitudes towards the stimulus formed by extramusical associations, taste, preference, and the testing situation. In addition, Harrer and Harrer (1980) suggested that active music performance gives rise to strong autonomic reactions that cannot be suppressed by deliberate detachment.

Experimental investigations have shown that (1) physiological changes are reflected in a highly idiosyncratic manner, and (2) music stimuli, within the concept of response stereotypes, can markedly affect these changes. The music therapist tries to determine the variables that influence the formation of psychophysiological responses in a client. The therapist must determine a client's arousal response, autonomic and emotional reactivity, current moods, attitudes, and preferences in response to certain music stimuli in order to provide meaningful psychological and physiological experiences for the client.

Situations in which certain physiological responses (especially autonomic) are deliberately elicited deserve special consideration. For example, several physiological measures, such as reduction of pulse rate, blood pressure, respiration rate, and muscular tension, are identified as general indicators of reduced stress and anxiety experiences. This relationship has been well documented in the clinical and research literature (Jacobson, 1974; Wolpe, 1965). The underlying principle might be summarized this way: Physiological relaxation is incompatible with anxiety, and the habit of responding with physiological tension blocks the habit of responding with anxiety, and vice versa (Marteniuk, 1976; Hernandez-Peon, 1961). When focusing on anxiety/stress reduction by influencing physiological responses, the music therapist seeks to establish a directional stimulus-response relationship. However, the selection of appropriate music stimuli again depends on the determination of individual reactivity patterns. Research documenting the use of music in relaxation training has shown support for music's efficacy in reducing anxiety and stress. Concise reviews of related research are provided by Abeles (1980) and Standley (1986). Contemporary researchers emphasize the importance of client preference in selecting music that supports the concept of individual reactivity patterns (Stratton & Zalanowski, 1984).

The foregoing discussion of idiosyncratic psychophysiological response patterns lends strong support to the inclusion of individual reactivity variables (such as preference) in future research. Too many studies still rely on general musical categories such as sedative versus stimulative, disregarding the evidence for idiosyncratic stimulus-response relationships. Music stimuli perceived as pleasant and relaxing may enhance physiological processes of tension reduction. In conclusion, music stimuli do elicit physiological responses within highly idiosyncratic response patterns, determined not only by the musical characteristics of the stimuli, but also by many variables within the individual. Only if information is provided on all relevant variables in this stimulus-response relationship will meaningful psychophysiological changes take place.

EFFECTS ON MOTOR LEARNING AND MOTOR REHABILITATION

Surprisingly, little attention has been devoted to the effects of music on motor responses. Three areas of research have emerged that document this particular relationship, i.e., the effects of music stimuli on (1) muscular activity, mainly through electromyograph (EMG) studies; (2) overt motor activity; and (3) motor performance, learning, and rehabilitation. The last area can be divided into (1) the use of music in general, especially the playing of musical instruments, to exercise certain gross and fine motor functions, and (2) the use of rhythm to facilitate aspects of motor performance.

The few studies investigating muscular activity through EMG measurements support the notion of muscular responses to music stimulation (Sears, 1952, 1958, 1960; Holdsworth, 1974; Oleron & Silver, 1963; Scartelli, 1982). Dainow (1977) and Abeles (1980) have reviewed studies documenting the influence of music on general motor activity. Although there is supporting evidence for a music-motor activity relationship (Brickman, 1940; Patterson, 1959; Stevens, 1971; Shatin, 1957; Reardon & Bell, 1971; Rieber, 1965), the nature of this relationship, in terms of directional effect of different types of music, is unclear. Inconsistent definitions of types of music and the use of different populations may have contributed to the ambiguity. Based on the earlier delineation of the concept of "individual response stereotypes," the directional ambiguity may actually result from the attempt to find general response tendencies rather than consistent intrasubject response patterns. However, considering the obvious effects of music stimuli on muscular responses, researchers might find a different paradigm to facilitate directional answers in the stimulus-response relationship in question.

Only a small research base exists in the motor-response area; it is concerned with the influence of music on motor learning, performance, and rehabilitation. The investigations described offer promising results for future research and clinical application.

To understand better the contribution that musical materials can make toward motor learning processes, the music therapist must view the psychological and physical properties of musically organized acoustic stimuli and related activities within the framework of functional and neural mechanisms for motor behavior. An analysis of those mechanisms following a neuropsychological model as, for example, proposed by Sage (1977), would evaluate the specific impact of musical stimuli on the neurological processes underlying motor behavior. Reception of stimulus cues, their translation into a motor program, and their command and feedback function in controlling the motor program would be the focus of investigation in this evaluation process. Four aspects of this research have been subject to much examination outside music therapy, and are invaluable to an assessment of musical materials in clinical practice. They are: (1) the effect of acoustic stimuli on motor neural activity, that is, the physiological basis for all motor behaviors; (2) the effect of rhythm, that is, the temporal structure of acoustic events; (3) the effect of the auditory modality on the temporal discrimination process in the central nervous system; and (4) the relationship between temporal perceptive processes in the central nervous system and the temporal components of motor learning and performance processes.

A fifth aspect, the feasibility of music materials (e.g., music instruments in rehabilitation exercises), has been documented in studies concerned with the effect of music-based rehabilitation programs for gross and fine motor functioning. Studies by Fields (1954), Cross, McLellan, Vomberg, Monga, and Monga (1984), and Cofrancesco (1985) document the efficacy of music-based rehabilitation programs on aspects of motor functions. Lucia (1987) has summarized many of these findings in regard to the work with head trauma and stroke patients. Motor aspects facilitated through music-based exercises include flexion-extension and rotation patterns in upper limbs, alternate and reciprocal limb patterns, gross motor movements using different lateral patterns, proprioceptive control of rhythmic gait, gross motor coordination, range of motion, and hand grasp strength. Clinical music-based techniques emphasize the feasibility and adaptability of working with music instruments and combining music and movement exercises to achieve therapeutic goals. The effect that playing instruments has on motor functions, physical disabilities, and clinical applications has been assessed by Sutton, (1984), Clark and Chadwick (1980), Moss Rehabilitation Hospital, Settlement Music School, and Therapeutic Music Program (1982), Farnan (1984), and Miller (1979).

The efficiency of music instruments in facilitating aspects of motor functions has been explained in several ways. Sutton (1984) has documented that gross and fine motor movements used in playing instruments reflect functional movements of joints and associated muscles. Berel, Diller, and Orgel (1971) have documented the efficiency of musical feedback by using tone-bars arranged in musical scales to facilitate visual motor sequencing tasks in children with cerebral palsy. As an adjunct effect, most studies report increased client motivation when music instruments are used in functional exercise programs. Two further rationales for using instruments and music-based activities in general have been mentioned in all reviewed studies: the motor-activating effect of appropriately selected music stimuli or playing on music instruments, and the facilitating effect of the temporal structure of music (i.e., rhythm) on motor performance.

Experimental studies, dealing specifically with rhythmic materials and handicapped populations, have been put forth by Staum (1983) and Thaut (1985). Safranek, Koshland, and Raymond (1982) have investigated the use of auditory rhythmic stimuli to aid neuromuscular coordination in gross-motor tasks. They found therapeutically beneficial changes in EMG measures under the rhythmic condition for increased duration, decreased variation, and co-contraction in muscular response patterns. Nonquantified clinical studies have been reported by Goellnitz (1975), Cotton (1965, 1974), and Cotton and Parnwell (1968). The literature strongly indicates the value of auditory rhythmic stimuli in facilitating aspects of motor performance in learning processes and remediation. Liemohn and Knapczyk (1947), in a factor analysis of components of gross motor skills, identified rhythmic quality as one factor, thus suggesting that rhythmic organization of movement might help to remediate aspects of motor functioning. The relevant question for music therapists is how to utilize external rhythmic (music) stimuli to shape timing and coordination in motor skill performance. Thaut (1983) has suggested a model of rhythmic auditory-motor integration in the attempt to validate the use of rhythmic aids in music-based motor rehabilitation. The basic findings will be presented in an abbreviated fashion.

A MODEL OF RHYTHMIC AUDITORY-MOTOR INTEGRATION

Research in motor development has dealt with the role of perception in motor learning, thereby focusing mainly on perceptual processes through vision and kinesthesis. Auditory perceptual processes, through language or music, have been given lesser attention. These processes are reported as tools for motivation or unspecific accompaniment of movement experiences.

However, a study by Smith (1957) indicates that temporal discrimination processes develop earlier through the auditory than the visual modality, and that there is transfer from the auditory to the visual but not the reverse. The potential effect of aurally perceived rhythmic stimuli on temporal accuracy in movement can be put forth quite logically, at least in theory, if the superior temporal discrimination process in the auditory mode can be translated into temporal muscular control. This translation process, which shall be called auditory-motor coordination or integration, has been investigated from very different viewpoints and through very different methodological approaches in the neurophysiological and behavioral research literature.

Motor Rhythm and External Rhythm

Motor rhythm usually refers to the temporal organization of serial muscle response, observable as the consistent and regularly recurring grouping of single motor acts. Rhythm, in this recurrence of events in time, constitutes the organization of temporal relationships. Auditory rhythm refers to the perception of a series of acoustic stimuli as a rhythmic pattern. The nature of the perceived grouping is influenced by objective characteristics of the stimulus series, e.g., intensities of its components, duration, and temporal spacing (Woodrow, 1951).

Studies that have tried to correlate verbal and motor responses have shown overwhelmingly that the ability to perceive and discriminate among rhythmic stimuli on verbal tests has no substantial relationship to the degree of motor rhythmic abilities (Bond, 1959; Lemon & Sherbon, 1934; Huff, 1972; Smith, 1957; Schwanda, 1969). The results indicate that the ability to synchronize motor rhythm patterns to an external rhythm is a separate skill, which seems to be dependent on training and exposure to rhythmic stimuli and movement. These results clearly contradict earlier notions that perception of rhythm is directly related to rhythmic motor responses because a kinesthetic or motor factor is already present in the perceptual process itself (MacDougal, 1902).

The literature leaves no other conclusion than that the kinesthetic or motor factor in the perceptual process still needs to be shaped or translated into a temporal muscular control scheme coordinated with external rhythmic stimuli before motor rhythmic performance can appear. Importantly, numerous studies have consistently shown that the auditory modality produces motor rhythmic responses that are less variable than do the visual, tactile, or combined auditory/visual presentation modes (Gault & Goodfellow, 1938; Haight, 1944; Huff, 1972; Lhamon and Goldstone, 1974; Rosenbusch & Gardner, 1968; Thomas & Moon, 1976; Cooper & Glassow, 1982).

Neurophysiological Aspects

Studies by Pal'tsev and El'ner (1967), Rossignol (1971), and Rossignol and Jones (1976) have shown that nerve pulses induced by sound signals—in particular, musical sound patterns—travel from the cochlear nuclei not only along the pathways ascending to the cerebral cortex, but simultaneously spread to the spinal cord via the alternate auditory pathway, where they raise the excitability of the motor nuclei. This process results in a shortening of the latent period of voluntary muscle reaction to strong sound signals by the time of the appearance of supraspinal influences of the segmental level. Furthermore, Rossignol, and Rossignol and Jones report that the effects of the motor neural potentiation through audio-spinal processes, when induced by repetitive auditory stimulation, result in a synchronization pattern between the neural activity and the external stimulus, thus facilitating timed muscular response patterns.

Automatization of Movement Patterns

Highly skilled movement performance seems to be associated with a preconceived, well-developed movement plan, established in the brain areas that are responsible for execution and control of motor activities (Singer, 1980). For example, a beginner needs to go through the steps in performing a task very consciously, attending to the various components of the movements and to all external guiding cues present. Conversely, an experienced performer seems to be able to complete the same sequence "unconsciously," without heavy reliance on external cues. A well-developed movement plan seems to provide built-in mechanisms for control and continuance of required activities.

In the development of the brain areas responsible for the control of motor behavior, the cerebral cortex plays an important role in any type of voluntary movement, and obviously in learning complex movements (e.g., athletic skills), whereas the cerebellum offers an automatic control function, being responsible for smooth, coordinated movement and for the execution of reflex-like movement patterns. Well-learned motor patterns, which presumably no longer require conscious control, might indeed become almost like reflex acts. This development would be connected to a shift in cortical areas from the cortex to the cerebellum, which is responsible for execution and control. Studies investigating the automatization process of motor patterns support the notion that the degree of anticipation displayed by the subjects performing the task is an important factor in the process of movement response automatization. Anticipation, however, seemed to be a variable, depending on the predictability of external response cues (Schmidt, 1968; Adams and Chambers, 1962). Experimental results show that a task that can be anticipated, in terms of serial ordering and reaction time, will require decreasing conscious control and attention over time, thus becoming automatized. Task performances cued by the predictable stimulus were superior to those in the unpredictable condition. The auditory stimulus always proved to elicit better responses than the visual.

Auditory cues, or sound events, if rhythmically organized, are predictable timing cues since they fall into consistent patterns. It is logical to assume, then, that auditory rhythmic stimuli can serve as predictable timing cues that facilitate the anticipation of a motor response, and that this response pattern gradually becomes automatized.

Muscular Fatigue and Recovery Time

Many studies have investigated the influence of the presence of musical stimuli on endurance in physical performance. There seems to be general agreement suggesting that physical endurance may be enhanced if movement is rhythmically coordinated with a musical stimulus (Bushey, 1966; Widdop, 1968; Harding, 1933; Anshel & Marishi, 1978; Stull & Kearney, 1974). Explanations for the advantageous effect of musical accompaniment on physical activity have been set forth by Marteniuk (1976), who suggests that due to the process of selective attention, the subject's perception of a pleasant auditory stimulus predominates over the attention to the less pleasant stimuli of physical exertion, and by Hernandez-Peon (1961), who contended that pleasurable sensory stimuli can facilitate electrical activity in one sensory pathway while blocking the transmission of other afferent pathways. Thus music may prolong physical endurance in the organism because it inhibits psychological feedback associated with physical exertion and fatigue.

Auditory Feedback and Proprioceptive Control

External auditory cues have been used successfully in a number of studies as an auxiliary feedback system for muscular control or contingent reinforcement of muscular control. Nonrhythmically organized acoustic stimuli, however, do not pertain directly to the temporal ordering process necessary for a motor rhythmic performance. They have been used instead to facilitate various other aspects of motor learning, mainly in terms of quantitative muscular control or as response feedback for short term motor retention. Adams, Marshall, and Goetz (1974) reported the use of combined auditory, proprioceptive, and visual feedback for learning and recalling a movement. The biggest retention loss was found for the condition with the least feedback present. Other studies have used auditory feedback to aid proprioceptive muscular control, such as in foot dragging (Spearing and Poppen, 1974) head osture (Wolfe, 1980), muscular functions in spastic conditions (Basmajian, 1979), and limb functions in hemiplegic conditions (Nafpliotis, 1956).

Temporal Predictability and Response Anticipation

Another quality of temporally predictable stimulus groups, besides their effect on the automatization of a response pattern, can be found in their impact on reaction time and quality of response. A shortening of the latency for volitional motor responses has already been suggested in the section on neurophysiological aspects.

Conrad (1956) has found that individuals, when given a choice, tended to organize response cues, presented at random time, in a consistent temporal structure. The influence of temporal consistency of the signal on the quality of response was statistically positive. Schmidt (1968), in surveying the literature on anticipation and timing in human motor performance, pointed out that anticipation and timing can be learned and that temporal and spatial predictability of the response cues seems to be the most potent determiner for anticipation. Furthermore, temporally predictable stimuli in the auditory mode produced better response quality (Cross, 1966; Trumbo, Noble, & Swink, 1967) and shorter response times than did stimuli in the visual or tactile modes (Adams & Boulter, 1964).

Wilson reported that the reaction time was significantly faster for rhythmic signal presentation than for nonrhythmic presentation. These findings seem to reinforce the view on movement response patterns to rhythmic stimuli, as discussed in the section on neurophysiological research. The observed rhythmicity of motor neural potentiation to auditory rhythms seems to support the notion that an optimal movement response time can be achieved best in a rhythmic presentation of auditory stimuli.

In summary, it is apparent that the auditory presentation mode produces consistently faster reaction times and better response qualities than the visual, tactile, or combined auditory/visual presentations.

Rhythmic Speech as Internal Movement Control

A crucial aspect in motor therapy is the maintenance of improved motor function. The question is whether an individual can maintain the motor rhythm accuracy once the cue is removed, after having learned to adjust the respective motor performance to an auditory timing aid. In this regard, Luria's (1961) investigations about the role of speech in regulation of behavior patterns are of great importance.

Meichenbaum (1977) has used the verbal-instructional training via self-talk, based on Luria's theories, to modify behavior in hyperactive children. Cotton (1965, 1974) reported on the technique of "rhythmic intention," which uses chants to direct and control volitional movement patterns in cerebral palsied children.

In summary, rhythmic speech (e.g., in chant form) actually seems to serve two purposes in regard to movement control: (1) It regulates the desired motor behavior through either the initiating action of speech itself or through semantic connections between movement and verbal accompaniment, depending on the individual's developmental level; and (2) it regulates the timing of the movement, that is, the correct serial ordering and time relationship of the motor acts involved, through its rhythmic structure, which can be anticipated as regularly recurring information.

A Model of Rhythmic Auditory-Motor Integration

The following model is introduced to summarize the findings of the previous discussion (Figure 2–1). This model depicts the delinated research factors as possible constituents of a relationship between auditory rhythmic stimuli and motor rhythmicity in performance underlying auditory-motor coordination processes.

Auditory rhythmic signals as external stimuli can facilitate temporal muscular control of movement patterns by:

1. influencing timing and potentiation of motor neural discharge;
2. decreasing muscular fatigue sensation;
3. facilitating automatized movement performance through the temporal predictability of their timing cues;
4. improving reaction time and response quality through facilitated response anticipation.

Rhythmic speech as an internal stimulus can facilitate muscular control of movement patterns by:

1. verbally guiding the conscious initiation or intention of the movement as well as the actual movement performance;
2. providing a regularly recurring (rhythmic) time structure for the verbal cues, thus regulating the timing relationship between conscious (cortical) control mechanisms and muscular activity within each movement pattern.

PRACTICAL APPLICATIONS

Clarification of Motor Patterns Through Chanting and Visual Modeling

Rhythmic organization is most useful in motor patterns that consist of a series of discrete motor events performed in a continuous manner, as found in gait patterns, upper extremity exercises (clasping hands, extending elbows, rotating shoulders, and stretching arms in various directions), and alternating reciprocal limb patterns. The music therapist should design chants that describe movement patterns in simple nouns or action words and should talk through those chants when visually modeling and/or physically assisting the clients. These techniques are similar to those of "rhythmic imitation" and "rhythmic stabilization" as used in proprioceptive neuromuscular facilitation, a therapy approach in physical dysfunction (Knott & Voss, 1968).

Figure 2–1.

A Model of Rhythmic Auditory-Motor Integration

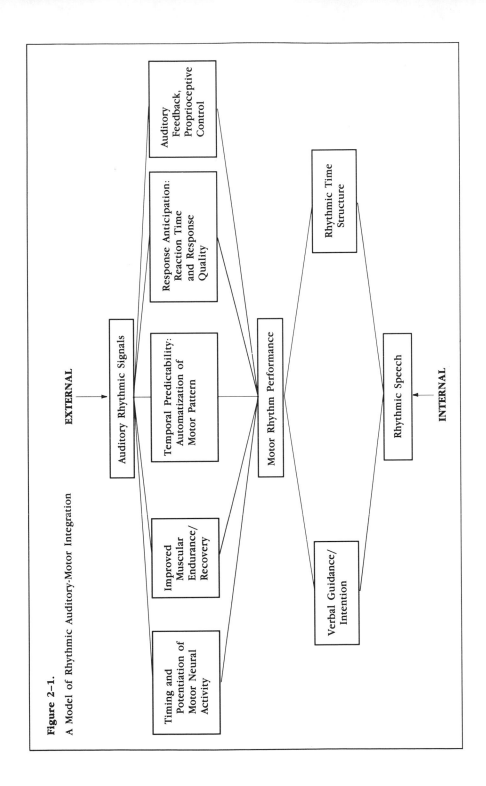

Use of Auditory Rhythm and Concurrent Rhythmic Chant to Make the Client Talk Through Motions

In a second step, the client should be encouraged to talk through the motions, with and without the therapist, without actually performing them. If the client is limited verbally, counting numbers may be used. In patients with certain brain lesions (e.g., left hemiplegic aphasic patients), a stronger emphasis on melodic components through singing instead of chanting might be a better rehearsal strategy (Lucia, 1987). The inclusion of a regularly recurring time structure for the movement pattern is important, even if the rhythmic distribution is not always even. The auditory rhythm should be provided from a live source so the therapist can adjust to performance variations. If the client plays music instruments that provide functional motor exercise, the auditory beat may be provided through the client's performance.

Synchronization of Speech and Stationary Gross Muscle Response Before Procedure to Locomotion

In order to learn to synchronize speech, external rhythm, and coincidental muscle response, one must proceed gradually through a system of levels, which facilitates the acquisition of skills from simple to more complex. Since locomotion requires a complex coordination of external and internal (proprioceptive) guidance and feedback systems in time and space, it is helpful to secure the rhythmic speech response as an internal guidance system first and integrate stationary muscle responses next before proceeding to locomotion.

Use of an Auditory Stimulus That Matches the Temporal Structure of the Motor Task

The rhythmic structure of the auditory stimulus should match exactly the temporal pattern of the movement. Intermediate accents on weak beats, elaborate melodies, and orchestration, which are often found in recorded instrumental pieces and songs, tend to confuse the desired auditory-motor match. Fully orchestrated pieces may be useful as background accompaniment to elicit unspecific movement responses. A simple rhythmic stimulus that clearly emphasizes and anticipates the beats on which motor responses are expected will facilitate the perceptual and synchronization process.

Rehearsal Strategies That Emphasize Coincident Motor Response to a Specific Timing Signal, One at a Time

It is evident from clinical experiences that successful rhythmic-based intervention techniques depend on rehearsal strategies to utilize rhythmic aids to their fullest potential. After rhythmic aids and motor response are introduced, it cannot be expected that the client will immediately be able to synchronize his motions to the external aids. The awareness of the external stimulus and the relationship between stimulus and response have to be taught, in a gradual process from multisensory modeling to increasingly independent functioning. Teaching the auditory-motor match is necessary for developing an internal template of a temporal motor plan. The plan will serve as a feedback system to guide the actual performance.

Use of High and Low Pitches to Match the Respective Space Levels of the Movement Sequence

Several other aspects of rhythmic stimuli can be used to accompany and guide desired movement. Often mentioned is pitch and melodic direction, which can illustrate space levels and spatial directions in movement patterns. For example, movements involving upward stretching may be accompanied by flowing ascending melodies, whereas the alternating of lower and upper limb movements may be accompanied by low and high pitched percussion instruments. However, it is important that these additional musical attributes only appear as long as required for the movement in question and do not diffuse the temporal structure of the rhythmic patterns.

The above-outlined principles have been documented in experimental studies or clinical reports for clients affected by head trauma and stroke, cerebral palsy, diffuse brain damage, and various motor problems best summarized by the term "minimal neural dysfunction" or "gross motor dysfunction." Crucial for clinical success in motor therapy is the creative and goal-oriented integration of music-based stimuli into functional rehabilitation exercises. On a more compensatory clinical level, or in less structured settings, the movement-activating and -regulating properties of music stimuli (especially rhythmic) may be still used, without emphasizing specific motor goals (e.g., facilitating and structuring movement experiences for psychiatric clients).

REFERENCES

Abeles, H. F. (1980). Responses to music. In D. A. Hodges (Ed.), *Handbook of music psychology* (pp. 105–140). Lawrence, KS: National Association for Music Therapy.

Adams, J. A., & Boulter, L. R. (1964). Spatial and temporal uncertainty as determiners of vigilance behavior. *Journal of Experimental Psychology, 67,* 127–131.

Adams, J. A., & Chambers, R. W. (1962). Response to simultaneous stimulation of two sense modalities. *Journal of Experimental Psychology, 63,* 198–206.

Adams, J., Marshall, P., & Goetz, E. (1974). The use of feedback in the reduction of foot dragging in a cerebral palsied patient. *Journal of Nervous and Mental Disease, 155,* 148–151.

Anshel, M., & Marisi, D. (1978). Effect of music and rhythm on physical performance. *Research Quarterly, 49,* 109–113.

Ax, A. F. (1957). The physiological differentiation between fear and anger in humans. *Psychosomatic Medicine, 15,* 433–442.

Basmajian, J. V. (Ed.). (1979). *Biofeedback—Principles and practice for clinicians.* Baltimore: Williams & Williams.

Berel, M., Diller, L., & Orgel, M. (1971). Music as a facilitator for visual motor sequencing in children with cerebral palsy. *Developmental Medicine and Child Neurology, 13,* 335–342.

Bond, M. H. (1950). Rhythm perception and gross motor performance. *Research Quarterly, 30,* 259–265.

Brickman, H. R. (1940). Psychiatric implications of functional music for education. *Music Educators Journal, 36,* 29–30.

Bushey, S. R. (1966). Relationship of modern dance performance to agility, balance, flexibility, and strength. *Research Quarterly, 37,* 313–316.

Clark, C. A., & Chadwick, D. M. (1980). *Clinically adopted instruments for the multiply handicapped. A sourcebook.* St. Louis: Magnamusic-Baton.

Cofrancesco, M. (1985). The effect of music therapy on hand grasp strength and functional task performance in stroke patients. *Journal of Music Therapy, 22,* 129–145.

Conrad, R. (1956). The timing of signals in skill. *Journal of Experimental Psychology, 51,* 365–270.

Cooper, J. M., & Glassow, R. B. (1982). *Kinesiology.* St. Louis: C. V. Mosby Co.

Cotton, E. (1974). Improvements in motor function with the use of conductive education. *Developmental Medicine and Child Neurology, 16,* 627–643.

Cotton, E. (1965). The institute for movement therapy and school of "conductors." Budapest, Hungary. *Developmental Medicine and Child Neurology, 7,* 437–446.

Cotton, E., & Parnwell, M. (1968). Conductive education with special reference to severe athetiod in a non-residential center. *British Journal of Mental Subnormality, 14,* 50–56.

Cross, K. (1966). *Discrete tracking proficiency as a function of temporal, directional, and spatial predictability.* Unpublished doctoral dissertation, Kansas State University.

Cross, P., McLellan, M., Vomberg, E., Monga, M., & Monga, T. (1984). Observations on the use of music in rehabilitation of stroke patients. *Physiotherapy Canada, 36,* 197–201.

Dainow, E. (1977). Physical effects and motor responses to music. *Journal of Research in Music Education, 25,* 211–221.

Diserens, C. M. (1923). Reactions to musical stimuli. *Psychological Bulletin, 20,* 183–199.

Farnan, L. A. (1984). Fine motor skills in music and adaptive instruments. In W. Latham and C. T. Eagle (Eds.), *Music therapy for handicapped children,* (pp. 96–101) Lawrence, KS: AMS Publishing.

Fields, B. (1954). Music as an adjunct in the treatment of brain damaged patients. *American Journal of Physical Medicine, 33,* 273–283.

Gaston, E. T. (1951). Dynamic music factors in mood change. *Music Educators Journal, 37,* 42–44.

Gault, R. H., & Goodfellow, L. D. (1938). An empirical comparison of audition, vision, and touch in the discrimination of temporal patterns and ability to reproduce them. *Journal of General Psychology, 18,* 41–42.

Goellnitz, G. (1975). Fundamentals of rhythmic psychomotor music therapy. *Acta Paedopsychiatrica, 41,* 130–134.

Haight, E. (1944). Individual difference in motor adaptations to rhythmic stimuli. *Research Quarterly, 15,* 38–43.

Harding, I. W. (1933). Rhythmization and speed work. *British Journal of Psychology, 23,* 262–278.

Harrer, G., & Harrer, H. (1977). Music, emotion, and autonomic function. In MacDonald Critchley and R. A. Henson (Eds.), *Music and the brain* (pp. 202–216). London: William Heinemann Medical Books.

Hernandez-Peon, R. (1961). The efferent control of afferent signals entering the central nervous system. *Annals of New York Academy of Science, 89,* 866–882.

Hodges, D. A. (Ed.) (1980). *Handbook of music psychology.* Lawrence, KS: National Association for Music Therapy.

Holdsworth, E. (1974). *Neuromuscular activity and covert musical psychomotor behavior: An electromyographic study.* Unpublished doctoral dissertation, University of Kansas.

Huff, J. (1972). Auditory and visual perception of rhythm by performers skilled in selected motor activities. *Research Quarterly, 43,* 197–207.

Jacobson, E. (1974). *Progressive relaxation.* Chicago: University of Chicago Press, Midway Reprint.

Knott, M., & Voss, D. E. (1968). *Proprioceptive neuromuscular facilitation.* New York: Harper & Row.

Lacey, J. I., & Lacey, B. C. (1970). Some autonomic-CNS interrelationships. In P. Black (Ed.), *Physiological correlates of emotion* (pp. 205–228). New York: Academic Press.

Lemon, E., & Sherbon, E. (1934). A study of the relationship of certain measures of rhythmic ability and motor ability in girls and women. *Research Quarterly, 5,* 82–85.

Lhamon, W. T., & Goldstone, S. (1974). Studies of auditory-visual differences in human time judgement: 2. More transmitted information with sounds than lights. *Perceptual and Motor Skills., 39,* 295–307.

Liemohn, W. P. & Knapczyk, D. (1947). Factor analysis of gross and fine motor ability in developmentally disabled children. *Research Quarterly, 45,* 424–432.

Lucia, C. (1987). Toward developing a model of music therapy intervention in the rehabilitation of head trauma patients. *Music Therapy Perspectives, 4,* 29–33.

Luria, A. R. (1961). *The role of speech in the regulation of normal and abnormal behavior.* London: Pergamon.

MacDougal, R. (1902). The relation of auditory rhythm to nervous discharge. *Psychological Review, 9,* 460–482.

Marteniuk, R. G. (1976). *Information processing in motor skills.* New York: Holt, Rinehart & Winston.

Meichenbaum, D. (1977). *Cognitive behavior modification: An integrative approach.* New York: Plenum Press.

Miller, K. (1979). *Treatment with music: A manual for allied health professionals.* Kalamazoo: Western Michigan University Printing.

Moss Rehabilitation Hospital, Settlement Music School, and Therapeutic Music Program (1982). *Guide to the selection of musical instruments with respect to physical ability and disability.* St. Louis: Magnamusic-Baton.

Nafpliotis, H. (1956). Electromyographic feedback to improve ankel dorsiflexion, wrist extension, and hand grasp. *Physical Therapy, 56,* 821–825.

Oleron, G., & Silver, S. E. (1963). Tension affective et effets dynamogniques dus à la musique. *Année Psychologique, 63,* 293–308.

Pal'tsev, Y. I., & El'ner, A. M. (1967). Change in the functional state of the segmental apparatus of the spinal chord under the influence of sound stimuli and its role in voluntary movements. *Biophysics, 12,* 1219–1226.

Patterson, C. H. (1959). *An experimental study of the effect of soothing background music on observed behavior indicating tension of third grade pupils.* Unpublished doctoral dissertation, University of Wisconsin.

Reardon, D. M., & Bell, G. (1971). Effects of sedative and stimulative music on activity levels of severely retarded boys. *American Journal of Mental Deficiency, 75,* 156–159.

Rieber, M. (1965). The effect of music on the activity level of children. *Psychonomic Science, 3,* 325–326.

Rosenbusch, M., & Gardner, D. (1968). Reproduction of visual and auditory rhythm patterns by children. *Perceptual and Motor Skills, 26,* 1271–1276.

Rossignol, S. (1971). Reaction of spinal motor neurons to musical sounds. *Proceedings XXV International Physics Congress IX,* abstract 480.

Rossignol, S., & Jones, G. (1976). Audio-spinal influence in man studied by the H-reflex and its possible role on rhythmic movements synchronized to sound. *Electroencephalography and Clinical Neurophysiology, 41,* 83–92.

Safranek, M., Koshland, G., & Raymond, G. (1982). Effect of auditory rhythm on muscle activity. *Physical Therapy, 62,* 161–168.

Sage, G. (1977). *Introduction to motor behavior: A neuropsychological approach.* Reading, MA: Addison-Wesley.

Scartelli, J. (1982). The effect of sedative music on electromyographic biofeedback assisted relaxation training of spastic cerebral palsied adults. *Journal of Music Therapy, 19,* 210–218.

Schachter, J. (1957). Pain, fear, and anger in hypertensive normotensives. *Psychosomatic Medicine, 19,* 17–29.

Schachter, S. (1964). The interaction of cognitive and physiologic determinants of emotional states. *Advances in Experimental Social Psychology, 1,* 49–80.

Schmidt, R. (1968). Anticipation and timing in human motor performance. *Psychological Bulletin, 70,* 631–646.

Schwanda, N. (1969). A study of rhythmic ability and movement performance. *Research Quarterly, 40,* 567–574.

Sears, W. W. (1952). Postural responses to recorded music. In E. G. Gilliland (Ed.), *Music therapy 1951* (pp. 197–198). Chicago: Allen Press.

Sears, W. W. (1958). The effect of music on muscle tonus. In E. G. Gaston (Ed.), *Music therapy 1957* (pp. 199–205). Lawrence, KS: Allen Press.

Sears, W. W. (1960). *A study of some effects on music upon muscle tension as evidenced by electromyographic recordings.* Unpublished doctoral dissertation, University of Kansas.

Shatin, L. (1957). The influence of rhythmic drumbeat stimuli upon the pulse rate and general activity of long-term schizophrenics. *Journal of Mental Science, 103,* 172–188.

Singer, R. (1980). *Motor learning and human performance.* New York: Macmillan.

Smith, O. W. (1957). Relationship of rhythm discrimination to motor rhythm performance. *Journal of Applied Psychology, 41,* 365–269.

Spearing, D., & Poppen, R. (1974). Response feedback and short-term motor retention. *Journal of Experimental Psychology, 92,* 82–95.

Standley, J. (1986). Music research in medical/dental treatment: Meta-analysis and clinical applications. *Journal of Music Therapy, 23,* 56–122.

Staum, J. (1983). Music and rhythmic stimuli in the rehabilitation of gait disorders. *Journal of Music Therapy, 20,* 69–87.

Stevens, E. A. (1971). Some effects of tempo changes on stereotyped rocking movements of low-level mentally retarded subjects. *American Journal of Mental Deficiency, 76,* 76–81.

Stratton, V. N., & Zalanowski, A. (1984). The effect of background music on verbal interaction in groups. *Journal of Music Therapy, 21,* 16–26.

Stull, A., & Kearney, J. (1974). Recovery of muscular endurance following rhythmic or sustained activity. *Journal of Motor Behavior, 6,* 59–66.

Sutton, K. (1984). The development and implementation of a music therapy physiological measures test. *Journal of Music Therapy, 21,* 160–169.

Thaut, M. H. (1983). *The use of auditory rhythm and rhythmic speech to aid temporal and quantitative muscular control in children with gross motor dysfunction.* Unpublished doctoral dissertation, Michigan State University.

Thomas, J. R., & Moon, D. H. (1976). Measuring motor rhythmic ability in children. *Research Quarterly, 47,* 20–32.

Trumbo, D., Noble, M., & Swink, J. (1967). Secondary task interference in the performance of tracking tasks. *Journal of Experimental Psychology, 73,* 232–240.

Weld, H. P. (1912). An experimental study of musical enjoyment. *American Journal of Psychology, 23,* 245–308.

Widdop, H. H. (1968). Effect of a ballet training program upon the physical performance of college freshman. *Research Quarterly, 39,* 752–754.

Wilson, D. (1959). Quickness of reaction and movement related to rhythmicity as nonrhythmicity of signal presentation. *Research Quarterly, 30,* 101–109.

Wolfe, D. E. (1980). The effect of automated interrupted music on head posturing of cerebral palsied individuals. *Journal of Music Therapy, 17,* 184–206.

Wolpe, J. (1965). *The practice of behavior therapy.* New York: Pergamon Press.

Woodrow, H. (1951). Time perception. In S. S. Stevens (Ed.), *Handbook of experimental psychology* (pp. 1224–1236). New York: Wiley.

Chapter 3

Music As Communication

Kate E. Gfeller

Despite the fact that musical sounds have no specific designative meaning, music has long been considered a form of communication. This belief is supported by psychologists and neurologists as well as musicians. For example, Pribram (1982) describes music as a language-like form by which humans express themselves and communicate with each other. Berlyne (1971, p. 59) states "if a work of art can be regarded as a system of symbols, we can go farther and conclude that art fulfills the additional criteria for being classed as communication." According to Kreitler and Kreitler (1972), there exists the broad assumption that a work of art is a vehicle for communicating meaning.

Communication of meaning is not a function of the stimulus or message alone. Rather, meaning comes from a relationship between the symbol, that to which it points, and the common observer (Meyer, 1956). A symbol must have similar meaning for both the originator and the recipient (Berlyne, 1971). Like speech, much of musical meaning is a function of cultural context. As a result, music of unfamiliar style may transmit little meaning to the listener.

Music as a form of auditory information is often compared to speech and language. Both are species specific, yet they differ greatly in function. One might question human need for two auditory forms of communication, especially since music appears to be unnecessary for existence (Roederer, 1982). Some scholars have taken an anthropological-historical approach to this question by examining the origins of music and speech.

MUSIC AND SPEECH

Although the study of music in primitive societies offers some insight into the origins of speech and music, the evolution of the two systems is primarily a matter of conjecture (Radocy & Boyle, 1979). Among those proposed explanations are Darwin's theory linking music to sexual instinct and mating and Nettl's theory of impassioned speech (1956). In this theory, music accentuates speech intonation during emotional expression.

It has also been suggested that early cultures used an undifferentiated method of communication that was neither speech nor music, but had common attributes of pitch, stress, and duration. According to Nettl (1975), language acquired words and consonants, while music acquired fixed pitches through gradual differentiation and specialization.

Bernstein (1976) suggests that initial auditory communication was sung. Pribram (1982) supports this view, noting that vocalization of nonhuman primates are essentially changes in pitch and duration while articulation is a characteristically human ability.

Although the evolution of speech and music remains a matter of speculation, obvious parallels and differences exist today in terms of syntax, semantics, and social context. Both language and music are forms of communication processed by the auditory system. Both systems have structural similarities in terms of pitch, duration, stress, and even listener expectations. In both, we are able to perceive (1) mistakes in content or structure, or (2) humorous intent as a result of learning and enculturation. These similarities have sparked the interest of linguists, musicologists, and psychologists alike.

In his published lecture series, "The Unanswered Question" (1976), Leonard Bernstein draws parallels between syntactical structure of music and language, based on linguist Noam Chomsky's model of surface and deep structure in language. This parallel has received mixed acceptance. For example, psychologist Diana Deutsch (1979) maintains that no fair comparison exists between music and the basic elements of speech, such as nouns and verbs. Further, music, unlike speech, does not refer to specific thoughts, ideas or events; rather it communicates embodied meaning (Deutsch, 1979; Benson, 1979).

In contrast, other scholars see comparison of language and music as productive (Campbell & Heller, 1981; Day, 1979), but suggest that past efforts may have failed as a result of invalid comparisons. For example, Campbell and Heller (1981) argue that conversation cannot be meaningfully compared to a musical performance.

For all the structural similarities that do exist (including a multitude of subfunctions within each system [Borchgrevink, 1982]), important differences remain that contribute to music's unique role within the therapeutic process. One difference is the prominence of pragmatic features such as variation and redundancy, which Pribram (1982) maintains is the key to meaning in music. Variations on musical patterns evoke dishabituation, while repetition results in habituation and recognition. These responses are associated with visceroautonomic responses and generation of feelings. According to Lathom (1971), the redundancy of music may also aid communication of clients whose verbal interactions have broken down.

Another feature of musical communication is its lack of dependence on rational or intellectual response. Altshuler, in describing the therapeutic uses of music states that music "offers the advantage of encountering few or no intellectual barriers, as words do" (1956, p. 120). Similarly Berlyne (1971) suggests that to some extent, appreciation of art may result from a privileged situation in which pressure from reason and rational thought is alleviated.

This reduction of rational response has therapeutic implications for those clients with limited intellectual capacity. Perhaps the most notable difference, however, is lack of referential meaning in music.

NONREFERENTIAL MEANING

Unlike words in language, musical pitches do not denote or refer to the extramusical world in a specific fashion (Meyer, 1956; Winner, 1982). The nondiscursive symbols in music are abstract in nature and not readily translatable (Kreitler & Kreitler, 1972; Winner, 1982). How then, is it possible for music to convey meaning without explicit denotation?

Scholars have long described what is called intrinsic or embodied meaning in music, which is derived from internal reference or intramusical organization. This embodied meaning is a function of our knowledge of musical style and expectations based on past listening experience (Winner, 1982; Meyer, 1956). This intramusical organization, while limited in referential semantics, is rich in meaning derived from pragmatic procedures (Pribram, 1982). Pragmatic procedures are based on structural qualities such as repetition, redundancy, variation, and deletions, which activate recognition, habituation, and dishabituation (Pribram, 1982).

While emphasis on internal structure may explain how music can convey meaning, the question still remains why an informational system unnecessary for survival is found in every culture known to man. In part, music's value emanates from its ability to "express the forms of vital experience which language is peculiarly unfit to convey" (Langer, 1953, p. 32). A loss of words in particularly poignant moments is not an uncommon phenomenon, even for the verbally eloquent. According to Gaston (1968), there would be no need for music if it were possible to communicate verbally that which is easily communicated musically.

Perhaps one of the reasons music, a nondiscursive form of communication, is cherished as unique and valuable is due to its common association with emotional response. Music, often referred to as the language of emotions (Winner, 1982), is commonly credited with the ability to evoke emotional response (Winner, 1982; Pribram, 1982; Meyer, 1956; Haack, 1980).

A number of studies (Smith & Morris, 1976; McFarland, 1984, 1985; Biller, Olson & Breen, 1974; Greenberg & Fisher, 1966; Fisher & Greenberg, 1972; Jellison, 1975; Elam, 1971) have examined how music influences affective response by comparing the effects of contrasting styles categorized through general descriptors such as stimulative, sedative, calming, or aversive. These studies have used both verbal report and physiological measures to indicate emotional response. While the data are not always consistent concerning what type of music will produce particular effects, it would appear that such contrasts in music do indeed influence mood (Abeles, 1980).

Fried and Berkowitz (1979) found that soothing or aversive music could significantly alter not only subject mood. They also found that subjects who have listened to "soothing," pleasant music showed significantly greater instances of helpful behaviors directly following the listening experience than did subjects who had been exposed to aversive music.

These studies suggest that music, even without explicitly referential content, communicates some type of information to the listener that influences human behavior. It is important to keep in mind, however, that the relationship between music and affective response is not a simple one of cause and effect.

A number of research studies (Cantor & Zillman, 1973; Wheeler, 1975; Eagle, 1971; Shantin, 1970; Fisher & Greenberg, 1972; Sopchak, 1955; O'Briant & Wilbanks, 1978) have investigated the influence of listener characteristics on musical response. In particular, these studies have examined the effect of prior mood and taste or preference on affective response to music. With the exception of the research by O'Briant & Wilbanks (1978), these studies have all supported Farnsworth's (1969) view that mood response to music is dependent upon many factors in addition to musical form, including the listener's mood set and attitude toward the music.

Given the ability of music both to influence and be influenced by the individual listener's mood, the skilled therapist can use music not only to evoke affective response and explore those emotions elicited through musical stimulus. It would also appear that the music can be utilized as a "canvas" upon which the client's prior feelings and attitudes are conveyed.

To what extent can the music therapist actually manipulate musical communication in order to focus on particular emotions relevant to the client's treatment? According to Winner (1982), listeners show remarkable agreement in categorizing music according to emotional labels. Studies by Trunk (1981) and Slattery (1984) note perception of emotional content in music occurring as early as the age of five. Greater accuracy and consistency of identification develop with increased age (Trunk, 1981). These findings are consistent with Roederer's (1982) belief that training and early exposure to culture-specific music shapes emotional response.

While perception of emotional content in music can certainly be attributed to training and enculturation, according to Nielzen and Cesarec (1981, 1982b), structural elements within the music itself play a crucial role in effectively transmitting emotional messages. These structural elements, though nonreferential, convey symbolic information and have the potential to evoke manifold meaning and flexible connotation.

MUSIC AS A SYMBOL

Unlike signs, which have relatively specific references, symbols evoke less specified and more subjective meaning (Kreitler & Kreitler, 1972). As an aesthetic and symbolic form, music transcends verbal expression and may evoke feelings.

According to Berlyne (1974), aesthetic objects are regarded as collections of symbols and are distinguished by two characteristics: (1) iconic properties, and (2) ability to communicate value properties. Symbols function in three ways to communicate values (Kreitler & Kreitler, 1972): (1) unification, or the unifying of discreet entities (such as man and nature, or man and society); (2) revelations, or reality revealed in deeper layers beyond logic; and (3) facilitating adaptation to reality, helping man to understand, interpret, organize, and universalize the human experience. All of these functions relieve tension through environmental orientation. While symbolism may be less easily accomplished in music than in visual art (Merriam, 1964), auditory patterns can take on symbolic meaning through association by contiguity, cultural convention, and iconic properties (Berlyne, 1971; Meyer, 1956).

Association By Contiguity

In some instances, musical materials and their organization become linked through repetition to a referential image. Over repeated encounters, connotations become habitual and automatic. Radocy and Boyle (1979) refer to this as the "Darling, they're playing our song" phenomenon in which a particular selection or style of music, through classical conditioning, becomes associated with a particular feeling. According to Roederer (1982), even a partial reinactment of neural activity that occurred during the storage act suffices to release strong associative recall.

Associative recall has potential within the therapeutic setting in a number of ways. One example is the use of familiar musical materials in reminiscence by geriatric or terminally ill patients (Bright, 1981; Munro, 1984). Reminiscence of important past events has been recommended as a therapeutic method for helping the elderly to review life events, to heighten awareness of past accomplishments, and to facilitate social interaction. Through associative recall, the music therapist can help the clients to access long forgotten events within their lives. The recalling of significant events may also be effective in psychiatric care in which the client is encouraged to work through past events and feelings.

Association by contiguity tends to be an individual response based on a personal experience. However, many musical themes and symbols are common to an entire culture, not just to an individual. Certain patriotic or religious musical themes, for example, have particular connotations that are based on cultural convention rather than classical conditioning.

Cultural Conventions

Just as verbal interaction becomes conventionalized so that people may communicate more effectively, so also does musical communication of mood and sentiments become conventionalized through standardized musical devices (Meyer, 1956). In Western music, for example, certain scales, harmonies, or timbres symbolize particular states of being (Merriam, 1964). Merriam cites television or film scores as the obvious example of how music evokes desired emotions through certain musical clichés. These connotations shared by a group of individuals within a culture are powerful factors in communicating symbolic meaning. Within the therapeutic process, the music therapist can take advantage of this factor, facilitating group cohesiveness or relative unity of response by presenting particular selections or a musical style that generally connotes a shared meaning (Plach, 1980). Some of these cultural conventions result in part from what Berlyne (1971) calls iconicity.

Iconicity

Iconicity implies similarity between auditory characteristics and some referential event, feeling, or idea. This is similar to the Gestalt idea of physiognomics, in which physical properties of the art object possess patterns similar to physical features (especially facial features) associated with particular emotions. Other examples of iconic meaning might be the use of particular auditory patterns that mimic a particular quality of sound in nature (e.g., sound of wind or birds) (Meyer, 1956; Roederer, 1982). For example, iconicity can facilitate motor activities in young children. The therapist may select music with specific characteristics such as slow, plodding music to represent the movement of elephants, or melodically and rhythmically disjunct music to encourage hopping movements.

No matter how symbolic meaning is derived, it gives music communicative potential within the therapeutic context. According to Kreitler and Kreitler (1972),

> confrontation with symbolic expression may give rise to insights which enable the individual to transcend the suffering, embarrassment, and dangers of specific situations ... [symbols] deal with problems of universal human significance, ranging from life and love to suffering and the fear of death. (pp. 323–324).

The extent of association, cultural convention, and iconic properties within music can, to greater or lesser extent, affect specific connotations from auditory stimuli. Despite these guiding factors, music still remains nonspecific in meaning. Ultimately, it is the listener who establishes meaning, based on cultural and individual experiences (Meyer, 1956).

This nonreferential abstraction allows for multiple organization and multidimensional meaning (Kreitler & Kreitler, 1972). According to Kreitler and Kreitler, works of art can be grasped, elaborated, and experienced in several systems of connected potential meaning. Aesthetic objects' capacity for more than one interpretation contributes to richness of meaning as well as wide appeal, thus providing a fusion between the general and specific meaning.

Berlyne (1971) believes that this ambiguity of meaning within art impels perceptual and intellectual effort of a pleasurable nature.

The multilevel meanings of art allow the observer to shift points of view, exchange one frame of reference for another, shift perceptual organization, or even attempt integration, viewing levels simultaneously (Kreitler & Kreitler, 1972). Shifting from one level to another has certain motivating factors. First, it overcomes a tendency toward satiation and subsequent lack of interest in the object. Second, there is the expectation that another level in a work of art may engage unresolved problems untouched on previous experience levels. Third, the most comprehensive level may provide the individual with significant and personal insights and suggestions, as well as new questions and answers to personal needs and problems (Kreitler & Krietler, 1972). In short, although music cannot specify and particularize connotations, it carries flexibility of connotation, including multiple meanings that allow the individual to view the human experience with unique insights (Meyer, 1956).

MUSIC IN CONJUNCTION WITH OTHER FORMS OF COMMUNICATION

While music stands alone as communication, it is often paired with poetry, prose, or art in serious and popular music as well as in advertising and other media. Historically, music has been utilized to intensify the emotional content or text of the art form with which it is paired. Consider, for instance, music reservata, text painting, and other techniques in which musical patterns reflect textual material. Early opera composers embarked upon this new musical form in part as an attempt to intensify the emotional impact of the libretto (Kamien, 1984). The practice of pairing music with other art forms is ubiquitous in contemporary music and musical theater as well. Is this phenomenon a matter of historical tradition alone, or is there some empirical basis for it?

In a number of studies, experimenters have investigated simultaneous processing of music and speech, with inconclusive results. Interpretation is no doubt complicated by the many variables that influence outcome. These include the subject's level of musical training, the type of verbal and musical stimuli, and the experimental methodology itself. Several explanations have been offered for simultaneous processing of speech and music.

Reineke (1981) hypothesizes that separate information-processing systems may be used for music and speech. Roederer (1982) believes that hemispheric specialization, (dominance of left- or right-brain hemisphere), while not absolute, is related to different processing strategies used for music and speech. Holistic analysis, so prominent in music, is a function of the right hemisphere while sequential processing takes place in the language (left) hemisphere.

Contrasting music and speech, Pribram (1982) describes language as primarily referential (i.e., semantic), and music as primarily evocative (i.e., pragmatic). He believes that referential and evocative types of information are subject to different types of neurological processing. Pribram explains this difference in the following way:

> Despite the severely limited information processing and resulting referential semantics, music is rich in meaning. This meaning is derived from pragmatic procedures which also enrich natural language, especially in their poetic usages. Pragmatic procedures are based on repetition, on variation of repetition, and on deletion of expected repetitions. It is the processes such as these which have been shown to be functions of the fronto-limbic formation of the forebrain generally thought to be involved in generation and control of feelings. (1982, p. 31).

Roederer (1982) suggests that elicitation of limbic function by the abstract sounds of music contributes to our emotional response to music. One might hypothesize that there is a neurological explanation for the historical practice of using music to intensify emotional content of other forms of communication. The music brings to the textual or visual information additional meaning of a feelingful nature.

Several empirical studies have investigated the result when visual and verbal communication is embedded in a musical setting. McFarland (1984) found that subject interpretations of ambiguous TAT pictures were significantly different in emotional content, depending on whether the listener heard tension-producing or calming music or no music. He found that subjects who listened to tension-producing music interpreted the picture with emotional reports of anxiety and frustration. In contrast, music categorized as calming tended to reduce negative effects expressed in response to the picture. Thus it would appear that music can either intensify or reduce affective response to visual information, depending upon the matching of emotional content of the music and visual stimulus.

A similar relationship between music and visual and verbal information was found by Wintle (1978) in his study of the emotional impact of music on television commercials. Wintle found that supporting background music routinely intensified the qualities (i.e., level of activity, pleasantness, or potency) positively characterized by a commercial, while "counteracting" background music diminished in intensity that quality that the commercial positively characterized.

In a study examining the effects of music on response to a film, Thayer and Levenson (1963) paired either "horror" music or more neutral "documentary" music with a stressful film. Both the physiological measures (autonomic responses) and the psychological measures (self-report) indicated that the contrasting musical styles were successful both in increasing reported distress (horror music) and in decreasing reported distress (documentary music). The authors hypothesized that the intensification resulting from the "horror" music was more than conditioned response to "stereotypic" music. They proposed that the music also provided the subjects with an effective auditory cue that helped them anticipate the period of threat within the film.

These studies suggest that music can intensify or alter emotional response to visual and verbal stimuli. A study by Parrott (1982) describes the effect of music on emotional response to paintings as essentially additive, depending upon the "goodness/badness" of the match between the music and the painting. Parrott found that emotional judgments of the music were influenced more strongly by the painting (particularly those paintings of a complex nature) than the music influenced judgments of the paintings. Therefore the interaction of two forms of communication may vary, depending on factors such as complexity and type of information.

Alteration or augmentation of emotional arousal is not the only psychological effect of music. Galizio and Hendrick (1972) agree that musical embedding of a verbal message can increase emotional arousal. However, the authors also found that instrumental accompaniment to the textual information resulted in significantly greater persuasion or acceptance of the message. It is interesting to note that a sung version of the text did not have the same impact as the instrumental accompaniment.

These studies indicate that music can, in some instances, alter or intensify the psychological and behavioral response to verbal and visual forms of communication. Either textual or visual media is commonly used in such therapeutic activities as lyric analysis, song writing, or combined media activities; therefore, this intensification has important implications for music therapy if the therapeutic intent includes focusing on, or increasing awareness of affective material.

These studies represent music as a form of communication (1) capable of transmitting emotional messages; (2) able to influence or reflect the mood of an individual; and (3) usable as a vehicle for intensification, amplification, or alteration of meaning of imbedded textual or visual information. As a result, music makes an effective tool for evoking or reflecting emotional response, identifying or heightening emotional awareness, and expressing or reflecting themes relevant to group processes.

Can the therapist assume that music will carry a similar message to psychiatric patients who suffer from disordered thought and affect? While the literature describing emotional effects of music in psychopathological states shows scattered and often imprecise results (Nielzen & Cesarec, 1982c), there are two primary viewpoints: (1) that the experience of music is comparable to that of normal subjects, and (2) that the musical experience is affected by the psychopathological state.

Studies by Biller (1973) and Giacobbe (1973) support the view that music conveys emotional meaning with some uniformity to both psychiatric patients and normal subjects. In addition, Biller noted a significant relationship between preferred music and the stated emotional mood for both groups. This finding is reminiscent of the iso-principle (Altschuler, 1948), well known in music therapy literature.

In examining the effects of pathological processes, Steinberg and Raith (1985) hypothesized that psychomotor differences resulting from depressive disorders may be identified through perception of musical tempo as measured through a motor task. The authors concluded that tempo perception (called intraindividual tempo) was stable not only in healthy people, but also in the greater majority of mentally disturbed patients.

In contrast, studies by Nielzen and Cesarec (1982a, 1982c) indicate some difference in emotional experience of music between mentally disturbed and nonhandicapped individuals. However, the authors point out that while the identifiable trends by diagnostic category tend to be weak, contrasting characteristic responses are presumed to be more apparent among subjects of differing diagnostic categories than when psychiatric patients are compared with normal subjects. These studies give little reason to assume that music communicates highly unusual or deviant emotional content for the mentally disturbed patient. Music appears to act as a viable form of communication, even for persons with psychological disorders.

SUMMARY

Music, while nondiscursive, does indeed transmit information, including emotional messages. Through association by contiguity, cultural convention, and structural properties (i.e., iconicity), it functions as a symbol capable of evoking feelings. Music's nonreferential nature renders it capable of manifold meaning and flexibility.

As a nondiscursive language, music transcends intellectual, rational thought and communicates readily through high levels of redundancy. It communicates human needs and values when words no longer suffice.

Because music can reflect, influence, and alter emotional response, it has particular merit as a therapeutic tool in those treatment processes that include identification, awareness, reflection, or expression of feelings and relevant issues. The ease with which music can be used in conjunction with textual or visual information further contributes to its value as a highly flexible therapeutic vehicle.

Naturally, the effectiveness of this therapeutic tool is dependent upon the skill of the music therapist. Within the context of music therapy processes such as song writing, improvisation, or lyric analysis, the therapist must manipulate this unique communicative form in a manner consistent with identified therapeutic goals, and be sensitive to the cultural and individual characteristics of the client.

REFERENCES

Abeles, H. F. (1980). Responses to music. In D. Hodges (Ed.), *Handbook of music psychology* (pp. 105–140). Lawrence, KS: National Association for Music Therapy.

Altshuler, I. M. (1948). A psychiatrist's experiences with music as a therapeutic agent. In D. Schullian and M. Schoen (Eds.), *Music and medicine* (pp. 266–281). New York: Henry Schuman.

Altshuler, I. M. (1956). Music potentiating drugs. In E. T. Gaston (Ed.), *Music therapy 1955*. Lawrence, KS: National Association for Music Therapy, 120–126.

Benson, W. (1979). Cited in Language and music as communication: A discussion. *Music Educators Journal, 65,* 68–71.

Berlyne, D. E. (1974). *Studies in the new experimental aesthetics.* New York: Wiley.

Bernstein, L. (1976). *The unanswered question: Six talks at Harvard.* Cambridge, MA: Harvard University Press.

Biller, O. A. (1973). *Communication of emotions through instrumental music and the music selection preferences of patients and nonpatients experiencing various emotional moods.* Unpublished doctoral dissertation, University of Arkansas.

Borchgrevink, H. M. (1982). Prosody and musical rhythm are controlled by the speech hemisphere. In M. Clynes, (Ed.), *Music, mind, and brain* (pp. 151–158). New York: Plenum Press.

Bright, R. (1981). *Practical planning in music therapy for the aged.* Lynbrook, NY: Musicgraphics.

Campbell, W., & Heller, J. (1981). Psychomusicology & psycholinguistics: Parallel paths or separate ways. *Psychomusicology, 2*(2), 3–14.

Campbell, I. G. (1942). Basal emotional patterns expressible in music. *American Journal of Psychology, 55*(1), 1–17.

Cantor, J. R., & Zillman, D. (1973). The effect of affective state and emotional arousal on music appreciation. *Journal of General Psychology, 89*(1), 97–108.

Day, R. (1979). Language and music as communication: A discussion. *Music Educators Journal, 65,* 68–71.

Deutsch, D. (1979). Language and music as communication: A discussion. *Music Educators Journal, 65,* 68–71.

Elam, R. W. (1971). *Mechanism of music as an emotional intensification stimulus.* Unpublished doctoral dissertation, University of Cincinnati.

Farnsworth, P. R. (1969). *The social psychology of music* (2nd ed.). Ames, IA: Iowa State University Press.

Fisher, S., & Greenberg, R. P. (1972). Selective effects upon women of exciting and calm music. *Perceptual and Motor Skills, 34,* 987–990.

Fried, R., & Berkowitz, L. (1979). Music hath charms . . . and can influence helpfulness. *Journal of Applied Social Psychology, 9*(3), 199–208.

Galizio, M., & Hendrick, C. (1972). Effect of musical accompaniment on attitude: The guitar as a prop for persuasion. *Journal of Applied Social Psychology, 2*(4), 350–359.

Gaston, E. T. (1968). (Ed.) *Music in therapy.* New York: Macmillan.

Giacobbe, G. A. (1973). *The response of aggressive emotionally disturbed and normal boys to selected musical stimuli.* Doctoral disseration, University of Georgia, Athens.

Greenberg, R. P., & Fisher, S. (1966). Some differential effects of music on projective and structured psychological tests. *Psychological Reports, 28,* 817–820.

Haack, P. (1980). The behavior of music listeners. In D. Hodges (Ed.), *Handbook of music psychology* (pp. 148–150). Lawrence, KS: National Association for Music Therapy.

Jellison, J. (1975). The effect of music on autonomic stress responses and verbal reports. In C. K. Madsen, R. Greer, and C. H. Madsen (Eds.), *Research in music behavior: Modifying music behavior in the classroom.* New York: Teachers College Press.

Kreitler, H., & Kreitler, S. (1972). *Psychology of the arts.* Durham, NC: Duke University Press.

Langer, S. (1942). *Philosophy in a new key.* New York: Mentor Books.

Lathom, W. (1971). Concepts of information theory and their relationship to music therapy. *Journal of Music Therapy, 13*(3), 111–116.

McFarland, R. A. (1984). Effects of music upon emotional content of TAT stories. *Journal of Psychology, 116*(2), 227–234.

McFarland, R. A. (1985). Relationship of skin temperature changes to the emotions accompanying music. *Biofeedback and Self Regulation, 10*(3), 255–267.

Merriam, A. P. (1964). *The anthropology of music.* Evanston, IL: Northwestern University Press.

Meyer, L. B. (1956). *Emotion and meaning in music.* Chicago: University of Chicago Press.

Munro, S. (1984). *Music therapy in palliative/hospice care.* St. Louis: Magnamusic-Baton.

Nettl, B. (1956). *Music in primitive culture.* Cambridge, MA: Harvard University Press.

Nettl, B. (1975). Music in primitive cultures: Iran, a recently developed nation. In Hamm, C., Nettl, B., & Byrnside, R., *Contemporary music and music cultures.* Englewood Cliffs, NJ: Prentice-Hall.

Nielzen, S., & Cesarec, Z. (1981). On the perception of emotional meaning in music. *Psychology of Music, 9*(2), 17–31.

Nielzen, S., & Cesarec, Z. (1982a). Aspects of tempo and perception of music in mania. *Psychology of Music, 10*(2), 81–85.

Nielzen, S., & Cesarec, Z. (1982b). Emotional experience of music as a function of musical structure. *Psychology of Music, 10*(2), 7–17.

Nielzen, S., & Cesarec, Z. (1982c). The effect of mental illness on the emotional experience of music. *Archiv fur Psychiatric und Nervenkrankheiten, 231*(6), 527–538.

O'Briant, M. P., & Wilbanks, W. A. (1978). The effect of context on the perception of music. *Bulletin of the Psychonomic Society, 12*(6), 441–443.

Parrott, A. C. (1982). Effects of paintings and music, both alone and in combination, on emotional judgements. *Perception and Motor Skills, 54*(2), 635–641.

Plach, T. (1980). *The creative use of music in group therapy.* Springfield, IL: Charles C. Thomas.

Pribram, K. H. (1982). Brain mechanism in music: Prolegomena for a theory of the meaning of meaning. In M. Clynes (Ed.). *Music, mind, and brain* (pp. 21–36). New York: Plenum Press.

Radocy, R., & Boyle, D. (1979). *Psychological foundations of musical behavior.* Springfield, IL: Charles C. Thomas.

Reineke, T. (1981). Simultaneous processing of music and speech. *Psychomusicology, 1*(1), 58–77.

Roederer, J. G. (1982). Physical and neuropsychological foundations of music. In M. Clynes (Ed.). *Music, mind, and brain* (pp. 37–48). New York: Plenum Press.

Shatin, L. (1970). Alteration of mood via music. A study of the vectoring effect. *Journal of Psychology, 75,* 81–86.

Slattery, W. S. (1985). *The effect of music and visuals on mood agreement under cue summation and channel interference conditions.* Unpublished doctoral dissertation, Boston University.

Smith, C. A., & Morris, L. W. (1976). Effects of stimulative and sedative music on cognitive and emotional components of anxiety. *Psychological Reports, 38*(3, Pt. 2), 1187–1183.

Sopchak, A. L. (1955). Individual differences in responses to music. *Psychology Monograph, 69*(11), 1–20.

Steinberg, R., & Raith, L. (1985). Music psychopathology: I-Musical tempo and psychiatric disease. *Psychopathology, 18*(5-6), 245–264.

Thayer, J. F., & Levenson, R. W. (1983). Effects of music on psychophysiological responses to a stressful film. *Psychomusicology, 3*(1), 44–52.

Trunk, B. (1982). *Children's perception of the emotional content of music.* Unpublished doctoral dissertation, Ohio State University, Columbus.

Wheeler, B. L. (1985). Relationship of personal characteristics to mood and enjoyment after hearing live and recorded music and to musical taste. *Psychology of Music, 13*(2), 81–92.

Winner, E. (1982). *Invented Worlds.* Cambridge, MA: Harvard University Press.

Wintle, R. R. (1978). *Emotional impact of music on television commercials.* Unpublished doctoral dissertation, University of Nebraska, Lincoln.

Chapter 4

Cultural Context As It Relates to Music Therapy

Kate E. Gfeller

Scholars from many disciplines, including anthropology, psychology, musicology, and physiology, have long questioned why music, which has no apparent survival value, should have remained in our behavioral repertoire for thousands of years (Hodges, 1980; Winner, 1982). Music's presence in every culture known to man suggests strongly that it grows out of some fundamental neurological process (Berlyne, 1971; Hodges, 1980; Merriam, 1964; Nettl, 1956b; Sloboda, 1985). Physiological investigation alone, however, does not fully explain the ubiquity of music in our lives; we are not simply passive respondents to auditory signals. As humans, we are "symbolizing, culture bearing, historical creatures who act in a frame of past and future, who can make sense or nonsense to themselves" (Smith, 1978, p. 33). Even our perceptual and cognitive processes are influenced by culturally laden beliefs and expectations (Meyer, 156b; Kreitler & Kreitler, 1972). This chapter will discuss music's function as a therapeutic agent from a historic perspective and within the cultural context of preliterate and industrialized societies.

THE PAST: A HISTORICAL VIEWPOINT

From records of early civilizations, we know that music has been attributed with power over physical and mental well-being. In ancient Egypt, priest physicians referred to music as "the physics of the soul," and included chant-therapies as part of medical practice (Feder & Feder, 1981). We also find Biblical references to music's soothing properties, and treatise of its influence on health and morality in ancient China (Tame, 1984).

Music was considered a special force over thought, emotion, and physical health in ancient Greece. In 600 B.C. Thales was believed to have cured a plague in Sparta through musical powers (Merriam, 1964). Healing shrines and temples included hymn specialists, and even then music was prescribed for the emotionally disturbed (Feder & Feder, 1981). This use of music for curing mental disorders reflects the belief that music could directly produce emotion and form character. Among the notables of Greece who subscribed to music's magic charms were Aristotle, who valued it as an emotional catharsis, Plato, who described music as the medicine of the soul, and Caelius Aurelianus, who warned against indiscriminate use of music to fight madness (Feder & Feder, 1981; Strunk, 1965).

While much of the splendor of classical Greece was lost with the Middle Ages, attitudes concerning the power of music were carried on by influential statesmen and philosophers, including Boethius who claimed that music either improved or degraded the morals of men (Strunk, 1965). During this time, we see a close tie between the power of music and religious and moral ideas. Cassiodorus, like Aristotle, saw music as a potent form of catharsis, and St. Basil saw it as a positive vehicle for sacred emotion (Strunk, 1965).

Music surfaces once again as a cathartic agent in medical writings of the Renaissance. It was believed to be the sovereign remedy for melancholy, despair, and madness. It gave ease to pain and a multitude of ills (Feder & Feder, 1981). This belief in cathartic value has even penetrated our century as a part of psychoanalytic theory. While Freud himself did not address music's therapeutic value, it is still discussed by his psychoanalytic disciples. They have described music as (1) a means of sublimation for channeling instinctual drives in a socially acceptable manner; (2) a vehicle for increased insight into the unconscious; and (3) a resource for strengthening the ego structure through mastery (Noy, 1967).

These are all examples of philosophical belief in the power of music from antiquity to the present. While this century has brought empirical examination of music's effect on man, we find that many of the same philosophies of music continue to exert influence, even in our age of scientific inquiry. To some extent, we may be viewing the power of historical tradition as well as the power of music. Historical tradition, however, does not provide a full explanation for the nascence of music's power within society.

MUSIC AS A CULTURAL PHENOMENON

While one can only speculate about the musical life of prehistoric man, one avenue of inquiry is the investigation of music in preliterate cultures. According to Nettl (1956a, 1956b), a knowledge of primitive musical style not only is helpful in understanding human response to music, it also provides insight into music as therapy in prehistoric times.

Of particular interest to the music therapy profession is (1) the common attribution to music of supernatural powers, with consequent use in religious and healing rituals; (2) music as an expression of emotions; and (3) music as a part of social institutions.

Music and Supernatural Powers

According to Nettl (1956a), members of primitive cultures believe in the power of music to affect human behavior. Often, this belief is related to music's relationship to the supernatural. For example, among such tribes as the Basongye, or some American Indian tribes, the songs used in important rituals are believed to come from superhuman or unearthly sources (Merriam, 1964; Sachs, 1965). These songs, thought to hold preternatural energies, are used for entreating the gods and controlling power for all activities requiring extraordinary assistance, such as religious or curing rites.

According to Berlyne (1971), music has been an essential accessory to religious practice throughout the world. The importance of its use is highlighted by the careful enforcement of ritualistic accuracy. For example, Sachs (1965) noted that any mistakes in musical performance during a ritual could undermine its power and divine acceptance. Such mistakes, therefore, may be punished by stern measures, even death.

The coupling of magical powers and music is commonly used in charms against sickness (Sachs, 1965). In many preliterate cultures, a medicine man or a shaman uses rattles, drums, and songs as an integral part of the ritual to heal and chase away evil forces.

Compare the role of music in ancient religious and healing rites to its use in contemporary music therapy. In modern society, music is still integrally related to spiritual values and practice (Gaston, 1968). In addition to their prominent role in religious services of many denominations, aesthetic works such as music can express moral values and acceptable behavior (Kreitler & Kreitler, 1972). The close relationship between music and religion may have particular therapeutic value in settings such as the hospice care, where the client may use music as a vehicle for expressing or reaffirming religious belief in preparation for death (Munro, 1984; Gilbert, 1977).

While music still has similar uses in contemporary religious practices as it had in the past, the uses of music in modern music therapy differ greatly from those of preliterate healing rituals. Nettl (1956a) points out a major difference: Primitive cultures attribute music's power to supernatural forces, whereas the contemporary music therapist attributes change to the direct effect of music on behavior conditioned by the individual's past experiences and physiological responses. While Nettl's observation is essentially true, there still exists a special relationship between these two belief systems. According to Meyer (1956a),

> just as belief in the significant and affective power of aesthetic experiences performs an important function in activating the psycho-physiological disposition to respond, so it would seem that a patient's belief in the efficacy and power of music to heal may be a significant element in the success of music therapy (p. 33)

We are only beginning to realize the importance of attitude in the healing process and the possible effects on physiological processes in the body. Past studies show the importance of patient attitude in treatment effectiveness. For example, in using music as a strategy for pain control, Melzack (1973) found that the subject's beliefs about music's effectiveness significantly affected tolerance for pain. In summary, our cultural tradition of music as a healing power to some extent contributes to music's effectiveness as a therapeutic agent.

Music As an Expression of Emotion

Examination of primitive cultures shows music to be an emotional outlet (Merriam, 1964). For example, within preliterate tribes such as the Tshui, the Maori, and the Futana, music is used to express emotion. However, the ethnomusicological literature is not clear on whether or not music can actually produce or arouse emotions (Merriam, 1964), a belief that contemporary culture holds to be true.

One feature common to both primitive and industrialized civilization, on the other hand is the use of the arts in a "safety value function" (Merriam, 1964). Within an aesthetic context, music is used to express publicly forbidden or taboo topics without censure. It would appear that content is subordinate to form: The aesthetic distance (see Chapter 5) provides a unique opportunity for expression. For example, in Western culture, many sexually explicit, forbidden, or politically sensitive topics are openly expressed within the format of popular music. Such opportunity for honest, and even emotionally sensitive communication has important connotations for individual and group psychotherapy (Plach, 1980).

We have also been enculturated to view the arts as an appropriate vehicle for emotional expression or response (Kreitler & Kreitler, 1972). According to Israel Zwerling, (1979), the creative arts therapies, through nonverbal media, tap emotional processes more directly and immediately than do more traditional verbal therapies. Therefore, musical context may allow a normally "reserved" or repressed individual to explore or express feelings of a sensitive or personal nature. Music can evoke feelings as well as offer alternative expression for clients who have difficulty in verbal expression (Plach, 1980).

As we consider music's affective nature, it is important to realize that the particular differentiation of emotional content within music is a cultural phenomenon that is learned. In addition, emotional response varies from culture to culture. It is critical for the therapist to use musical materials that will be culturally meaningful (Meyer, 1956a; 1956b).

Music Within Social Institutions

Music's social nature is apparent when we consider that music is

> used both as a summatory mark of many activities and as an integral part of many others which could not be properly executed, or executed at all, without music . . . There is probably no other human cultural activity which is so

all-pervasive and which reaches into, shapes, and often controls so much of human behavior (Merriam, 1964, p. 218).

Music, which is species specific, takes us from cradle to grave: from our first lullaby to the requiem Mass, music fills our life with enjoyment and social structure. It expresses our deepest emotions and contributes to our cultural stability (Merriam, 1964). Within complex stratified cultures, music can act as a "social marker" or symbol of group affiliation. Listener preference for particular styles such as country music, rock, jazz, or opera is often associated with different classes, lifestyles, and ethnic groups (Abeles, 1980; Haack, 1980; Radocy & Boyle, 1979). Music has provided a unifying focal point for many social phenomena, from rebellious youth protest to concern for the handicapped. For example, isolation has been described as more debilitating to the aged than physical deterioration (Bright, 1980). Unsatisfactory or inappropriate social relationships are prominent within most emotional disturbances (Paul, 1982). Learning to socialize in an appropriate manner is a major goal for the mentally retarded (Carter, 1982). It follows, therefore, that improved social interaction is a primary concern in many treatment programs. Even within psychoanalysis, where the intimate interaction of psychiatrist and patient is paramount, ability to relate on a group level within the treatment milieu has been emphasized (Boenheim, 1968; Kohut, 1956).

In addition to rhythmic structure, music has other characteristics that lend themselves to social opportunities. First, and most important, music is readily recognized as a social art. The individual comes to the music experience with a "preparatory set" (see Chapter 5) that he is engaged in a social event (Meyer, 1956b; Berlyne, 1971; Kreitler & Kreitler, 1972). Second, music offers unique communication: Verbal skills are minimized within musical creation. Thus music gives handicapped individuals with poor verbal skills an alternative for interaction. Third, music is not a "monolithic" skill, but rather a collection of subskills (Sloboda, 1985). The individual can participate with a wide range of abilities, from listening to adept performance.

For the individual with no musical skills, involvement is possible through listening activities in which the listener is encouraged to respond. Because of music's infinite variety of style and form, most musical tastes generally can be accommodated to make the experience more meaningful. Even within musical performance, the skilled music therapist can modify musical materials to accommodate the individual level of experience and cognitive development. This flexibility in form gives music tremendous potential for integrating a widely varied group of individuals in a common endeavor.

Early writings about music in hospitals described social activities centered around music as a diversion or entertainment (Van de Wall, 1936). Within the chronic-care model of the past, this was an appropriate use for music. In today's world of short-term treatment and community health centers, music as diversion has a limited role. Rather, it provides a flexible resource for integrating the handicapped into the fabric of social existence. According to

Zwerling (1979), one of the primary offerings of the creative arts, including music, is the ability to involve patients in intrinsically social- and reality-based activities that require interaction and optimal functioning. Music offers an opportunity to put into practice those insights that have been discussed at an intellectual level in traditional verbal therapy.

In group therapy, music stimulates verbalization and socialization as it provides a common theme or focal point for discussion and personal work (Plach, 1980). As an aesthetic form, music imparts meaning on a variety of levels (Kreitler & Kreitler, 1972). For example, in conjunction with lyrics, music can communicate denotative information while acting simultaneously on a connotative level. As symbolic expression, music can relate ideas that are meaningful to an entire culture; yet as nondiscursive information, it allows individual involvement and interpretation. Because music relates meaningful and affective information on both individual and group levels, it provides an excellent vehicle for group therapy.

In summary, satisfactory human relationships are of major concern in contemporary health care. Music, through its infinite variety and adaptability, as well as its potent historical and cultural tradition, is a powerful therapeutic resource for emotional expression and reality-based socialization.

REFERENCES

Abeles, H. (1980). Responses to music. In D. A. Hodges (Ed.), *Handbook of music psychology* (pp. 105–140). Lawrence, KS.: National Association for Music Therapy.

Berlyne, D. E. (1971). *Aesthetics and psychobiology.* New York: Appleton-Century-Crofts.

Boenheim, C. (1968). The position of music and art in contemporary psychotherapy. *Journal of Music Therapy, 5*(3), 85–87.

Bright, R. (1980). *Music in geriatric care.* Lynbrook, NY: Musicgraphics.

Carter, S. A. (1982). *Music therapy for handicapped children: Mentally retarded.* Lawrence, KS.: National Association for Music Therapy.

Feder, E., & Feder, B. (1981). *The expressive arts therapies.* Englewood Cliffs, NJ: Prentice-Hall.

Gaston, E. T. (1968). (Ed.). *Music in therapy.* NY: Macmillan.

Gilbert, J. P. (1977). Music therapy perspectives on death and dying. *Journal of Music Therapy, 14*(4), 165–171.

Haack, P. (1980). The behavior of music listeners. In D. A. Hodges (Ed.) *Handbook of music psychology.* (pp. 141–182). Lawrence, KS.: National Association for Music Therapy.

Hodges, D. A. (Ed.) (1980). *Handbook of music psychology.* Lawrence, KS: National Association for Music Therapy.

Kohut, H. (1956). Some psychological effects of music and their relations to music therapy. In E. T. Gaston (Ed.) *Music Therapy 1955* (pp. 17–20). Lawrence, KS: National Association for Music Therapy.

Kreitler, H., & Kreitler, S. (1972). *Psychology of the arts.* Durham, NC: Duke University Press.

Melzak, R. (1973). *The puzzle of pain.* Middlesex, England: Penguin Education.

Merriam, A. P. (1964). *The anthropology of music.* Evanston IL: Northwestern University Press.

Meyer, L. B. (1956a). Belief and music therapy. In E. T. Gaston (Ed.), *Music therapy 1955,* (pp. 26–33). Lawrence, KS: National Association for Music Therapy.

Meyer, L. B. (1956b). *Emotion and meaning in music.* Chicago: University of Chicago Press.

Munro, S. (1984). *Music therapy in palliative/hospice care.* St. Louis: Magnamusic-Baton.

Nettl, B. (1956a). Aspects of primitive and folk music relevant to music therapy. In E. T. Gaston (Ed.), *Music therapy 1955* (pp. 36–39). Lawrence, KS: National Association for Music Therapy.

Nettl, B. (1956b). *Music in primitive cultures.* Cambridge, MA: Harvard University Press.

Noy, P. (1967). The psychodynamic meaning of music. Part V. *Journal of Music Therapy, 4,* 117–125.

Paul, D. W. (1982). *Music therapy for handicapped children: Emotionally impaired.* Lawrence, KS: National Association for Music Therapy.

Plach, T. (1980). *The creative use of music in group therapy.* Springfield, IL: Charles C. Thomas.

Radocy, R. E., & Boyle, J. D. (1979). *Psychological foundations of musical behavior.* Springfield, IL: Charles C. Thomas.

Sachs, C. (1965). *The wellsprings of music.* (ed. by Jaap Kunst). New York: McGraw Hill.

Seashore, C. E. (1941). *Why we love music.* Philadelphia: Oliver Ditson Company.

Sloboda, J. A. (1985). *The musical mind: The cognitive psychology of music.* Oxford: Clarendon Press.

Smith, B. (1978). Humanism and behaviorism in psychology: Theory and practice. *Journal of humanistic psychology, 18,* 27–36.

Strunk, D. (1965). *Source readings in music history.* New York: W. W. Norton.

Tame, D. (1984). *The secret power of music.* New York: Destiny Books.

Van de Wall (1936). *Music in initiations.* New York: Russell Sage Foundation.

Winner, E. (1982). *Invented worlds.* Cambridge, MA: Harvard University Press.

Zwerling, I. (1979). *The use of creative arts in therapy.* Washington, D.C.: American Psychological Association.

Chapter 5

The Function of Aesthetic Stimuli in the Therapeutic Process

Kate E. Gfeller

Music has been described as the language of emotion, a generator of social fellowship, a source of intellectual satisfaction, an expression of joy, and an activity that takes us out of the humdrum and into the realm of the ideal (Seashore, 1941). This belief in the inherent value of music is evident in music therapy literature that advocates aesthetic experiences for the handicapped as a source of gratification, self-actualization, and normalization (Gaston, 1955; Lathom, 1981). According to Nordoff and Robbins, "the right music, perceptively used, can lift the handicapped child out of the confines of his pathology and place him on a plane of experience and response, where he is considerably free of intellectual or emotional dysfunction" (1971, p. 238).

Speculative aesthetics,[1] the belief in the intrinsic value of the arts, is prominent in much music therapy literature. In 1955, S. B. Sterne, a clinical psychologist, described this viewpoint as stimulating, inspirational, but of a primarily subjective nature. He recommended more objective and empirical substantiation of music's benefits as a therapeutic tool.

Since 1955, there has been encouraging growth in research examining physiological and psychological response to musical stimuli, which has implications for music in therapy. This includes an alternative view of the aesthetic experience, focusing on its stimulative properties and how they relate to psychobiological processes.

The purpose of this chapter is to analyze the therapeutic potential of music in view of Meyer's theory of expectations, Berlyne's experimental aesthetics, Gestalt psychology, and Kreitler and Kreitler's cognitive theory of aesthetic response. These theories will be examined as they pertain to (1) focus, (2) perception, (3) cognition, and (4) affect in the therapeutic process.

FOCUS

Berlyne (1971), a champion of experimental aesthetics, suggests that art can stimulate properties that effectively control attention and reinforcement; this,

---

1. Berlyne (1971) describes speculative aesthetics as that branch of aesthetic philosophy which is heavily dependent on deduction from definitions of concepts, self-evident principles, generally accepted propositions, and the author's beliefs and experiences.

70

in turn, promotes many kinds of learning. The ability to stimulate attention is of major concern in therapeutic processes that require establishing and maintaining attending behaviors. For example, clients with poor eye-contact, limited attention span, or low level of motivation (e.g. those in infant stimulation programs, the severely handicapped, and some emotionally impaired) will fail to benefit from therapeutic intervention unless initial focus is obtained. Considerable research over the past two decades demonstrates the ability of music to reinforce attending behaviors in various handicapped clients (Carter, 1982). While we know that music can act as a reinforcement, we must also examine why. The answer may be related in part to focus. In establishing focus, or attention, aesthetic stimuli can aid through (1) dishabituation, (2) preparatory set, and (3) exploratory behavior.

Dishabituation

Habituation is the result of either monotonous regularity or possibly too much contrasting and novel stimuli, both of which can be unpleasant, and diminish response to sensory signals (Berlyne, 1971). In situations such as institutionalization or low sensory and intellectual functioning, reaction to familiar objects becomes automatic and unconscious (Kreitler & Kreitler, 1972). Through the use of novel stimuli such as attractive musical sounds, psychological and physiological readiness can result (Hodges, 1980; Altshuler, 1956). Shklovskij (quoted by Ehrlich, 1965, pp. 150–51) sees art as a new way of experiencing the world, thus facilitating dishabituation.

Because the easily manipulated variables of rhythm, melody, and harmony can provide optimal combinations of novel and familiar or redundant stimuli, music provides a flexible resource for establishing attention, even in low-functioning individuals. Musical stimuli of a moderate level have been found more pleasing than music that is either too low or too high in complexity or novelty. The music therapist has the task of selecting and arranging musical stimuli of appropriate complexity for the client's level of functioning and interest. A basic knowledge of the client's developmental level, as well as an understanding of musical development, can provide essential information in this area.

Preparatory Set

In addition to dishabituation, aesthetic forms such as music can further aid attention through what is called "preparatory set" (Meyer, 1956; Kreitler & Kreitler, 1972). As listeners, we bring to the auditory experience not only the raw acoustic material but our own beliefs about music's value. Generally, individuals believe that aesthetic experience should be both interesting and unique. This belief contributes to music's usefulness as a contingency in behavioral programs. An essential ingredient in successful operant conditioning is the selection of a valued reward or reinforcement. Music's usefulness as a reward is strengthened by cultural attitudes that perceive aesthetic forms as valuable commodities.

Preparatory set causes both conscious and unconscious adjustments in the listener that facilitate and condition response to the expected musical sounds (Meyer, 1956). This encourages attention and elicits behavioral responses to the stimuli (Kreitler & Kreitler, 1972).

Exploratory Behavior

A third effect of aesthetic stimuli is encouragement of exploratory behavior, which helps in orientation to the environment. Such orientation, when it manifests itself as identification of food sources or potential sources of danger is necessary for survival. But humans also demonstrate an orienting behavior known as diversive exploratory behavior, in response to aesthetic stimuli. Exploratory behavior is, as far as we know, unnecessary to human survival. This behavior is particularly strong in extended periods of low environmental stimulation.

Because, to some extent, aesthetic objects are a source of learning, they encourage exploratory behavior: in fact, any opportunity to learn about the world can contribute to more effective coping mechanisms. In addition, extensive research shows that contact with and exploration of novel stimuli may be intrinsically rewarding, providing incentive for new responses (Kreitler & Kreitler, 1972). For aesthetic objects, this exploration may be further motivated by the hedonic value—the pleasingness—of an art form (Berlyne, 1972).

While eliciting focus has value in drawing a client out of isolation and into the therapeutic experience, it is only a starting point. Simple awareness of stimuli is inadequate for transmission and encoding of information. Therefore, we must consider the next step: perception.

PERCEPTION

Perception is a selective process; we cannot absorb the vast world of competing stimuli. Instead we filter, select, and organize information for further processing. To some extent, what we perceive is related to personal attitude, preference, and expectation based on previous experience.

In addition to these intrasubject factors, the organizational structure of the external stimuli plays a role in how readily information is perceived. According to Gestalt psychologists, the organization of incoming sensory stimuli is facilitated through patterns or groupings known as "good Gestalts." Although this term has not been specifically defined, organizational attributes believed to contribute to a "good Gestalt" include regularity, similarity, proximity, symmetry, and simplicity (Berlyne, 1971). While the bulk of Gestalt theory focuses on visual perception, similar principles of organization also can be applied to auditory stimuli (Meyer, 1956; Berlyne, 1971; Kreitler & Kreitler, 1972; Sloboda, 1985).

In music, the components of rhythm, melody, and harmony provide temporal organization of sound, which introduces order and allows the listener to "parse" acoustic information (Berlyne, 1971). Rhythm, for example, provides temporal distribution in recurrent spacial/temporal organization, acting as an external stimuli for the structuring of time. This rhythmic organization, in addition to facilitating perception of musical information, is believed to aid memory and the understanding of incoming stimuli, including verbal information (Sloboda, 1985; Berlyne, 1971; Gfeller, 1982).

Gestalt psychologists consider perceptual organization a natural part of neurological processes. The organizational structure of music has implications for individuals such as the developmentally or learning disabled who suffer from poor short-term memory or difficulty in informational encoding. In addition to pure structural organization, however, one should also consider the effect of learning and of human development on the ability to perceive and encode information. For example, while Meyer (1956) would agree that some musical patterns are more readily perceived than others, he attributes part of the value of "good Gestalts" to learning. He suggests that we have been taught or conditioned to perceive particular patterns within our environment.

Additionally, according to the Piagetian theory, perception is related to the stages of child development. For example, some patterns may be inaccessible until conservation skills are in place. In terms of therapeutic practice, this would suggest that while the organizational structure of music has potential value in aiding clients to perceive incoming stimuli, the therapist must consciously evaluate previous musical experiences and learning along with the developmental level in selection of appropriate materials.

While there can be little doubt that the perceptual process is enhanced through structural properties of music, some aesthetic psychologists would argue that organizational properties alone cannot account for the psychological impact of aesthetic objects in terms of symbolism or musical meaning (Kreitler & Kreitler, 1972). We must look further to the process of cognition.

COGNITION

The role of cognition in aesthetic meaning and enjoyment is explored in two principal aesthetic theories: Kreitler and Kreitler's theory of cognitive orientation (1972) and Leonard Meyer's theory of expectations (1956).

Cognitive Orientation

According to Kreitler and Kreitler (1972), behavior in relation to an aesthetic object is not simply a result of the perceptual organization of the stimulus.

Behavior is also directed by the knowledge and beliefs about that object, which are based on judgments and evaluations.

By experiencing an art work through cognitive orientation, we can view reality with heightened awareness. The art form provides a special view of reality, an "as if" or alternative conceptualization, not a replica (Kreitler & Kreitler, 1972). Through this unique, symbolic view, we may perceive new solutions to old problems or realize new problems.

According to Kreitler & Kreitler (1972), the art form provides a favorable context for expanding cognitive orientation and confronting new ideas because of the intermingling of novel stimuli with the familiarity of either referential objects or structural elements. This blending of the unfamiliar (and thus novel source of high arousal) with the familiar (a source of arousal moderation) replaces boredom of habituation with interest, curiosity, and exploration at a level of arousal palatable to the individual.

In those schools of psychotherapy that emphasize insight as an important goal of therapy, expanding cognitive orientation has real therapeutic potential. An example in clinical practice would be the music therapy procedure known as lyric analysis. With this procedure, the therapist introduces a song in which the lyrics present a situation or emotional expression on a topic related to the client's personal problems. As the client listens to the lyrics, he may recognize a familiar dilemma, situation, or feeling within the song. The song may tell of everyday feelings or problems, but through the novelty of the musical context, the listener is able to bring new meaning and perhaps new insights to his own situation.

But while cognitive orientation may modify opinions or provide new insights, it does not necessarily result in corresponding behavioral changes (Kreitler & Kreitler, 1972). An insight facilitated through an aesthetic experience is only one step in the therapeutic process. It would appear that the therapist must further guide the individual in integrating insights into meaningful behavioral adjustments.

While cognitive orientation draws heavily from a referentialist, or extramusical, perspective, Meyer's theory of expectation explores primarily embodied meaning derived from the structural elements of the musical sounds themselves.

Theory of Expectation

Meyer's (1956) theory of expectation exemplifies an expressionistic position in aesthetic circles. According to this theory, musical meaning is a function of our knowledge of a style, and subsequent expectations about what sounds we anticipate. From listening to musical stimuli, we begin to notice certain musical groupings or clichés that occur frequently in a particular style. We develop expectations by comparing incoming sensory information with past listening experiences. These expectations facilitate effective processing of new information, and help us to develop internal reference among the musical elements. Because of the role of experience in this process, we may derive little meaning from music of an unfamiliar style.

Meyer (1956) notes that expectation frequently involves a high order of mental activity including judgement and cognition of both the stimuli and the context in which the stimuli appear. This mental process can occur very rapidly at a conscious or unconscious level. Since our listening experiences are organized in part by memories, the memory process is critical to expectation. In fact, Meyer states that "without thought and memory there could be no musical experience" (1956, p. 87).

Meyer's theory is particularly interesting in relation to musical response of mentally subnormal individuals. These people, who make up approximately one third of the clientele served by music therapists in the United States, are commonly reported to be very responsive to musical stimuli (Carter, 1982). In fact, music is often used as a reinforcement in behavioral management programs since it is viewed as enjoyable and intrinsically rewarding for this population. In view of the poor short-term memory capacity generally associated with mental retardation, one might question if complex music is truly meaningful to the more profoundly retarded, who suffer particularly debilitating memory deficits.

According to Sloboda (1985), musical capacity (production and ability to comprehend) includes many independent subskills that, he hypothesizes, are processed in different anatomical locations within the brain. Higgs and McLeish (1966) have also pointed to the subskills of music, noting that the educationally sub-normal may perform well on pure discrimination of structural elements but fall below age group norms in those musical skills that require memory and meaningful comparisons. Thus the mentally retarded individual may be responding to music using subskills that are relatively functional. (It is also important to note that there are mentally retarded with splinter skills in music or the exceptional cases such as the idiot savant [Winner, 1982].)

If, indeed, expectations are an integral part of meaning in music, this would explain why very simple and redundant music can maintain a high level of interest for the moderately retarded individual even after what seem to be infinite repetitions. Meyer's theory would suggest the careful selection of music that facilitates recall and understanding through much melodic, rhythmic, and harmonic redundancy for those individuals with limited memory capacity. For the most profoundly retarded individuals, musical stimuli might be utilized as precisely that novel sound that can elicit attention. More complex and extensive musical materials may lack meaning.

AFFECT

While musical appreciation can be an intellectual endeavor, for the greater majority of naive listeners, music has a close tie with affect or emotional response. Music has been described as the language of emotions (Winner, 1982), evoking physiological and psychological reactions associated with mood and emotion (Hodges, 1980).

Beyond our subjective observations that music affects or expresses mood, psychological studies have investigated claims that music expresses emotions by determining the degree of consensus about moods transmitted in musical samples. Most of these studies, according to Winner (1982), have shown remarkable agreement in mood identification, in both naive and trained listeners.

According to Langer (1953), musical stimuli do not result in direct emotions, but, rather, they act as symbols for emotions. Since nondiscursive musical symbols do not translate literally, they can capture the flux of sensation and emotion perhaps more effectively than ordinary language (Winner, 1982). While Winner and Langer both ascribe emotional response to music's embodied elements, Altshuler (1956) attributes this response to the images and mental associations that music evokes. These two viewpoints exemplify the expressionistic and referentialist schools of aesthetic philosophy.

INTRINSIC CHARACTERISTICS OF MUSIC AND EMOTION: AN EXPRESSIONISTIC POSTURE

From an expressionistic viewpoint, the acoustic elements of music are responsible for music's emotional expressiveness. According to Winner (1982), the structure of music mirrors the structure of emotional experiences: "Music sounds the way moods feel. Music is structured in terms of tension and release, motion and rest, fulfillment and change" (1982, p. 211).

The ability of nonreferential information within music to evoke mood is also at the heart of Meyer's (1956) theory of expectation.

Meyer's Theory of Music and Emotion

Meyer's belief about music and emotion is based on John Dewey's conflict theory of emotions, which states that "emotion or affect is aroused when a tendency to respond is arrested or inhibited" (Meyer, 1956). According to Meyer (1956), music arouses both consciously and unconsciously expectations that may or may not be directly or immediately satisfied. When an expectation is not satisfied, the tendency to respond is inhibited, and emotion or affect is aroused. Therefore, on an unconscious, nonintellectual level, music evokes a feeling response. While Meyer (1956) acknowledges the occurrence of emotional response through referential processes, his theory of embodied emotions is one of the most prominent in aesthetic philosophy.

Berlyne's Theory of Arousal and Hedonic Value

Like Meyer, Berlyne (1971) focuses on structural features of music, which he calls collative properties, as a source of emotional response. Berlyne's theory is based on empirical investigation of psychobiological response to formal elements in aesthetic objects. He views affective response as the result of arousal and hedonic value (elements that are beautiful or pleasurable in the art work). The combined features, such as complexity versus simplicity, or redundancy versus novelty, contribute to arousal in the observer. Pleasure is said to result from an optimal level of arousal which emanates from one of the following conditions: (1) moderate rise in arousal from a point of low arousal; (2) reduction of arousal from a state of unpleasantly high arousal; or (3) arousal jag, which is an initial intense build in arousal followed immediately by reduction, resulting in pleasure. He further links arousal activity to centers of the brain that house emotional activity.

Kreitler and Kreitler's Homeostatic Model of Motivation

This model incorporates Berlyne's theory of arousal, addressing the role of optimal level of stimulation (homeostatic balance) in efficient human functioning. The balance can be disrupted by either too much or too little stimulation. In either case mobilization restores equilibrium and, consequently, pleasurable feelings. Musical properties such as rhythm, consonance and dissonance, and melodic Gestalts (goodness of organization) can evoke tension and relief as the listener follows the unfolding thematic material.

Kreitler and Kreitler further maintain that participation in aesthetic experiences is motivated by potential tension reduction:

> It is our contention that a major motivation for art is tensions which exist in the spectator of art to his exposure to the work of art. The work of art mediates the relief of these preexisting tensions by generating new tensions which are specific. Our hypothesis that preexisting tensions are involved in the process assumes that tensions may long persist and can be transferred from one domain to another ... Since all too often a person may be prevented from performing the action appropriate for the reduction of tension, evoked tensions are not reduced and may persist (1972, p. 19).

When obstacles to reduction of tensions arise, one may displace aggression by transferring tension from one domain to another. Thus an individual may discharge tension through an activity similar to the activity that has been obstructed.

Further, Kreitler and Kreitler (1972) maintain that unresolved tensions persist in the form of diffuse, directionless tension expressed in restlessness and emotionality, including a readiness to overreact. Diffuse tensions can be absorbed into the more specific and directed tensions of an art work. These specific tensions are resolved through aesthetic means.

Emotional response to embodied properties of music is representative of the expressionistic school of aesthetic philosophy. Probably more prevalent in music therapy practice is the referentialist view, which states that musical meaning comes from music's reference to extramusical concepts or actions.

EXTRAMUSICAL ASSOCIATIONS

A common example of extramusical association in affective response to music is classical conditioning, or association by contiguity. In certain instances, musical stimuli evoke emotional response not because of the music's structural properties, but because the music has, in the past, accompanied stimuli with emotional effects. The "spine-tingling" music we associate with a horror movie provides a classic example of this phenomenon (Berlyne, 1971).

A second type of extramusical association is produced by resemblances in which some physical structure within the music "mimics" similar properties of a nonmusical event or feeling. For example, the depressed motor responses of sadness might be represented musically through slow tempo or descending passages (Berlyne, 1971).

In all the aforementioned examples, general moods seem to be a more characteristic response than specific emotions, even though such general mood responses may evoke reminiscence of specific past events (Kreitler & Kreitler, 1972). This leads to an important point: It is quite difficult to trace the relationship between specific musical stimuli and resulting imagery (Meyer, 1956). The listener can attach very private and seemingly inappropriate imagery to music as a result of the music's association with a personal experience. In addition, affective experiences themselves may evoke memories that in turn arouse further images. One image may follow another, not because of the music, but because of the subjective content in the listener's mind (Meyer, 1956).

Within any cultural context, however, there are so-called collective responses common to an entire group. Individuals tend to agree as to the mood elicited by certain types of musical stimuli (e.g., descending chromatic passages in Western music are often associated with grief or despair (Meyer, 1956; Radocy & Boyle, 1979).

Whether music evokes emotional response through intrinsic or extramusical events, its ability to transport the listener into the affective domain gives it a special place among therapeutic modalities. As Zwerling (1979) points out, a major goal of many forms of psychotherapy is to increase affective awareness and expression. He maintains that the ability of the arts to tap directly the affective domain makes them a particularly potent tool in psychiatric care (as opposed to predominately intellectual means).

While some might criticize the authenticity of musical expression of emotion due to music's nondesignative nature, this lack of denotative meaning provides freedom of individual projection and identification in music therapy

(Kreitler & Kreitler, 1972). One aesthetic object can take on unique, individually relevant meaning while providing a more general symbolic message (Kreitler & Kreitler, 1972). Musical stimuli permit multiple interpretations, and the listener enjoys the freedom of defining what the music means. Kreitler and Kreitler (1972) suggest that the subtle economy of art, which does not provide full disclosure, obliges the observer to supplement meaning with personal experience and projection of individual needs. Even in more cognitively oriented approaches to therapy, which emphasize intellectual rather than affective growth, the lack of designative meaning in musical stimuli provides opportunity for exercise in problem solving, decision making, evaluation, and observation (Corey, 1986), (e.g., rational-emotive and reality therapy models).

Whatever the therapeutic application of music, the therapist must consider the importance of selecting music that is meaningful in terms of past experience and expectations, as well as in its potential for eliciting extramusical association. It is unrealistic to assume that a music therapist can systematically guide a specific cognitive or emotional response through the selection of a particular music excerpt. Responses will differ among individuals. The music therapist must be sensitive to the relative sophistication of the client, selecting music that is accessible and thus meaningful to that individual. In general, the music therapist should take pains to familiarize himself with the musical tastes of the individuals in a group, taking into consideration age and other cultural differences (see Chapter 3). The therapist should also select music that readily evokes nonmusical associations, through structural "mimicry," musical styles, selections associated with events of personal significance, or lyrics that are pertinent to client concerns.

Music's ability to evoke mood makes it a powerful resource for therapy. However, Kreitler and Kreitler (1972) identify additional features common to most aesthetic experiences, which contribute to the therapeutic value of music: (1) preparatory set, (2) aesthetic distance, (3) feeling into, or empathy, (4) identification, and (5) multileveledness.

SPECIAL PROPERTIES OF AESTHETIC OBJECTS

One reason that aesthetic experiences may contribute to the therapeutic process is that personal involvement is characteristic of the arts. The following properties are believed to contribute to this involvement (Kreitler & Kreitler, 1972).

1. *Preparatory set.* This feature, previously discussed as part of eliciting focus, may also increase readiness for emotional involvement. Because society views art as a special, and generally emotionally laden experience, it sets expectations for emotional response.

2. *Aesthetic distance.* One feature characteristic of most art is disinterestedness, or aesthetic distance. This may result, in part, from the physical

remoteness built into many art experiences (such as frames around pictures, staging, and concert hall structure) as well as art's separation from practical needs and ends. Aesthetic distance not only tends to inhibit the usual motor response to affect what we experience in reality (for example, we do not run on stage to accost the villain in a play), but also facilitates emotional involvement. The observer, even though involved, can view the situation in a more objective, removed fashion.

This intensified involvement, coupled with some level of objectivity, promotes insight and examination into personal problems or concerns without the subjective, emotional reaction that may hamper judgment in real life (Kreitler & Kreitler, 1972). As in the case of expanded cognitive orientation, this characteristic of the aesthetic experience may be a useful tool in insight-oriented therapy models.

3. *Feeling into*. This characteristic, sometimes called empathy, makes possible intensification and personalization of elicited tensions through the reflection of emotions represented or implicit in the work of art. The empathic response is an attenuated rather than realistic form of emotional response.

4. *Identification*. Repressed or ungratified wishes and imaginary fulfillment are activated through sublimation, projection, or identification.

5. *Multileveledness*. The richness and symbolic nature of art allows multiple (even simultaneous or contradictory) interpretations of the aesthetic event. This feature, (which is discussed in greater detail in Chapter 4) in part explains why one art work can be meaningful to so many people, and take on very personal meaning for each observer. Multileveledness is particularly helpful in terms of group therapy settings. For example, the therapist or group facilitator may select musical stimuli either as a focal point for a theme-centered interaction, or to represent a common group tension (Plach, 1980).

In conclusion, aesthetic stimuli have therapeutic potential in terms of focus, perception, cognition, and affect, when these properties are manipulated by a skilled music therapist. While musical experiences in and of themselves may provide pleasure and feelings of well-being, the systematic usage of musical stimuli is of real importance to specific therapeutic direction. Without this direction, the music has no more specific or extended therapeutic value than the music in a concert or on the radio.

REFERENCES

Altshuler, I. M. (1956). Music potentiating drugs. In E. T. Gaston (Ed.), *Music therapy 1955*. Lawrence KS: National Association for Music Therapy, 120–126.

Berlyne, D. E. (1971). *Aesthetics and psychotherapy*. New York: Appleton-Century-Crofts.

Carter, S. B. (1982). *Music therapy for handicapped children: mentally retarded*. Lawrence, KS: National Association for Music Therapy.

Corey, G. (1986). *Theory and practice of counseling and psychotherapy* (3rd ed.). Monterey, CA: Brooks/Cole Publishing Company.

Ehrlich, V. (1965). *Russian formalism* (2nd ed.). New York: Humanities.

Gaston, E. T. (1968). *Music in therapy.* New York: Macmillan.

Gfeller, K. E. (1982). *The use of melodic-rhythmic mnemonics with learning disabled and normal students as an aid to retention.* Unpublished doctoral dissertation, Michigan State University.

Higgs, G., & McLeish, J. (1966). *An inquiry into the musical capacities of educationally sub-normal children.* Cambridge, England: Cambridge Institute of Education.

Hodges, D. A. (1980). Neurophysiology and musical behavior. In D. A. Hodges (Ed.), *Handbook of music psychology* (pp. 195–224). Lawrence, KS: National Association for Music Therapy.

Kreitler, H. & Kreitler, S. (1972). *Psychology of the arts.* Durham, NC: Duke University Press.

Langer, S. K. (1953). *Feeling and form.* New York: Scribners.

Lathom, W. B. (1981). *Role of music therapy in the education of handicapped children and youth.* Lawrence, KS: National Association of Music Therapy.

Meyer, L. B. (1956). *Emotion and meaning in music.* Chicago: University of Chicago Press.

Nordoff, P., & Robbins, C. (1971). *Music therapy in special education.* New York: The John Day Company.

Plach, T. (1980). *The creative use of music in group therapy.* Springfield, IL: Charles C. Thomas.

Radocy, R. E., & Boyle, J. D. (1979). *Psychological foundations of musical behavior.* Springfield, IL: Charles C. Thomas.

Seashore, C. E. (1941). *Why we love music.* Philadelphia: Oliver Ditson Company.

Sloboda, J. A. (1985). *The musical mind: The cognitive psychology of music.* Oxford: Clarendon Press.

Sterne, S. B. (1956). The validity of music as an effective group psychotherapeutic technique. In E. T. Gaston, Ed., *Music therapy 1955* (pp. 130–140). Lawrence, KS: National Association for Music Therapy.

Winner, W. (1982). *Invented worlds.* Cambridge, MA: Harvard University Press.

Zwerling, I. (1979). *Creative arts therapies.* Washington, D.C.: American Psychological Association.

PART TWO

MUSIC THERAPY IN THE CLINICAL SETTING

The five chapters in Part Two of this volume are included as an introduction to and a summary of some clinical practices in music therapy. The profession of music therapy has been developed over the past 45 years. Clinical techniques have been scrutinized and redeveloped over a long period and have been stabilized to the level where there is now an identifiable common practice among music therapy professionals.

Chapter 6, on psychosocial and neurophysiological aspects of music therapy, bridges the material from Part One, Chapters 1 and 2, to music therapy clinical practice.

Chapter 7 focuses on music therapy practice in a variety of settings. Chapter 8 presents music therapy in the framework of several psychotherapeutic models. Chapter 9 specifies the relationship between the use of psychotropic medication and music therapy, along with other psychosocial therapies, in the rehabilitation of the client.

Chapter 10 deals with the music therapist's responsibility in assessment of client needs and presents the current models of music therapy assessment and evaluation materials and treatment judgments. For example, when several techniques for relief of a symptom are recommended, the therapist chooses the one most appropriate for a particular patient. The setting may determine individual versus group choices. Only primary techniques are suggested; others are potentially useful for certain patients. All programs and techniques can be used on a variety of levels. Improvisation technique, for example, can be precisely structured or highly creative and free; progressive muscle relaxation can be guided and structured, or it can be practiced under complete control of the client.

Effective treatment is a consequence of good timing in the selection and use of interventions to stimulate in the patient the development of improved behaviors and improved health.

Chapter 6

Psychosocial and Neurophysiological Aspects of Music Therapy Interventions

Michael H. Thaut and Roger A. Smeltekop

Music therapy has come to be an established therapy modality in the field of mental health care. The efficacy of music therapy is defined through the unique mode of action of music as a therapy medium. The psychophysical, structural, and associated psychological properties of music stimuli, unlike other therapy modalities, influence the human personality and behavior in their psychosocial dimension—for example, affective and cognitive behavior domains—and on a measurable neurophysiological response level. It has been a longstanding observation throughout history that sound has an inherent quality that tends to elicit psychological and physiological responses, such as pleasure, fear, muscular tension, sensations of pain, and feelings of energy and arousal (Wolberg, 1977). Research has shown how sounds influence both cortical and subcortical areas, affecting the central and autonomic nervous system. Music therapy interventions can affect the entire human personality and the multifold psychophysical interactions within the nervous system.

Based on the previously outlined psychomusical foundations (Part One), specific areas of clinical concern in psychiatric music therapy will be highlighted briefly to illustrate the unique mode of action of music as therapy.

Clinical experience shows that music elicits mood/emotional responses that can range from pleasure and excitement to sadness, fear, and apprehension, depending on past associations and present symbolic significances. Roederer (1974) suggests neurophysiological explanations for the ways in which music evokes meaningful and emotional responses on a psychological level. He contends that mood/emotional responses are based on neural information processing and are likely due to engagement of the limbic system by music processing. The mood/feeling response to music is used in therapy to engage the patient in an active feeling and thinking process that can be directed towards achieving therapeutic goals. For example, music listening techniques can be used effectively in clinical settings to alter existing moods of clients.

Research has shown that the thought and feeling response elicited by

85

music is always accompanied by definite, individually determined changes in physiological measures. An individual's psychophysiological response pattern depends on the musical characteristics of the stimulus as well as personal attitudes toward and associations with the stimulus. This rather idiosyncratic response system is employed in various ways in psychiatric music therapy with psychotic and neurotic patients, to achieve change in thinking, feeling, and interpersonal behavior. For example, a music therapist, understanding a verbally withdrawn patient's particular response pattern to music, can stimulate productive activity through knowledgeable applications of musical stimuli.

Music is used successfully in clinical settings to encourage and guide social interaction among patients. The interaction is manifested in such behaviors as verbalization of thoughts and feelings, contributions to a group effort, cooperation with others, or observing and responding to the needs of others. Music listening techniques can be used effectively to deal with affective interpersonal interaction situations (Ridgeway, 1976).

Music activities can function effectively as psychotherapeutic agents to improve patients' self-concepts (Henderson, 1983). For example, instrumental group improvisation or group singing therapy activities provide sensory and social feedback as well as success experiences that can be used to develop appropriate self-worth and identity. Structured movement techniques, dances, and physical exercise with supportive and facilitating music accompaniment are used effectively to promote body awareness and establish ego boundaries.

The cognitive aspects of functional behavior in the mentally ill patient are utilized and enhanced by music stimuli and experiences. The structure of music follows organizational principles that are based in objective reality. The fact that music is ordered in a time frame helps and requires a patient to perceive and respond to it in an organized manner as external reality. Basic sensory information, such as high and low pitch or fast and slow tempo, must be conceptualized with a degree of accuracy for adequate musical response.

The mathematical nature of rhythm, the spatial relationships in notation, the temporal sequence of musical events, and the logic of musical form are all used to aid in reintegrating the disorganized thinking of the mentally ill patient. Additionally, the cognitive skills of memory, concentration, learning, processing sequential information, and logical problem-solving are all exercised in music activity.

Music affects anxiety states, as measured by both verbal reports and physiological measures. It is generally suggested that stimulative music tends to increase anxiety while sedative music tends to decrease anxiety. Clinical studies show that music can be used effectively to reduce feelings of anxiety, promote muscle relaxation, and release motor tension. Important, however, for the relaxation-supportive function of music is the concept of preference.

Sound stimuli, and in particular rhythmic stimuli, exert an influence on a person's motor system. Strong sound signals raise the excitability of the motor nuclei of the spinal cord and bring the motor system into a state of perceptual alertness and readiness to move. The potential of music to stimulate and structure motor activity is of paramount clinical importance in psychiatric settings to promote mental and physical alertness, body awareness, and acceptance, to release energy and tension, and to act as bridge to greater social participation.

The six areas briefly mentioned—(1) eliciting mood/feeling response and altering feeling states, (2) aiding interpersonal interaction, (3) improving self-concept, (4) promoting cognitive mental organization, (5) reducing anxiety states, and (6) stimulating perceptual and motor activity—are in the main focus of every treatment and rehabilitation setting in mental health care. Music works in each area on the psychological and neurophysiological response levels, and thus constitutes a therapy modality that affects the entire human personality in an objective and measurable manner.

REFERENCES

Gaston, E. T. (1968). *Music in therapy*. New York: Macmillan.

Henderson, S. M. (1983). Effects of a music therapy program upon awareness of mood in music, group cohesion, and self-esteem among hospitalized adolescent patients. *Journal of Music Therapy, 20,* 14–20.

Kanas, N., Rogers, M., Kreth, E., Patterson, L., & Campbell, R. (1980). The effectiveness of group psychotherapy during the first three weeks of hospitalization: A controlled study. *Journal of Nervous and Mental Disease, 168,* 483–492.

Pattison, E., Briserdeh, A., & Wohl, T. (1967). Assessing specific effects of inpatient group psychotherapy. *International Journal of Group Psychotherapy, 17,* 283–297.

Priestley, M. (1975). *Music therapy in action*. London: Constable & Co.

Ridgeway, C. L. (1976). Affective interaction as a determinant of musical involvement. *The Sociological Quarterly, 17,* 414–438.

Roederer, J. (1974). The psychophysics of musical perception. *Music Educators Journal, 60,* 20–30.

Tyson, F. (1966). Music therapy in private practices: Three case histories. *Journal of Music Therapy, 3,* 8–18.

Watson, J., & Lacey, J. (1974). Therapeutic groups for psychiatric inpatients. *British Journal of Medical Psychology, 47,* 307–312.

Wheeler, B. (1983). A psychotherapeutic classification of music therapy practices: A continuum of procedures. *Music Therapy Perspectives, 1,* 8–16.

Wolberg, L. R. (1977). *The technique of psychotherapy*. New York: Grune & Stratton.

Yalom, I. D. (1983). *Inpatient group psychotherapy*. New York: Basic Books.

Chapter 7

Music Therapy in Hospital and Community Programs

Brian L. Wilson

FROM INSTITUTIONALIZATION TO DEINSTITUTIONALIZATION

Over the last 30 years many changes have occurred in the types and methods of delivery of services for adult psychiatric clients. The catalysts to reform the mental health system have come from several directions. The introduction of psychotropic medications in the mid-1950s made the patient more accessible to treatment and gave evidence that treatment, or at least maintenance, of emotional problems could be done quickly and efficiently and outside the institutional setting. In 1963 Congress passed the Community Mental Health Center Act (PL 8-164), which would establish approximately 1,200 community mental health centers across the nation and thereby depopulate state institutions. New innovative programming ideas for the mentally ill, such as out-patient care, small community-based inpatient units, and after-care services in local mental health centers, were seen as replacements for previous long-term hospitalizations. Social changes of the 1960s also affected mental health care. In the early 1960s Congress passed legislation giving all Americans the right to psychiatric treatment regardless of their social, economic, racial, or ethnic background. These principles reflected a new awareness of patient's rights both in and out of the institution (Solomon, Gordon, & Davis, 1984).

Although it was expected that many state hospitals would close as more community-based services were implemented, that has not been the case. Many chronic patients were unable to be discharged at all or not as early as planned, while the rate of admissions has continued to rise. Unquestionably, the census of state hospitals has been dramatically reduced (by about 75 percent since 1955), and the length of time patients spend in the hospital has steadily declined. Concommitant with these decreases has been the quadrupling of outpatient care episodes in community-based outpatient treatment centers. The contribution of the hospital to the economy of small towns and the strength of employee unions have also contributed to the phasing down rather than phasing out of public hospitals (Solomon, et al 1984). Whether public hospitals survive remains to be seen. However, hospitalization, rather than being eliminated, will probably remain as a viable option in the overall package of mental health services. What is questionable is how many appropriate avenues for treatment will continue to be available as financial cutbacks lead to further retrenchment in programming.

Recent media coverage has called attention to the deplorable living conditions of many former patients who have slipped through the protective umbrella of social/rehabilitation programs or who have been simply "deinstitutionalized" and therefore are not eligible for further services. Some states have resorted to desperate measures, including "Greyhound therapy" (a one-way bus ticket out-of-state), in order to reduce the case loads. The number of homeless mentally ill has also increased substantially since the onset of deinstitutionalization, averaging three to four times greater than that of the homeless population in general (Appelby & Desai, 1985). The recent shift in emphasis from public to private responsibility for treatment is partly due to the accessibility of federal reimbursement (Medicaid and Medicare) to private programs. This may lead to the eventual elimination or substantial cutback of programs that are ineligible for federal support as states continue to look for ways to reduce their budgets. The proposed implementation of Diagnostic Related Groups (DRGs) or similar cost-containment plans to mental health programs further threatens the existence and quality of care available to those in need by strictly limiting reimbursement for hospitalization based on diagnoses alone (Scovel, 1986; MacLean, 1987).

PREPARING THE CLIENT FOR INDEPENDENT LIVING

The continuing attempt to eliminate the need for long-term hospitalization has led recently to the development of decentralized networks of services. The following model, made up of three major components, purports to provide public patients with a network of services capable of responding to their needs at all levels of disability and illness:

1. Community-based services (community residences, after-care programs, and outpatient clinics) designed for individuals capable of living in the community.
2. Community hospitals (community mental health centers and general-hospital inpatient units) designed for those who are temporarily unable to function in community programs.
3. Other forms of sheltered settings for those who cannot function independently in the community but refuse traditional services (Mollica, 1983, p. 367).

The high rate of recidivism among chronic mental patients (35-50 percent within one year after discharge) indicates that many current deinstitutionalization procedures have not been entirely successful (Anthony, Cohen, & Vitalo, 1978; Lamb, 1980). One possible method of deterring this "revolving door" syndrome is to provide the client with a community liaison team and a "linking" program between institution and community resources. Rosenfield, Caton, Nachumi, and Robbins (1986) found that discharge planning teams that had positive and ongoing relationships with providers of community services to mental patients were able to reduce significantly the rehospitalization rates for their chronic mental patients.

Certain types of services have also been identified as necessary for the psychiatric client to achieve a successful transition to the community after discharge. Besides appropriate living arrangements and financial support, newly discharged clients need medical care, vocational rehabilitation, counseling, and leisure time activities. In a longitudinal study of 550 patients (Solomon, et al. 1984), an assessment of post-discharge service needs revealed that counseling and leisure-time activities were second only to medical care. The inpatient social workers' assessments ranked appropriate use of leisure time as the poorest functioning area for their clients, with almost 75 percent needing assistance. The same social workers reported that they assumed that for approximately one-half of their clients, the need for counseling and leisure time planning would *not* be met after discharge. Although the clients themselves generally perceived less need for services, nearly three-fourths reported needing individual counseling and over one-third needed activity therapy. In a similar study of discharge outcomes for 505 after-care clients, social isolation, unoccupied time, and troubled interpersonal relationships were reported by most subjects. Six months after discharge, the subjects reported that loneliness and boredom were their most difficult problems and continued to be problems for two years post discharge (Goering, Wasylenki, Lancee, & Freeman, 1984).

MUSIC THERAPY: EVOLVING ROLES

The pairing of music with the treatment of mental illness has been documented since the origins of man and well described in the professional literature (Boxberger, 1961; Tyson, 1981; Peters, 1987). The early use of music in mental hospitals (1920–1950) was primarily educational in nature and often for entertainment. Many institutions established their own bands and choruses along with talent shows, drum and bugle corps, and holiday pageants. After World War II, music therapy became an accepted treatment modality in many Veterans Administration and state hospitals. As music began to be recognized for its unique contribution to treatment, the use of music in therapy began to shift from recreational and educational to more therapeutic and rehabilitative orientations. By the 1960s a research base in music therapy was developing that scientifically supported the previously observed effects that music had on human behaviors.

In the first published survey of the clinical practices of music therapists, Michel (1965) discovered that the state hospital was the largest employer of music therapists. At that time patients were most often referred to music therapy by a physician because of the patient's "interest" rather than for "therapeutic reasons." Besides record listening, approximately 50 percent of the survey respondents included chorus and holiday and seasonal programs among the activities used in their work. Later studies (Braswell, Maranto, & Decuir, 1979; Lathom, 1982: McGinty, 1980) reveal that music therapy services have reflected the ongoing changes in mental health care. In addition to offering a greater diversity in activity offerings, contemporary music thera-pists are doing fewer performance-based activities (chorus, band, chamber groups, etc.) and more activities emphasizing a multidimensional approach to treatment (creative movement, discussion groups, guided imagery, sports, and arts and crafts activities). It would seem from this diversity in program-ming that the music therapist's skills and competencies have also broadened. Current music therapy interventions are goal-directed and based on the psy-chological, behavioral, and social needs of the client, in both the institutional or community settings.

Even though adult psychiatric clients are still the most frequently reported population served by music therapists, the range of employment settings has grown from primarily state and federal mental hospitals to include private hospitals, community-based programs, and private practice. The need to ad-dress cost containment and quality assurance issues has also meant that music therapists in all of these settings are being asked to document the *unique* effect of their treatment interventions. Guidelines to help the clinician achieve this formidable task are currently being developed (Furman, 1988).

Music therapy has been shown to have a positive influence on adult psy-chiatric clients in a variety of ways. Music therapy "offers an element of the human experience that direct psychotherapy—regardless of how well it is done—cannot offer" (Graham, 1980, p. 39). As an expressive therapy, music therapy encourages the client to take steps towards reeducation and recon-struction in a supportive environment without complete dependency on ver-balization.

Wheeler (1983) further breaks down the music therapy experience in psychotherapy into three distinct categories: (1) music therapy as an activity therapy, (2) insight music therapy with reeducative goals, and (3) insight music therapy with reconstructive goals. The first level of intervention is closely allied to a behavioral approach in which the clients' impulses are suppressed "in favor of more adaptive behaviors which are structured by the therapist, rather than the exploration of instincts and impulses" (p. 10). In preparing the client for reintegration into the community, this level of music therapy intervention is particularly well suited for reducing inappropriate behaviors (i.e., poor attention span, inability to follow directions, and inap-propriate verbal or motor interaction) that may interfere with such place-ment. For example, Cook and Freethy (1973) used contingent piano playing to eliminate complaining behavior in a chronic schizophrenic female, while Williams and Dorow (1983) successfully reduced the same behavior in a chronic depressed male by using interrupted music and verbal feedback.

Carroccio, Latham, and Carroccio (1976) found that rate-contingent guitar rental decelerated stereotyped head/face-touching of an adult psychiatric patient. Hauck and Martin (1970) used time-out from music to decrease rates of rocking, finger-flicking, and pacing in a chronic schizophrenic female.

Furthermore, these studies support the finding that reductions in undesirable behavior in the music therapy session can be positively transferred to the client's behavior in other environments. Wheeler (1987) later surveyed 148 music therapists working with adult psychiatric clients in order to test her three-level system in clinical practice. It is interesting to note that two goals, developing appropriate leisure-time skills and improving confidence, did not factor at the activity therapy level as Wheeler expected, even though she found general agreement regarding goals represented at each level. These findings may indicate a need for music therapists, when working toward their clients' reintegration into the community, to align their treatment objectives more closely with those most commonly acknowledged as necessary for a successful transition.

The development of community-based programs in music therapy has mirrored the growth of other community-based services for the mentally ill over the last 20 years. Tyson (1968, 1973, 1981), a pioneer in private community music therapy, has identified important contributions that such a program of services can offer to newly discharged mental health patients. She stressed that music therapy can provide needed avenues for expression and continued awareness of feelings that may not be available through more traditional methods. She also cautioned that music therapy acquires "deeper dimensions" in community practice than it does in institutional programs, due to the client's total life situation. This level of client-therapist interaction may differ from that in the hospital milieu, where the large number of rehabilitation services available may lead to a more superficial interaction between the client and the music therapist. In the community setting, the music therapist becomes more of a central, rather than adjunctive, part of the client's therapy, with all of the accompanying responsibilities. Several case studies detailing practice and effectiveness of this approach have appeared in the literature (Tyson, 1987, 1981).

In the public community mental health program, the role and responsibilities of the music therapist are often similar. The music therapist may be delegated as a "primary therapist" and have sole responsibility for designing and evaluating the majority of the client's treatment program. Music therapy interventions must be responsive to client problems that are associated with community, not hospital, adjustment. Even when clients in outreach programs are initially unmotivated and resistant to change, implementation of music therapy procedures that provide immediate and continued success in performance may encourage the sharing of common experiences and problems, further helping the client to cope with the environment (Rubin, 1973, 1975).

Another resource for the adult psychiatric client is the community music school. Although these programs are often geared toward children, services may be available for adults (Steele, 1972). The charges for sessions are generally on a sliding scale based on the individual's ability to pay. The community music school with a music therapy program can assist the adult psychiatric client in both making a successful transition from hospital to community and maintaining "wellness" once established in the community.

Private practice by music therapists is a growing aspect of the discipline, although there is a paucity of information in the literature about the unique clinical parameters of this approach. In her survey of 466 music therapists Lathom (1982) reported that 4.1 percent worked in private practice, a slight increase from the 2.77 percent reported a few years earlier (Braswell et al. 1979). Crocker (1968) has described the procedures necessary for assessing and evaluating private clients for either rehabilitative or preventative programming. Her published case studies, however, have been restricted to children. Interest in establishing a private practice has led to the publication of "how-to" guidelines that, unfortunately, do not include descriptions of clinical philosophy or methodology (O'Brien & Goldstein, 1985; Henry, Knoll, & Reuer, 1982).

REFERENCES

Anthony, W. A., Cohen, M. R., & Vitalo, R. (1978). The measurement of rehabilitation outcome. *Schizophrenia Bulletin, 4,* 365–383.

Appleby, L., & Desai, P. (1985). Documenting the relationship between homelessness and psychiatric hospitalization. *Hospital and Community Psychiatry, 36*(7), 732–737.

Boxberger, R. (1961). Historical basis for the use of music in therapy. *Music therapy 1961.* Lawrence, KS: National Association for Music Therapy.

Braswell, C., Maranto, C., & Decuir, A. (1979). A survey of clinical practice in music therapy: Part I. *Journal of Music Therapy, 16*(1), 2–16.

Carroccio, D., Latham, S., & Carroccio, B. (1976). Rate-contingent guitar rental to decelerate stereotyped head/face-touching of an adult male psychiatric patient. *Behavior Therapy, 7,* 104–109.

Cook, M., & Freethy, M. (1973). The use of music as a positive reinforcer to eliminate complaining behavior. *Journal of Music Therapy, 10*(4), 213–216.

Crocker, D. B. (1968). Music therapy in a private music studio. In E. T. Gaston (Ed.), *Music in therapy* (pp. 202–207). New York: Macmillan.

Ficken, T. (1976). The use of songwriting in a psychiatric setting, *Journal of Music Therapy, 13*(4), 163–172.

Furman, C. (Ed.). (1988). *Effectiveness of music therapy procedures: Documentation of research and clinical practice.* Washington, DC: National Association for Music Therapy.

Goering, P., Wasylenki, D., Lancee, W., & Freeman, S. (1984). From hospital to community: Six-month and two-year outcomes of 505 patients. *Journal of Nervous and Mental Disorders, 172*(11), 667–672.

Graham, R.(1980). Music therapy: The state of the field. *NAPPH Journal, 11*(2), 32–39.

Hauck, L., & Martin, P. (1970). Music as a reinforcer in patient controlled duration of time-out. *Journal of Music Therapy, 12*(2), 43–53.

Henry, D. J., Knoll, L. D., & Reuer, B. L. (1986). *Music works: A handbook of job skills for music therapists.* Stephenville, TX: Music Works.

Lamb, H. R. (1980). Therapist-case managers: More than brokers of services. *Hospital & Community Psychiatry, 31,* 762–764.

Lathom, W. (1982). Survey of current functions of a music therapist. *Journal of Music Therapy, 19*(1), 2–27.

MacLean, B. (1987). DRGs: What they are and how they impact treatment in the psychiatric setting. *Arts in Psychotherapy, 14,* 249–253.

Michel, D. (1965). Professional profile: The NAMT member and his clinical practices in music therapy. *Journal of Music Therapy, 2*(4), 124–129.

Michel, D. (1985). *Music therapy: An introduction* (2nd ed.). Springfield, IL: Charles C. Thomas.

McGinty, J. (1980). Survey on duties and responsibilities of current music therapy positions. *Journal of Music Therapy, 12*(3), 148–166.

Mollica, R. (1983). From asylum to community: The threatened disintegration of public psychiatry. *New England Journal of Medicine, 308*(7), 367–373.

O'Brien, N., & Goldstein, A. (1985). A systematic approach to developing a private practice in music therapy. *Music Therapy, 5,* 37–43.

Peters, J. (1987). *Music therapy: An introduction.* Springfield, IL.: Charles C. Thomas.

Rosenfield, S., Caton, C., Nachumi, G., & Robbins, E. (1986). Closing the gaps: The effectiveness of linking programs connecting chronic mental patients from the hospital to the community. *Journal of Applied Behavioral Science, 22*(4), 411–423.

Rubin, B. (1975). Music therapy in a community mental health program. *Journal of Music Therapy, 12*(2), 59–66.

Rubin, B. (1973). Music therapy as an outreach station of the Milwaukee County Mental Health Center. *Journal of Music Therapy, 10*(4), 201–204.

Scovel, M. (1986). DRGs: A prospective payment system of reimbursement. In K. Gfeller (Ed.), *Fiscal, regulatory and legislative issues for the music therapist* (pp. 9–14). Washington, DC: National Association for Music Therapy.

Solomon, P., Gordon, B., & Davis, J. (1984). *Community service to discharged psychiatric patients.* Springfield, IL.: Charles C. Thomas.

Steele, A. L. (1972). The community music school: Flexibility and accessibility. *Journal of Music Therapy, 9*(3), 111–118.

Tyson, F. (1968). The community music center. In. Gaston, E. T. (Ed.), *Music in therapy* (pp. 382–388). New York: Macmillan.

Tyson, F. (1973). Guidelines toward the organization of clinical music therapy programs in the community. *Journal of Music Therapy, 10*(3), 113–124.

Tyson, F. (1981). *Psychiatric music therapy.* New York: Creative Arts Rehabilitation Center.

Tyson, F. (1987). Analytically oriented music therapy in a case of generalized anxiety disorders. *Music Therapy Perspectives, 4,* 51–55.

Wheeler, B. (1983). A psycho-therapeutic classification of music therapy practice: A continum of procedures. *Music Therapy Perspectives, 1*(2), 8–12.

Wheeler, B. L. (1987). Levels of therapy: The classification of music therapy goals. *Music Therapy, 6*(2), 39–49.

Williams, G., & Dorow, L. (1983). Changes in complaints and non-complaints of a chronically depressed psychiatric patient as a function of an interrupted music/verbal feedback package. *Journal of Music Therapy, 20*(3), 143–155.

Chapter 8

Music Therapy Within the Context of Psychotherapeutic Models

Mary A. Scovel

Music therapists work within a framework of many psychotherapeutic models. This is a strength of this particular discipline because music therapists aren't restricted to one philosophical orientation but rather base treatment on eclectic models. It also signifies that the therapist has versatile skills and utilizes those skills in designating specific music activities that compliment the particular psychotherapeutic model. The music therapist assesses the client's strengths and weaknesses, and establishes the treatment intervention and the rationale for treatment in order to design appropriate musical and nonmusical goals for the client. Each music activity is designed to help the client reach his fullest potential. The same music activity may be used in more than one psychotherapeutic approach. What is done with musical activity and why it is done distinguishes one approach from another (Wheeler, 1981).

A model is a device for generating ideas, for guiding conceptualization, and, therefore, for generating explanation (Reed, 1986). Models aid scientific understanding and guide therapeutic methods. There are so many kinds of abnormality that it is unlikely that one particular model will explain all mental disorders. No matter what model is used, one first identifies a syndrome (using several Axis-DSM III-R), searches for an etiology, and then sorts out numerous possibilities before trying various treatments. When this process is completed, the therapist communicates the results of the activity in the language of the prospective theoretical model. The five major models commonly used are biomedical, behavioral, psychodynamic, cognitive, and humanistic (see Table 8–1). Sometimes these models are complementary, but often they are competitive in their attempts to understand and cure abnormality. A sixth model, the holistic-wellness model, is included in this chapter because of the strong influence of the holistic movement, with its emphasis on consideration of all relative information about the life of an individual as a biological, psychological, social, and spiritual organism.

BIOMEDICAL MODEL

The biomedical model defines abnormality as being an illness of the body. Biomedical researchers consider three possible causes for an illness: germs, genes, and biochemistry (Rosenhan & Seligman, 1984).

Medical model theories tend to place the nature and cause of mental illness in the person's biological nature. It is believed that behind the symptoms of abnormal behavior are organic, physiological, or biochemical processes that cause the person's abnormal behavior (Ruud, 1980).

In determining the etiology of psychological abnormalities, psychologists and psychiatrists who use the biomedical model search for an organic basis to the abnormality. They look for a germ that is causing the syndrome, then they study the family history to see if the patient's germs might be the cause. They then explore the biochemistry, specifically the brain, for any further insights that might influence the abnormality. Once an etiology is discovered, some biological treatment, usually a drug, will be used to mitigate the abnormality.

Psychological disorders involve several levels of malfunctioning. For a patient who is chronically depressed and who has symptoms of sleeplessness and loss of weight, the therapist would focus on the symptoms that relate to the biological process. There is some accepted evidence that the chemistry of a patient's brain changes when the patient is depressed (Rosenhan & Seligman, 1984). Presently, therapists are asking whether these biochemical factors are the cause of the depression. In order to counteract the biomedical factors, chemical therapies or drugs might be prescribed. In the case of depression, the biological treatments are tricyclic antidepressants, monoamine oxidase inhibitors, and electroconvulsive shock therapy. Peach (1984) compared subjects' pre- and post-test skin temperatures with their perceived ability to relax and with production of images in a relaxed state. It was found that persons taking antidepressants may be among those who can benefit most from music and a multisensory approach to imagery in the therapy process. She reports that some property of the drug, as the drug allows the depressive feature to go into remission, may also enhance receptivity to imaginative processes (Peach, 1984).

Within this model, the therapist's role is to study the etiology, work toward understanding the diagnosis, and recommend treatment based on an understanding of the illness. To help understand an illness, one might acknowledge that the disease can be treated by connecting the biochemical and neurophysiological processes (Reed, 1984).

When working with a depressed person, a music therapist might use music in conjunction with muscle relaxation training. See Taxonomy VI, *Music and Relaxation,* A. "Music with Progressive Muscle Relaxation Training," for an explanation of this technique. During relaxation training the client will learn to discriminate between relaxation and tension responses and to substitute acquired relaxation responses for anxiety-stress conditions. Using anxious

TABLE 8–1 PSYCHOTHERAPEUTIC MODELS

	Biomedical	Behavioral	Psychodynamic
Major Contributors	Richard von Kraft-Ebing (1840–1915) Paul Ehrlich (1854–1915)	B.F. Skinner (1904–) Ivan Pavlov (1849–1936) Edward I. Thorndike (1874–1949) J. Wolpe	Sigmund Freud (1856–1939) Alfred Adler (1870–1937) Carl Jung (1875–1961) Harry S. Sullivan (1892–1949) Erick Fromm (1900–1980) Erik Erickson (1902–)
Definition	Illness of the body germs, genes, biochemistry	Learn through conditioning to be abnormal	Abnormality is driven by hidden conflicts within the personality
Therapist Role	Understand and recommend treatment based on diagnosis.	Active & directive: Provide a means to attain a goal	Foster a transference
Therapist Techniques	Connect the biochemical and neurophysiological process	Token economics, self-management	Dream analysis, free association
Evaluate Change	Find the germ, genes, or biochemistry causing the disturbance	Unlearn old maladaptive patterns and learn new adaptive habits	Insight of causality leads to personality change
Terminology	Medical model, chemical therapies	Operant conditioning, positive-negative reinforcer	Id, ego, superego, transference, defense mechanism, resistance

subjects and Spielberger's State-Trait Anxiety Inventory, Stoudenmire (1975) found that relaxing music can be as effective a method for state anxiety reduction as is muscle relaxation training.

Another study suggests that music listening may be used as a technique to alter body chemistry. Because of the close relationship between adrenal corticosteroids (stress hormones) and the immune system, data suggest a relationship between muscle/relaxation techniques and physical health (Rider, Floyd, & Kirkpatrick, 1985).

Hanser examined music therapy and stress reduction and found that the presence of background music significantly affected behavioral manifestations of tension in specific areas of the body as well as verbalizations associated with pain. The behavioral measures supported patients' verbal

Cognitive	Humanistic	Holistic
Albert Ellis (1913–) Aaron T. Beck (1921–) Donald Meichenbaum (1940–) Maxie Maultsby (1932–) William Glasser (1925–) Eric Berne (1910–1970)	Carl Rogers (1902–) Viktor Frankl (1905–) Abraham Maslow (1908–1970) Frederick Perls (1893–1970)	Jan Christiaan Smuts (1870–1950)
Abnormality comes from disordered thinking about self and others	Abnormality is the outcome of failure to grow, to find meaning, and to be responsible for self	Abnormality exists when body, mind, and spirit are not in harmony or "in tune" with the natural and social environment and with the cosmos
Act as a guide and challenge self-defeating ideas that client sees as truth	Focus on here-and-now, offer total acceptance	Educate, become emotionally involved, share experience
Homework to test assumptions, change of language	Honest expression to help client move to a higher level of personal functioning	Provide information on nutrition, stress management, physical fitness, environmental stressors, Yoga, meditation, visualization
Eliminate problems by changing thoughts that promote them	Client identifies factors that block his freedom	See self as a growing, changing person who can take charge of life, manifested in increased inner peace and harmony
Crooked thinking, unconditional shoulds, absolutistic musts	Self-directed, values, choice, autonomy, self-responsibility	Wellness, inner healing, imagery, energy balance, psychic abilities, awareness

reports of music's effectiveness in assisting relaxation (Hanser, 1985, p. 201).

To effect a change in a person's condition, the therapist working in a biomedical model evaluates whether it is the germ causing the syndrome or the genetic make-up and background of the person's biochemistry and anatomy, specifically the brain, that determine the cause of the disturbance.

Terminology used in this model might include the following: medical model, genetic, germs, biochemistry, and chemical therapies.

BEHAVIORAL MODEL

The behavioral model holds that human beings learn through conditioning to be abnormal and can, therefore, unlearn these maladaptive behaviors. Skinner's model is based on reinforcement principles and has the goal of identifying and controlling environmental factors that lead to behavioral change (Corey, 1986). Skinner's view of controlling behavior is based on the principles of operant conditioning, the assumption being that changes in behavior are brought about when that behavior is followed by a consequence. Skinner contends that learning occurs only when some kind of reinforcement, either positive or negative, is paired with the learning. Another behavior therapy that follows a classical conditioning model is based on the work of Joseph Wolpe.

The therapist's role is to provide a means for the client to attain the goal. The therapist assumes an active and directive role in treatment that might include setting up a contingency to help change any maladaptive behavior. This framework is useful for the music therapist since he is concerned with manipulating the musical stimuli to effect a behavior change.

A technique used in music therapy suggests that music itself is the operant conditioner, reinforcing the altered behavior. Music therapists may use behavior analysis techniques and design individual treatment programs to meet the needs of the people they serve, i.e., observing, identifying the behavior, establishing a baseline, determining strategy for change, implementing, evaluating, and recording changes in behavior (Hanser, 1983). The opportunity to play an instrument can be used as a contingency for improved client behavior. See Taxonomy I, *Music Performing,* E. "Individual Instrumental Instruction (product oriented)," for an explanation of this technique.

In addition, the client may seek to exercise and improve an existing musical skill or to learn and develop a new musical skill. The therapist instructs the client in playing techniques using materials or the appropriate learning level, and assigns practice tasks of which the client is capable. The therapist may include positive reinforcement for desired behavior, nonmusical and/or musical. One case in the literature involved time away from music as a contingency. This strategy was effective in reducing the inappropriate mannerisms of a woman diagnosed as schizophrenic (Hauck & Martin, 1970).

Other techniques used in this model are relaxation training, token economies, modeling methods, systematic desensitization, assertion training, and self-management programs.

One criterion for evaluating change is to create new conditions for learning. It is essential that the old maladaptive behaviors that the client must unlearn and the new adaptive ones that the client must learn be quantitatively observed and measured.

Terminology utilized in this model might include these terms: Pavlovian or classical conditioning, operant conditioning, conditioned response, stimulus, cause and effect, extinction, positive and/or negative reinforcer, selective punishment, biofeedback, and avoidance situation.

PSYCHODYNAMIC MODEL

The psychodynamic model treatment approach is based on Freudian theory; however, more modern views of psychoanalysis exist today. This model holds that abnormality is driven by hidden conflicts within the personality. The client is helped to be more aware of his unconscious conflicts and desires, focusing on the relationship between early childhood experiences and present functioning. Treatment interventions are designed to identify and work through the emotional conflicts of the client.

The therapist's role is to demonstrate qualities such as self-confidence and controlled emotional warmth. These traits enable the therapist to offer the client a pattern of action, personal participation, that arouses expectations of help and facilitates attitude change (Frank, 1961). As the therapist attempts to foster a transference relationship, (e.g., client's displacement of feelings for significant people in one's childhood onto the physician or therapist [Rowe, 1989]), he encourages more self-awareness, more honesty, and the resolving of personal relationship issues. He also encourages dealing with anxiety in a realistic way and gaining control over impulsive and irrational behavior (Corey, 1986).

The therapist's role changes from that of an analyst to that of an ally and active supporter who encourages the patient to learn, mature, and grow emotionally by working through problems on a more realistic level (Tyson, 1981, p. 20). Other techniques include interpretation, dream analysis, free association, analysis and interpretation of resistance, and analysis and interpretation of transference techniques.

In a music therapy setting, one technique used would be the introduction and use of music instruments to provide a structured, nonverbal mode for the expression of unconscious thoughts and feelings.

According to Jung, performing music requires all four functions of the psyche: thinking, to turn the notes into music; feeling, to give the music expression; sensation, in the person's proprioceptive (position awareness) feedback from his body when playing an instrument or singing; and intuition, to get into the very essence of the composer's inspiration (Priestly, 1975, p. 18). See Taxonomy I, *Music Performing,* G. "Individual Music Improvisation/Interaction (process oriented)," for an explanation of this technique. The client learns to use the instrument as an emotional outlet and to release feelings of tension and anxiety. The therapist provides elementary musical forms in which the client learns to express himself freely.

In this model, change is achieved by modifying the client's character structure through making the unconscious conscious, and by strengthening the ego so that behavior is based more on reality and less on instinctual cravings (Corey, 1986). The focus is on using a therapeutic method to bring out the unconscious material, which can then be worked through.

The terminology used in this model might include: defense mechanism, libido, life instincts, aggressive drives, id, ego, superego, oral stage, phallic stage, latency period, genital stage, oedipus complex, penis envy, castration, anxiety conflict, free association, and transference.

COGNITIVE MODEL

The cognitive model holds that abnormality springs from disordered thinking about oneself and the world. Rational Emotive Therapy (RET), a form of cognitively oriented behavioral therapy, is the forerunner of the cognitive therapies. The others are Maultsby's rational behavior therapy, Beck's cognitive therapy, Meichenbaum's cognitive behavior modification, Glasser's Reality Therapy (cognitive/behavioral), and Berne's Transactional Analysis (affective/cognitive/behavioral). They all stress the importance of cognitive processes as determinants of behavior. The cognitive school is an outgrowth of and reaction to the behavioral school. The cognitive psychologist contends that disordered cognitive processes cause psychological problems and, by changing these conditions, the psychologist can alleviate and perhaps even cure the disorder.

RET is based on the assumption that human beings are born with a potential for both rational, straight thinking and irrational, crooked thinking (Corey, 1986). RET stresses that a person's emotions stem from his beliefs in, evaluations and interpretations of, and reactions to life situations. Clients learn skills that help them identify and then dispute any acquired irrational beliefs that are being prolonged by habit and/or self-indoctrination. They learn how to think effectively and rationally and, as a result, to change former emotional reactions to more positive reactions of their own choosing.

An important component of the RET conceptualization of human behavior is the detection of irrational beliefs. The key to detection is examination of one's thinking for the "musts" and "shoulds." These words reveal unrealistic and irrational thinking that often involves self-imposed demands (e.g., the young clarinetist who says that he or she must make first chair or feel like a complete failure [Bryant, 1987, p. 29]).

The therapist's role is that of a guide. Within that framework, the therapist facilitates the client's efforts to encounter, express, and resolve conflicts, helping him become aware of the irrational shoulds, oughts, and musts he expresses in life. The self-defeating ideas he had come to accept as truth are challenged by the therapist. The client is then assisted in adopting new, healthy responses.

A therapist might use the technique of structuring the music experience to guide the processing of individual and/or group reactions and facilitate the verbal processing of the material. According to Maultsby (1977), music functions both as a stimulus and a reinforcer. Maultsby maintains that learning is created when emotional reactions are reinforced by repetition of the lyrics;

ultimately the lyrics become associated with the actual logical, emotional, and physical action (Bryant, 1987, p. 30). In Taxonomy II, *Music Psychotherapy*, B. "Interactive Music Group and/or Individual Psychotherapy," the primary activities are the various forms of guided music listening that may lead to discussion of lyric content, the music's mood, and associations with past experiences of personal relevance to the individual's conscious conflicts. In addition, music selections might express and reflect themes and issues that are relevant to the group's process and thus serve as a focal point for theme-centered interaction.

Other techniques used in this model include homework to test new assumptions, modifying "shoulds," changing language, open-ended questions, role playing, and imagery.

In order to evaluate change, the therapist and client must work together to dispute irrational beliefs that cause negative emotional reactions. Change is noted when a style of thinking that manifested itself in unrealistic, immature, and demanding ways has changed to a way of thinking and behaving that is realistic, mature, and logically empirical. Thus the client will have developed the ability to react more appropriately to life situations that demand a feeling response.

The terminology used for this model includes: unconditional shoulds, absolutistic musts, self-defeating, self-indoctrination, judging, deciding, analyzing and doing, crooked thinking, and new self-statements.

HUMANISTIC MODEL

The humanistic approach to abnormality has been described as an outcome of the failure to grow, find meaning, and be responsible for oneself and others. The humanistic/existential model holds that disorder results when an individual fails to confront successfully the basic questions of life. What is the meaning of life? How can I live up to my fullest potential? How can I face death (Rosenhan & Seligman, 1984)?

Humanistic theories are concerned with defining the needs that are central to human functioning. Humanistic psychologists are often concerned with the positive aspects of living, or, more simply, one's passion (Rosenhan & Seligman, 1984). Abraham Maslow, one of the early and influential humanistic thinkers, described human needs in terms of a pyramid, a hierarchy of needs ranging from basic biological needs to self-actualization. Frederick (Fritz) Perls developed Gestalt therapy, a form of existential (grounded in the here-and-now) therapy based on the premise that people must find their own way in life and accept responsibility if they hope to achieve maturity (Corey, 1986). Carl Rogers developed a therapy based on unconditional positive regard and therapist empathy. Additionally, Rogers developed techniques to evaluate the effectiveness of client-centered therapy.

In this model, the therapist's role is to be immediately present and accessible to the client and to focus on the here-and-now experience created by the relationship. The therapist's attitude is just as critical as the techniques, knowledge, or theory. If the therapist demonstrates genuine caring, respect, acceptance, and understanding, the client is helped to release defenses and rigid perceptions and move to a higher level of personal functioning. For example, a therapist choosing musical improvisation as a nonverbal tool for communication would not guide the client in any specific direction, but would support and reflect the client's improvisation both verbally and musically (Wheeler, 1981).

The techniques must be an honest expression of the therapist; they cannot be used self-consciously, for then the therapist would be acting incongruently. The therapist helps the client to think, feel, and explore in order to develop an internal frame of reference. A music therapist might provide ego support through musical accomplishment and improve musical and interpersonal skills for a personal expressive outlet. This model is generally concerned with the self-actualization process, in which the individual is viewed as a purposeful creature of plans, strategies, and choices. A person's thoughts and feelings are critically important to what he says and does. Through music performance activities and the support of the therapist, the client gains awareness of the polarities between his thinking and attitudes and his actual music performance. See Taxonomy I, *Music Performing,* F. "Individual Vocal Instructor (product oriented)," for an explanation of this technique. It may help the individual to learn to accept the responsibility of practice as a self-imposed task and relate effort to an aesthetically satisfying musical result.

Change is evaluated by determining whether a client has achieved greater independence and integration of his personality. Thus change is determined when the client is taking responsibility for his actions and demonstrates an ability to identify factors that block his freedom and spontaneous expression of feelings.

Terminology used in this model is: experiential, relationship oriented, vocabulary of freedom, choice, values, personal responsibility, autonomy, purpose, and meaning.

HOLISTIC MODEL

The holistic model is based on the assumption that the individual is an integrated whole with resources to promote personal health (Reed and Sanderson, 1980). The word holistic (sometimes spelled wholistic) stems from the Greek "holos," meaning whole or entire, which relates to the words heal and health.

Unity of mind, body, and spirit is the fundamental principle of the holistic health philosophy. It demands treating the individual rather than the disease (Mattson, 1982). The person is seen as a whole comprised of these three interrelated dimensions, and change in one part brings about shifts in other parts. Illness, then, is a disturbance of the unified functioning of the whole and not just an isolated cause or effect (Deliman & Smolowe, 1982, p. 9).

America's loss of faith in the medical establishment gave a strong symbolic push to the paradigm shift from institutional help to self-help (Naisbett, 1982). Naisbett states that three major trends have emerged from this new way of thinking. They are: (1) new habits that actualize one's new-found responsibility for health; (2) self-care that illustrates self-reliance in areas not genuinely requiring professional help; and (3) the triumph of the new paradigm of wellness, preventive medicine, and holistic care over the old model of illness, drugs, surgery, and treating symptoms rather than the whole person.

The trend toward a wide variety of experiential therapies has emerged in the latter half of the twentieth century, their purpose being inner growth and self-actualization. Although the movement is in an embryonic stage, it is growing fast. Disillusioned people are looking for alternatives to the care provided by organized medicine.

The holistic health approach has opened up a new area in the search for health and wellness: the human mind (Naisbett, 1982). The belief that any disease can be diminished through the powers of the mind and a positive attitude is evidenced in this model. Even traditional medicine has acknowledged that the mind has a role in the prevention and healing of disease, as was demonstrated by Norman Cousins' recovery from an incurable illness through what was reported as a combination of his determination, Vitamin C, laughter, and help from his doctor. The emphasis of the holistic approach is on refocusing health care toward the individual as a unique, whole, priceless being. The holistic model seeks to concentrate on obtaining and maintaining health, which includes adopting a life style that focuses on health.

Health professionals are being exposed to the broad spectrum of approaches within holistic principles. Viewed as the "new consciousness," the new therapies embrace mysticism, occultism, spiritism, parapsychology, and altered states of consciousness, to name a few of the approaches (Mattson, 1982). They emphasize new ways in which people see themselves, the universe, and especially the supernatural realm. Probably the hardest holistic principle to accommodate in clinical practice is the spiritual dimension and belief in the concept of energies (Mattson, 1982). Advocates of the holistic way of life state that the spiritual component is necessary for healing, but to the traditional mind, this component is often still neglected. Although presently there are no objective standards or guidelines for treatment and no accepted consensus as to the holistic model's role in medicine and society, forthcoming research will likely expedite the acceptance of these healing alternatives.

The therapist views himself as an educator. Knowledge is freely shared on the assumption that understanding will enable the client to be more active in the healing process. The therapist shares his own experiences, creating a more equal therapist-client relationship. The therapist is also willing to become emotionally involved, which creates an opportunity to "evolve one's consciousness." The therapist's techniques not only help the client find information but promote techniques to develop self-responsibility, better nutrition, stress management, and physical fitness, and to counteract environmental stressors.

The techniques used in this model encourage the client to look within for his own healing. They might include acupuncture, rolfing, meditation, shiatsu, bodywork, homeopathy, herbology, applied kinesiology, chiropractic therapy, imagery and visualization, psychosynthesis, and psychic healing. See Taxonomy II, *Music Psychotherapy*, D. "Catalytic Music Group and/or Individual Therapy," for an explanation of this technique. The emphasis is to encourage the client to reach and explore altered states of consciousness for the purpose of allowing imagery, symbols, and latent feelings to surface from the inner self. The aim is to help the client to develop self-awareness, clarify personal values, release blocked psychic energy sources, enrich group spirit, bring about deep relaxation, and foster religious experience (Bonny & Savary, 1973).

Pianist Arthur Rubinstein struggled to define what he called "this thing in us, a metaphysical power that emanates from us." He had often felt it in his concerts, he said, this tangible energy reaching out into the audience. "It is something floating, something unknown that has no place to disappear to" (Ferguson, 1980).

Change would be evidenced in a client's reduction of stress level and removal of pain or dysfunction. The client would see himself as a growing, changing person who can take charge of life. Changes would manifest themselves in an alteration of affect and a demonstration of more patience, harmony, and peace.

Terminology used in this model would include: inner healing, imagery, psychic abilities, awareness training, self-responsibility, eclectic, practitioners, self-care, self-examination, and self-healing.

CONCLUSION

Many theories exist in the treatment of psychiatric clients. An eclectic approach that draws from more than one theory is often used. There are a multitude of differences, especially in points of emphasis within each of these theories.

Ideally, all therapies may be designed to alleviate somatic dysfunctions, psychosocial maladaptation, or existential anxieties. The therapist should use every medical, environmental, and psychosocial means to relieve somatic distress, and every form of influence to encourage patients to explore more satisfactory and useful styles of conduct. The therapist might also assist patients in developing a philosophy of life in which they can find more satisfying qualities of well-being, creativity, security, and serenity (Karasu, 1984).

All the models discussed try to affect change and growth. Growth means an enlarging and expansion of one's horizons and boundaries, outwardly in perspective and inwardly in depth (Wilbur, 1981). Music therapy activities selected for specific theoretical models might be interchanged and used in other models. The language and/or terminology would differ in the explanation of the processing and evaluation of the activity.

Music therapists are educated to define treatment and communicate in the language of the various theoretical models. However, procedures within the field of therapy with music ought to be judged, not on the basis of whether they are "humanistic," "true," or "scientific," but on the basis of their consequences (Ruud, 1988).

REFERENCES

Bonny, H., & Savary, L. (1973). *Music and your mind.* New York: Harper & Row.

Bryant, D. (1987). A cognitive approach to therapy through music. *Journal of Music Therapy, 24*(1), 27–34.

Corey, G. (Ed.). (1986). *Theory and practice of counseling and psychotherapy.* Pacific Grove, CA: Brooks/Cole.

Deliman, T., & Smolowe, J. (1982). *Holistic medicine.* Reston, VA: Reston Publishing Co.

Ferguson, M. (1980). *The Acquarian conspiracy.* Boston: Houghton Mifflin.

Frank, J. (1961). *Persuasion and healing.* Baltimore, MD: Johns Hopkins University Press.

Hauck, L. P., & Martin, P. L. (1970). Music as a reinforcer in patient controlled duration of time-out. *Journal of Music Therapy, 7,* 43–53.

Hanser, S. (1983). Music therapy: A behavioral perspective. *The Behavior Therapist, 6*(1), 5–8.

Hanser, S. (1985). Music therapy and stress reduction research. *Journal of Music Therapy, 22*(4), 193–203.

Karasu, T. B. (Ed.). (1984). *The psychosocial therapies, Part II of the psychiatric therapies.* Washington, D.C.: American Psychiatric Association.

Mattson, P. (1982). *Holistic health in perspective.* Palo Alto, CA: Mayfield Publishing Co.

Maultsby, M. (1977). Combining music therapy and rational behavior therapy. *Journal of Music Therapy, 14*(2), 89–97.

Naisbitt, J. (1982). *Megatrends.* New York: Warner Books.

Peach, S. (1984). Some implications for the clinical use of music facilitated imagery. *Journal of Music Therapy, 21*(1), 27–34.

Priestly, M. (1975). *Music therapy in action.* London: Constable.

Reed, K. (1984). *Models of practice in occupational therapy.* Baltimore, MD: Williams & Wilkins.

Reed, K., & Sanderson, S. (1980). *Concepts of occupational therapy.* Baltimore, MD: Williams & Wilkins.

Rider, M., Floyd, J., & Kirkpatrick, J. (1985). The effect of music, imagery, and relaxation on adrenal corticosteroid and the re-entrainment of circodian rhythms. *Journal of Music Therapy, 22*(1), 46–57.

Rosenhan, D., & Seligman, M. (1984). *Abnormal psychology.* New York: W. W. Norton.

Rowe, C. J. (1989). *An outline of psychiatry.* Dubuque, IA: Wm. C. Brown.

Ruud, E. (1980). *Music therapy and its relationship to current treatment theories.* St. Louis: Magnamusic-Baton.

Stoudenmire, J. (1975). A comparison of muscle relaxation training and music in the reduction state and trait anxiety. *Journal of Clinical Psychology, 31,* 490–492.

Tyson, F. (1981). *Psychiatric music therapy.* New York: Creative Arts Rehabilitation Center.

Wheeler, B. (1981). The relationship between music and theories of psychotherapy. *Music Therapy, 1*(1), 9–15.

Wilber, K. (1981). *No boundary.* Boston: New Science Library.

Chapter 9

Music Therapy and Psychopharmacology

Roger A. Smeltekop and Becki A. Houghton

Psychiatric treatment is most often provided in a milieu of several types of interventions. These essentially include a structured environment, a regime of medication, a variety of psychotherapeutic interventions, and a program of activity therapies. Effective treatment depends on a coordinated effort by the staff of these areas; each patient may derive primary benefit from one or another of them.

Psychotropic medications function to alleviate many of the major symptoms of mental illness that interfere with successful daily life functioning, as well as to help relieve the accompanying psychological distress. They also aid the patient in maintaining psychological equilibrium when coping with the stresses of the environment after satisfactory functioning has been restored by treatment. This chemical intervention serves to render the patient accessible to psychosocial therapeutic treatment (Spiegel & Aebi, 1981). The effectively medicated patient is receptive and able to work in the psychotherapeutic situation, since medication provides an avenue to the patient's capacity to change overt behavior and disordered thinking. The term "psychoactive" is sometimes used for this group of medications; however, this term also commonly includes street drugs, as well as medications legitimately prescribed for psychological treatment.

HISTORICAL DEVELOPMENT

Forty years ago a major breakthrough occurred in the treatment of patients with mental disorders. Henri Laborit, a French anesthesiologist, sought a drug to use in the prevention of surgical shock (Caldwell, 1970). In testing one drug preoperatively, he found an unexpected sedation in patients, an effect which he described as a "euphoric quietude." Thinking this might be helpful in treating mental patients, Laborit recommended it to some of his psychiatrist colleagues. This drug was the immediate forerunner of chlorpromazine, which revolutionized the treatment of schizophrenia (Swazy, 1974). Chlorpromazine not only reduced stress and agitation in schizophrenics, but it also caused a significant reduction in their auditory hallucinations and delusional thinking. For the first time, many of these patients were able to begin to function in the world outside the sheltered hospital environment.

Although medication made a remarkable difference, it alone did not give the schizophrenic a normal life. Patients who had been hospitalized for many years had lost the skills necessary to survive in the world outside of the hospital. Consequently, shortly after the introduction of chlorpromazine and other similar drugs, mental patients began to return to the local communities, and local mental health agencies were developed to address the unique needs of these deinstitutionalized mental patients. Community Mental Health agencies offered a spectrum of services, including individual psychotherapy, outpatient medication clinics, vocational rehabilitation, and partial hospitalization or day treatment, which addressed the psychosocial and community adjustment needs of the more independent, noninstitutionalized patient (see Chapter 7).

Chlorpromazine was the first psychoactive drug. Soon other drugs were developed that assisted in the treatment of other major psychiatric illnesses such as major depression and bipolar disorders. None of the drugs cure mental illness. Approximately 20 percent of mental patients do not respond to medication. However, the use of psychoactive drugs has drastically improved the outlook for the mentally ill. Some patients may still experience symptoms upon leaving the hospital, but although they may occasionally hear voices, experience some delusional thinking, and perhaps be suspicious of others, the symptoms are no longer severely debilitating. Effectively medicated patients can generally live in an independent, or semi-independent environment, and perhaps hold jobs. At times, even when a patient seems well controlled on medication, the stable condition can deteriorate and lead to rehospitalization. The psychiatrist then must re-evaluate the patient to determine whether there is a need for an increase in medication, a change in medication, or perhaps a combination of medications to control the symptoms. However, this decompensation is often caused when the patient himself, after being stabilized on medication, decides he no longer needs medication and discontinues its use. Often, when this occurs, psychotic symptoms reappear.

ANTIPSYCHOTIC MEDICATIONS

Antipsychotic medications are classified in families (e.g., Phenothiazines) according to their common chemical derivations. The generic names of individual drugs (e.g., chlorpromazine) reflect their chemical compositions as well. Trade names (e.g., Thorazine) are given by the drug manufacturers for purposes of success in marketing, and easier, more familiar reference. Physicians have traditionally used the trade names for prescribing and administering psychotropic medications; however, some clinics use only generic

TABLE 9–1 ANTIPSYCHOTIC TRANQUILIZERS (NEUROLEPTICS)*

Family	Generic Name	Trade Name	Usual Daily Dose
I. Phenothiazines			
A. Aliphatic	chlorpromazine	Thorazine, Promopar	200–800 mg
	promazine	Sparine	500–1000 mg
	triflupromazine	Vesprin	50–100 mg
B. Piperidine			
	thioridazine	Mellaril	100–600 mg
	piperacetazine	Quide	30 mg
	mesoridazine	Serentil	50–100 mg
C. Piperazine			
	acetophenazine	Tindal	30–120 mg
	fluphenazine	Prolixin HCl	2–10 mg
		Prolixin Enanthate	Long acting,
		Prolixin Deconoate	injectable
	perphenazine	Trilafon	8–16 mg
	prochlorperazine	Compazine	75–100 mg
	trifluoperazine	Stelazine	4–15 mg
II. Thiozanthines			
	chlorprothixene	Taractan	50–400 mg
	triothixene	Navane	5–10 mg
III. Butyrophenone			
	haloperidol	Haldol	2–5 mg
IV. Dihydroindolone			
	molindone	Moban, Lidone	50–100 mg
V. Dibenzoxazepine			
	loxapine	Loxitane	50–75 mg

* These drugs are often referred to as major tranquilizers, neuroleptics, or antipsychotic drugs. Since tranquilizer implies that sedation is the primary effect, the terms antipsychotic or neuroleptic are preferred (Bassuk & Schoonover, 1977).

names for accuracy and impartiality towards drug companies. Table 9-1 lists the antipsychotics by family, generic name, trade name, and usual daily dosages. Table 9-2 shows two sets of drug groupings based on common features including potency and effects on the patient.

There is general agreement among psychiatrists today on the theory of how most of the psychotropic drugs work. The most prominent theory involves neurotransmitters, chemical substances that transmit messages across synapses, or gaps between nerve cells in the brain. Different neurotransmitters have different functions and pathways, and are associated with different behavioral states (Kety, 1978). In schizophrenia, for instance, the neurotransmitter dopamine is secreted by nerve cells in the brain. It then crosses a synapse and activates the receptors on nearby nerve cells. The limbic system, where thoughts, feelings, and moods are processed, is the location of many dopamine receptors. Once the activation has occurred, the dopamine is normally reabsorbed into the nerve cell from which it came.

It is speculated that the disordered thinking and behavior in schizophrenia is caused by one of the following: (1) the neurotransmitter dopamine is

TABLE 9–2 PROMINENT FEATURES OF THE NEUROLEPTICS

Generic Name	Trade Name	Prominent Features
chlorpromazine	Thorazine*	
promazine	Sparine	
triflupromazine	Vesprin	Lower potency, higher dose
thioridazine	Mellaril	Fewer extrapyramidal side effects
chlorprothixene	Trilafon	More sedation
prochlorperazine	Compazine	More hypotension
acetophenazine	Tindal	
fluphenazine	Prolixin	
trifluoperazine	Stelazine	Higher potency, lower dose
thiothixene	Navane	More extrapyramidal side effects
haloperidol	Haldol	Less sedation
molindone	Moban	Less hypotension
loxapine	Loxitane	

* These drugs are often referred to as major tranquilizers.

reabsorbed too slowly; (2) too much of the neurotransmitter is initially released; or (3) the receptors are overly sensitive to the neurotransmitters. Theoretically, psychotropic medications attach themselves to the receptors and block the action of the neurotransmitters. There are also receptors in the areas of the brain that control motor responses. It is thought that the cause of many side effects from the psychotropic medications are the result of the actions of the medications on the neurotransmitters and receptors in those areas of the brain that control motor responses.

Side Effects of the Neuroleptics

Side effects are not uncommon in treatment with psychotropic drugs. Most common are the central nervous system side effects. Parkinson-like symptoms may develop, which consist of muscular rigidity, tremors, and difficulty in walking. In addition, restlessness, muscle twitching, and tardive dyskinesia may occur. All except the latter are easily treated with anti-Parkinson medications. Tardive dyskinesia consists of abnormal involuntary movements in other parts of the body (Jeste & Wyatt, 1980). Tardive dyskinesia is causing concern as the incidence seems to be rising, and in some patients it has been found to be irreversible (Jeste & Wyatt, 1980). The current methods of minimizing tardive dyskinesia are to prescribe psychotropic medications only when the indication is absolutely clear, to use the minimal effective dose, to examine frequently for the onset of symptoms, and to discontinue use when there is adequate hope that a patient may continue symptom-free without medication. Table 9-3 lists common side effects of the neuroleptic medications, including the effects on the functions of the autonomic nervous system and the central nervous system.

TABLE 9–3 COMMON SIDE EFFECTS OF THE NEUROLEPTICS*

A. AUTONOMIC NERVOUS SYSTEM SIDE EFFECTS
    Note: These side effects usually disappear after a period of time on medication

 1. *Anticholinergic Effects*

    dry mouth, blurred vision, constipation, nasal congestion

 2. *Cardiovascular Effects*

    postural hypotension, dizziness, or blackouts when rising suddenly
    tachycardia (fast heart rate)
    hypo- or hypertension (low or high blood pressure)
    agranulcytosis (white blood count lowered)

 3. *Weight Gain*

    common side effect of long term phenothiazine treatment

 4. *Photosensitivity*
    skin may sunburn easily

B. CENTRAL NERVOUS SYSTEM SIDE EFFECTS
    Note: See section on treatment of extrapyramidal side effects

 1. *Parkinson-like syndrome*
    muscle rigidity in legs, arms, and face
    tremors of hands and extremities
    pill rolling—finger and thumb rotation
    excess salivation/drooling
    stooped posture and reduced mobility
    cogwheel rigidity (an extremity moves in a series of jerks when flexed & relaxed)

 2. *Dystonias*

    facial grimacing and distortions
    muscle spasms of neck, face, body, and extremities
    staring, eye rolling

 3. *Akathesia*

    restlessness, inability to sit still
    pacing
    fidgeting
    internal sensation of muscles quivering

 4. *Tardive Dyskinesia (Jeste and Wyatt, 1980)*

    rhythmical involuntary movements of face, tongue, and jaw
    sucking and smacking lip movements
    rapidly sticking out tongue
    puckering lips, puffing of cheeks
    head jerking

---

* While this is not an exhaustive list of all possible side effects, it does identify the most common from neuroleptics.

Treatment of Extrapyramidal Side Effects

Extrapyramidal side effects can usually be reduced or eliminated by decreasing the dose of the neuroleptic. At times the medication cannot be lowered enough to eliminate the side effects without a recurrence of psychotic symptoms. When decreasing the dose is not an effective solution, additional anti-Parkinson medication to control the side effects is administered. The most common anti-Parkinson medications are benztropine mesylate (Cogentin) or trihexyphenidyl (Artane). The average daily dose for Cogentin is 2-6 mg/day, and Artane is 2-10 mg/day (Shader & Jackson, 1975). Tardive dyskinesia is not generally responsive to these medications.

MOOD-STABILIZING MEDICATIONS

During the same time that chlorpromazine was first being used on schizophrenics, it was discovered that lithium carbonate helped to control the symptoms of mania. Originally tested as a sedative, lithium was found to prevent the occurrence of manic episodes. Lithium seems to behave chemically in the brain in much the same manner as the neuroleptic medications, by reducing the activity of the dopamine receptors. It also appears to have an effect on another neurotransmitter, serotonin.

The administration of lithium carbonate (Eskalith, Lithane, Lithonate) requires careful monitoring by medical personnel. Generally a 600 mg loading dose is given and blood serum lithium levels are measured frequently thereafter to check for a therapuetic blood level and to prevent lithium toxicity. The generally accepted therapeutic range for lithium serum levels is 0.6 to 1.2 mEg/L. Levels are measured approximately 12 hours after the last dosage of lithium has been administered (Bernstein, 1983). During an acute manic phase 1500–2400 mg is a normal daily dose. For maintenance doses 300–1500 mg is generally recommended. Because there is a lag period of 4-10 days before lithium reaches a therapeutic level, often one of the neuroleptics is given during this period to sedate a patient who is in an acute manic episode (Bassuk & Schoonover, 1977).

Lithium is indicated for control of an acute manic episode, as a mood-stabilizing agent in the manic and depressive patient (lithium helps reduce the frequency and severity of mood swings), and as an antidepressant in the depressed phase of a bipolar disorder.

Table 9-4 lists the common side effects of lithium. Any warning signs of toxicity or intoxication warrant immediate medical attention. Patients on lithium should maintain normal salt intake to assure stable lithium blood levels. Regular fluid intake and output are also necessary to maintain stable lithium levels (Bassuk & Schoonover, 1977).

ANTIDEPRESSANT MEDICATIONS

Tricyclic Antidepressants

The discovery of the group of antidepressants called tricyclic antidepressants dates before 1900. However, it was not until the discovery of chlorpromazine in the 1950s that the tricyclics were given consideration for use with psychi-

TABLE 9–4 COMMON SIDE EFFECTS OF LITHIUM

nausea (usually just initially)
fine tremor of the hands
excessive urination
excessive thirst

Caution: Warning signs of toxicity

coarse tremors of hands/feet
pronounced lack of muscle coordination
muscular weakness
unusual drowsiness
diarrhea (for longer than 24 hours)
vomiting
headache
tinnitus (ringing in the ears)

Serious intoxication

slurred speech
blurred vision
persistent drowsiness
muscular twitching
convulsions
stupor
coma

atric patients. When it was observed that the chemical structure of the tricyclics was quite similar to that of chlorpromazine, the tricyclics were tried with schizophrenic patients. The tricyclics had little effect on them, except that at times the antidepressants seemed to raise the spirits of the patients.

Most psychiatrists now believe that a functional deficiency in one or both of the neurotransmitters, serotonin and norepinephrine, is the cause of most forms of depression. The tricyclic antidepressants appear to block the nerve reuptake of both neurotransmitters, which increases their availability at receptor sites in the brain (Bernstein, 1983).

The tricyclic antidepressants appear to be most effective with patients over age 35 with signs of endogenous or psychotic depression. These symptoms include severe weight loss, early morning awakening, pessimism, suicidal thoughts, and psychomotor agitation or retardation (Klerman, 1978). Because the tricyclic antidepressants are more effective and less toxic than the monoamine oxidase (MAO) inhibitors, they are more often the drugs of choice in the treatment of depression. There are six different compounds in the tricyclic group (see Tables 9-5 and 9-6). Some of the tricyclics have sedative and hypnotic effects, and are best used with patients who are agitated, anxious, or unable to sleep. Other tricyclics are more stimulating, and while not useful for an agitated patient, are helpful for a patient with motor retardation or apathy (Klerman, 1978).

Several very important related facts to remember about the tricyclic antidepressants are:

TABLE 9–5 TRICYCLIC ANTIDEPRESSANTS

Generic Name	Trade Name	Usual Daily Dose
amitriptyline	Elavil	75–300 mg
	Endep	75–300 mg
desipramine	Norpramin	75–200 mg
	Pertofrane	75–200 mg
doxepine	Sinequan	75–300 mg
imipramine	Tofranil	75–300 mg
	SK-Pramine	75–300 mg
	Janimine	75–300 mg
nortriptyline	Pamelor	40–100 mg
	Aventyl	40–100 mg
protriptyline	Vivactyl	30–60 mg

1. It can take 7–14 days for the therapeutic effect of the tricyclic medication to become apparent. It may take even longer for the full effect to be realized.

2. Even a relatively small overdose of a tricyclic can be fatal. Caution must be used in dispensing the medication to a suicidal patient.

3. The withdrawal of the tricyclic drug should be gradual, as nausea, vomiting, and other side effects can occur when the drug is discontinued too abruptly.

4. During a switch from tricyclic antidepressants to MAO inhibiters, a drug-free period of 14 days is recommended, to avoid the danger of medication interactions and to observe accurately the effects of each drug.

TABLE 9–6 SIDE EFFECTS OF TRICYCLIC ANTIDEPRESSANTS

Anticholinergic (see Table 9–3)

Postural hypotension (see Table 9–3, Cardiovascular Effects)

Sedation
  most sedation—amitriptyline and doxepin
  intermediate—imipramine
  least sedation—desipramine, nortriptyline, and protriptyline (Bassuk and Schoonover, 1977)

Other
  increased sweating
  increased heart rate
  weight gain
  cardiac arrhythmias
  fine tremors
  insomnia, restlessness, agitation

Monoamine Oxidase Inhibitors

During the 1950s doctors discovered that a new drug, iproniazid, which was used in the treatment of tuberculosis, caused emotional excitement in some patients. Other drugs were found for the treatment of tuberculosis, but iproniazid began to be used in psychiatry for its effectiveness in the treatment of depression (Klein & Davis, 1969). In the brain, an enzyme, monoamine oxidase inactivated the neurotransmitter serotonin, which affects mood. Iproniazid blocks or inhibits the activity of the enzyme monoamine oxidase—hence the name monoamine oxidase (MAO) inhibitors (see Table 9-7). MAO inhibitors have serious side effects (see Table 9-8).

ANTI-ANXIETY MEDICATIONS

Anxiety is a part of everyday life for each individual. It can prove to be helpful (as a motivator or signal of threat), or it can be harmful (as an immobilizing and debilitating response to nondangerous circumstances). We can experience anxiety when we are in danger, when we are afraid, or when we are in new situations. It can be a specific, focused anxiety, or a general, free-floating anxiety. It can be a phobic anxiety or a simple situational anxiety. Anxiety can be crippling, causing a patient to stay home, avoid friends and work, and impair relationships. The treatment of anxiety requires that the physician be clearly aware of the type of anxiety the patient is experiencing. The symptoms for anxiety and depression may be quite similar, and if a depressed patient is given an anti-anxiety agent, rather than an antidepressant, the patient could become more depressed, and perhaps even suicidal.

One of the earliest treatments of patients with serious anxiety was the use of alcohol for its calming effects. Alcohol is frequently still used by anxious individuals to medicate themselves. Today a thorough understanding of the patient's anxiety is needed to determine which of a vast array of anti-anxiety agents will be most beneficial. Additionally, other drugs may be used to treat anxiety (see Table 9-9). For instance, if it is determined that the patient has an anxious depression, the more sedative tricyclic antidepressants, such as amitriptyline or doxepin may be used (see Table 9-5). In a patient with a psychotic terror, one of the neuroleptics would be indicated (see Table 9-1) (Shader & Greenblatt, 1975).

TABLE 9–7 MAO INHIBITORS

Generic Name	Trade Name	Usual Daily Dose
isocarboxazid	Marplan	10–50 mg
phenelzine	Nardil	15–75 mg
tranylcypromine	Parnate	20–40 mg

TABLE 9–8 SIDE EFFECTS OF THE MAO INHIBITORS

vasodilation (headache, flushed feeling)
dry mouth, constipation
agitation, tremor
postural hypotension (see Table 9–3, Cardiovascular Effects)
increased sweating
hypertensive crisis (see following information)

CAUTION: Dangerously high blood pressure can develop if the MAO inhibitors are mixed with certain foods containing the amino acid typramine. The following foods should be avoided while taking MAO inhibitors:

avocado
beer
cheese (aged)
chicken livers
chocolate
figs, dates, raisins
pickled herring
sour cream
wine (Chianti)
yeast extracts

ADDITIONAL CAUTION: Any patient taking an MAO inhibitor should first consult with the physician who prescribed it before taking any other medication. In particular, the patient should not use nasal decongestants, cough syrups, nose drops, cold remedies, diet pills or other stimulant drugs (Bernstein, 1983).

TABLE 9–9 ANTI-ANXIETY DRUGS

Generic Name	Trade Name	Usual Daily Dose
A. *Barbiturates*		
amobarbital	Amytal	45–200 mg
butabarbital	Butisol	45–200 mg
phenobarbital	Luminal	45–200 mg
B. *Propanediols*		
meprobamate	Equanil	1.2–1.6 mg
C. *Benzodiazepines*		
chlordiazepoxide	Librium	15–100 mg
diazepam	Valium	6–40 mg
oxazepam	Serax	30–120 mg
chlorzepate	Tranxene	11.25–60 mg
D. *Antihistamines*		
hydroxyzine	Atarax	30–200 mg
	Vistaril	30–200 mg
E. *Azaspirodecanedione*		
buspirone HC1	Buspar	20–30 mg

The most widely used drugs for anxiety are in the benzodiazepine group. They are generally the most effective, but even when taken at a therapeutic dosage the patient is at risk of addiction. Barbiturates and meprobamate were the drugs used most often in the treatment of anxiety prior to the discovery of the benzodiazepines. They are still used today, although their potential for abuse and lethal overdose is greater than that of the benzodiazepines. Another class of drugs used for the treatment of anxiety is the autonomic sedative anti-anxiety type, the antihistamines. However, they also do not appear to be as effective as the benzodiazepines. The most common side effect of the anti-anxiety agents is drowsiness.

In 1986 physicians began to recognize the anti-anxiety property of a non-benzodiazepine anxiolytic, Buspar (buspirone HCl). Active marketing of this product, emphasizing its superiority over the benzodiazepine medications, began in 1987. Treatment with buspirone HCl has several significant advantages. Clinical trials indicate that buspirone HCl causes no more drowsiness than a placebo (Newton, 1986). This is particularly important when a patient needs to stay alert, as most other anti-anxiety agents cause drowsiness (Moskowitz & Smiley, 1982). Again, unlike benzodiazepines, buspirone HCl does not impair motor skills, or potentiate the effects of alcohol (Mattila, 1982). Whereas the benzodiazepines often create dependency needs and increase the likelihood of abuse, buspirone HCl has no apparent abuse liability, because it does not produce the euphoria that often accompanies many abused drugs (Cole, Orzak, Beake, Bird, & Bar-Tal, 1982). Therefore buspirone HCl is not a controlled substance. Additionally, buspirone HCl has no withdrawal syndrome even upon an abrupt discontinuation of treatment (Rickels, Weisman, Norstad, Singer, Stoltz, Brown, and Danton, 1982).

Buspirone HCl must be given regularly for full therapeutic effect. Although a reduction in anxiety may be apparent in 7–10 days, full therapeutic effect may take 3–4 weeks, and treatment should continue through that period of time. Whereas the introduction of certain drugs may block the withdrawal syndrome of the previous drug, buspirone HCl will not block the withdrawal syndrome that generally accompanies the discontinuation of benzodiazepine therapy. Therefore, careful and complete withdrawal from benzodiazepines should be achieved before the introduction of buspirone HCl.

Side effects of buspirone HCl are relatively minor and have low incidence of occurrence. They include: dizziness, nausea, headache, nervousness, lightheadedness, and excitement. Rate of occurrence is 2–12 percent.

Research is ongoing in the area of psychopharmacology. A drug called L-Dopa is being tested to determine whether or not it can prevent tardive dyskinesia. Clonidine, a medication that controls high blood pressure, is being used for patients with Tourette's syndrome as well as patients with panic phobias. A blood test, the dexamethasone suppression test, has been developed to test for clinical depression. Researchers are continuing to investigate the use of neuroleptic medications with schizophrenics to determine the adequate blood levels of medication for the effective treatment of psychotic symptoms.

MUSIC THERAPIST RESPONSES TO MEDICATION SIDE EFFECTS

Psychoactive medications affect patients both biochemically and psychologically. The primary biochemical effects, or actions, are largely intended and desirable. The resulting improvement in mood, thinking, and behavior is usually welcomed by the patient. Emotionally the patient may feel relieved, nurtured, hopeful, and secure. However, when these emotions are accompanied by undesirable side effects, the therapist must adjust treatment to reduce the patient's psychological distress and physical difficulties.

Some of the physical side effects, such as constipation, urinary retention, weight gain, amenorrhea, and sexual dysfunction, primarily require medical and nursing care interventions. Many of the Autonomic Nervous System side effects will disappear after the patient has been on the medication for a period of time, and Central Nervous System (extrapyramidal) side effects can be controlled by reductions in dosage or administration of additional medications such as Artane or Cogentin. But there is frequently an interval during which all caregivers must assist the patient in maximizing therapeutic gain in the face of these intruding side effects.

Common-sense precautions and accommodations dictate how to respond to many side effects, such as excessive thirst, urination, sweating, or salivation. Precautions should also be taken to avoid overexposure to the sun for patients on phenothiazines and to monitor diet for those taking MAO inhibitors. The therapist should carefully observe and limit strenuous activity for patients who experience hypertension, tachycardia, or cardiac arythmias. Movement activities that involve postural shifts should be avoided by patients with orthostatic hypotension.

The music therapist must take into account the specific physical side effects when considering choices of music activity. The anticholinergic effects of dry mouth and nasal congestion could cause difficulty in playing most wind instruments and, to some degree, could influence the patient's comfort in singing activities. Blurred vision limits success in tasks requiring music reading and visual-motor accuracy. Alternate choices should be made available to allow for successful performance. For example, activities employing rote performance and auditory and tactile skills can be used.

Extrapyramidal side effects, most of which involve neuromuscular activity, require adjustments by the music therapist in the areas of activity choice and flexible expectations of performance. Muscle rigidity may respond to relaxation exercises and movement exercises emphasizing smooth and relaxed motor activity. Patients experiencing akathesia may benefit from movement and dance and instrumental playing, which can provide a purposeful focus and a diversion from the sensations of restlessness and muscular quivering. In tardive dyskinesia the voluntary inhibition of the movements in one body area exacerbates the movements in another (Bassuk & Schoonover, 1977). Music activity can be a source of productive movement substitutes for the otherwise purposeless motor activity. Fatigue and emotional tension tend to increase the movements of dyskinesia, as well as Parkinsonian tremors (Bassuk & Schoonover, 1977). The use of supportive music therapy interventions and relaxing music stimuli will help reduce the prevalence of these symptoms. Similarly, stimulating music and motor activity are useful for increasing arousal and interest to counteract the side effects of drowsiness. For the most part, an attitude of matter-of-fact acceptance by the therapist of the side effects and the resulting limitations in performance will help reduce preoccupation with and disruption from these symptoms. It is also useful to remind the patient that the side effects and the adjustments to them are temporary and that return to usual functioning is expected.

Negative psychological responses to side effects also require supportive interventions. Loss of motor control is a source of great anxiety, frustration, and anger in many patients. In spite of the knowledge that these losses are predictable and most often temporary, some patients experience strong fears that they will be permanent. Music experiences designed to structure and organize motor responses can give the patient a sense of control over his movements. Side effects that appear and feel health-threatening, such as tachycardia and hypotension, often cause anxiety and preoccupation. Many physical side effects result in mild reactions of discomfort, irritation, or annoyance; however, these too can influence the effectiveness of psychosocial therapies. In the case of tardive dyskinesia, the symptoms of which are not appreciably reversible, the patient will be facing a psychological adjustment of greater intensity and longer term.

The music therapist can facilitate and support the patient's acceptance of these transient side effects and assist in the resolution of the resulting emotional reactions while continuing to implement the specific music therapy treatment program. This supportive type of therapeutic intervention can take several forms. The therapist should:

1. acknowledge the reality of the occurrence of common side effects;
2. accept the validity of the feeling responses of the patient;
3. reinforce factual information as to the source of the symptoms (side effects) and the expected course of their occurrence, to reduce the distortions caused by confused and psychotic thinking;
4. provide encouragement and reassurance that the symptoms are transient;
5. facilitate appropriate verbal and nonverbal outlets for expression of the distressing feelings, through music psychotherapy, performing, movement, or other expressive arts;

6. convey a firm and consistent message that, with the therapist's support, the patient can continue to work in therapy despite the side effects, by diverting attention to musical tasks of performing, movement, recreational music, or relaxation;

7. report complaints of side effects to the treatment team to avoid overlooking symptoms of other potentially significant pathology and to monitor for possible drug toxicity.

Often patients show initial resistance to participation in some or all aspects of the therapeutic setting. Chemotherapy is frequently distrusted or feared, sometimes perceived as an invasion of the body or as a relinquishing of control. Music therapy, by adding pleasant stimuli to the setting and by offering nonthreatening, often nonverbal, activity to the patient, can lend a relaxing and anxiety-reducing effect. The music therapist also actively promotes an attitude of cooperation with other aspects of treatment. A study by Linn, Caffery, Klett, Hogarty, and Lamb (1979) of schizophrenic patients who were being discharged from V.A. hospitals found that those assigned to day treatment plus drug therapy showed less symptomatology and longer delayed relapses than those given drug therapy alone. The most successful day treatment programs emphasized activity therapy and sustained nonthreatening environments.

MEDICATION AND PSYCHOSOCIAL THERAPIES COMBINED

Psychosocial rehabilitation occurs through talk-based therapies, such as individual, group, or family psychotherapy, on a variety of levels from supportive to analytic, and through activity-based therapies, also ranging from supportive to psychodynamic levels. These approaches provide secure settings in which the patient can examine, relearn, and practice new behavior and thinking patterns. Kanas and Barr (1983) attributed improvement of hospitalized schizophrenic male patients to the addition of group therapy to their neuroleptic medications. Similar conclusions were drawn by Spiegel and Aebi (1981) when they reviewed studies involving nonhospitalized schizophrenics.

The necessity for both chemical and psychosocial interventions can be illustrated in the treatment of schizophrenia. Hallucinations, delusions, and incoherent thinking have long been regarded as the primary features of symptomatology, as they are the most glaring, bizarre, and disruptive. Current theorists suggest that the less dramatic "deficit" symptoms, such as disturbances in affect and volition, are equally debilitating and possibly interfere more with the overall functioning of the schizophrenic patient (Boffey, 1986). There appears to be general agreement that the former, more florid, manifestations of the disease respond to psychotropic medications, while the latter, deficit symptoms, are not appreciably affected.

Target Symptoms Responding to Medication	Target Symptoms Not Responding to Medication*
combativeness/aggressiveness	lack of insight
hallucinations	lack of judgment
delusions	impaired memory
restlessness/agitation	
social withdrawal	

* (Bassuk and Schoonover, 1977; Spiegel and Aebi, 1981). Whether or not affective symptoms respond to psychotropic medication is not clearly supported. Spiegel and Aebi (1981) suggest that neuroleptics improve affective blunting and indifference. However, many practicing clinicians have observed that medication alone does not seem to effect affective change to a great degree.

Music therapy, as one of the psychosocial therapeutic disciplines, is effective mainly in this latter "deficit" area, thus complementing medication by treating symptoms that medications do not reach. The music therapist engages the client in music experiences that stimulate growth, insight, or behavioral change in the areas of affective expression, perceptual-motor behavior, interpersonal communication, and social interaction.

Specifically, the schizophrenic client with blunted affect is treated with music therapy techniques that utilize listening and movement experiences to elicit feeling responses. The client is subsequently provided with opportunities for appropriate and safe expression of the feelings through instrumental playing, singing, or movement. For the apathetic client, music is frequently a pleasant and attractive medium that stimulates interest and promotes involvement in goal-directed activities in music performing or movement, on a level appropriate to the client's abilities. Frances and Clarkin (1981) stated that ". . . drugs and psychotherapy seem to work in separate areas (drugs for symptoms, psychotherapy for social rehabilitation and interpersonal functioning) and to have independent and additive beneficial effects, especially for schizophrenic, affective, and pain disorders." They concluded that "drug treatment without some psychotherapy (even if of low intensity) almost never makes sense." (p. 542).

In addition to treating areas that are not affected by medication in schizophrenic illnesses, music therapy, through deliberately and specifically constructed experiences, complements the desirable primary effects of medication in other psychiatric disorders. For example, a patient who experiences a successful musical/interpersonal effort feels increased self-worth and brighter affect, and the effect of antidepressant medication is thereby enhanced. A patient achieving increased relaxation in a secure, supportive music setting finds relief of body and psychological tension, which adds positive benefit to the effects of antianxiety medication. In encountering a structured task linked to a predictable music stimulus, a patient organizes thinking and responding, a process frequently made possible by the action of antipsychotic medication.

In summary, music therapy contributes, with other psychosocial therapies, to the rehabilitation component of treatment that is potentiated by administering psychotropic medication to the psychiatric patient. Music therapy provides treatment in aspects of psychiatric illness that chemotherapy does not treat. Additionally, the music therapist encourages compliance with the necessary psychopharmacological interventions and serves to aid in creating a supportive atmosphere in the therapeutic setting.

REFERENCES

Bassuk, E. L., & Schoonover, S.C. *The practitioner's guide to psychoactive drugs*. New York: Plenum.

Bernstein, J. G. (1983). *Handbook of drug therapy in psychiatry*. Boston, John Wright—PSG.

Boffey, Philip M. (1986, March 16). Schizophrenia: Insights fail to halt rising toll. *The New York Times*.

Caldwell, A. E. (1970). *Origins of Psychpharmacology: From CPZ to LSD*. Springfield, IL: C. Thomas.

Cole, J. O., Orzak, M. H., Beake, B., Bird, M., Bar-Tal, Y. (1982). Assessment of the abuse liability of buspirone in recreational sedative users. *Journal of Clinical Psychiatry, 43* (12, Sec. 2), 69–74.

Frances, A., & Clarkin, J. (1981). Differential therapeutics: A guide to treatment selection. *Hospital and Community Psychiatry, 32:8*, p. 537–546.

Jeste, J. V., & Wyatt, R. J. (1980). Tardive dyskinesia: The syndrome. *Psychiatric Annals, 10,* 16–25

Kanas, N. & Barr, M.A. (1983). Homogeneous group therapy for acutely psychotic schizophrenic inpatients. *Hospital and Community Psychiatry, 34,* 257–259.

Kety, S. S. (1978). The biological bases of mental illness. In J. P. Bernstein (Ed.), *Clinical psychopharmacology*. Littleton, MA.: PSG Publishing Co.

Klein, D. F., & Davis, J. M. (1969). *Diagnosis and drug treatment of psychiatric disorders*. Baltimore: Williams & Wilkins.

Klerman, G. L. (1978). Psychopharmacologic treatment of a depression. In J. P. Bernstein (Ed.), *Clinical psychopharmacology* (pp. 63–79). Littleton, MA: PSG Publishing Co.

Linn, M. W., Caffery, E. M., Klett, C. J., Hogarty, G. E. & Lamb, H. R. (1979). Day treatment and psychotropic drugs in the aftercare of schizophrenic patients. *Archives of General Psychiatry, 36,* 1055–1066.

Mattila, M. J., Aranko, K., & Seppala, T. (1982). Acute effects of buspirone and alcohol on psychomotor skills. *Journal of Clinical Psychiatry, 43* (12, Sec 2), 56–60.

Moskowitz, H., & Smiley A. (1982). Effects of chronically administered buspirone and diazepam on driving-related skills performance. *Journal of Clinical Psychiatry, 43* (12, Sec 2), 45–55.

Newton, R. E., Marunycz, J. D., Alderice, M. T., & Napoliello, M. J. (1986). A review of the side effect profile of buspirone. *American Journal of Medicine, 80* (3B), 17–21.

Rickels, K., Weisman, K., Norstad, N., Singer, M., Stoltz, D., Brown, A., & Danton, J. (1982). Buspirone and diazepam in anxiety: A controlled study. *Journal of Clinical Psychiatry, 43* (12, Sec 2), 81–86.

Schildkraut, J. J., & Klein, D. F, (1975). The classification and treatment of depressive disorders. In R. I. Shader (Ed.), *Manual of psychiatric therapeutics.* Boston: Little, Brown.

Shader, R. I. (Ed.). (1975). *Manual of psychiatric therapeutics.* Boston: Little, Brown.

Shader, R. I., & Greenblatt. D. J. (1975). The psychopharmacologic treatment of anxiety states. In R. I. Shader (Ed.), *Manual of psychiatric therapeutics* (pp. 27–38). Boston: Little, Brown.

Shader, R. I., & Jackson, A. H. (1975). Approaches to Schizophrenia. In R. I. Shader (Ed.), *Manual of psychiatric therapeutics* (pp. 63–100). Boston: Little, Brown.

Spiegel, R., and Aebi, H. J. (1981). *Psychopharmacology.* Chichester, England: Wiley.

Chapter 10

Assessment of Adult Psychiatric Clients: The Role of Music Therapy

Brian L. Wilson

The recognition that music therapists should be able to assess the needs of their clients as well as evaluate the effectiveness of their therapeutic interventions is an indication of the maturation of the music therapy discipline over the past 40 years. Early proponents of music therapy appeared to be more interested in providing a positive musical experience for their patients than in specifying treatment goals and objectives. Van de Wall (1946) stated that "the general objective of any hospital music program is to provide the patients with pleasurable musical experiences of a comforting and encouraging nature" (p. 41). Offerings typical of hospital music programs during this period (group singing, instrumental activities, musical theatricals, and religious services) were routinely prescribed for patients, with limited attention given to patient needs. In contrast, Braswell (1959) recommended that "every music therapy activity, group or individual, should be structured in such a way that during the activity some pre-determined goal, or group of goals, will either be accomplished or partially accomplished" (p. 50). However, in his survey of 339 music therapists, Michel (1965) found that the majority of respondents failed to identify specific methods for either involving or evaluating patients in their music therapy programs.

Later investigations of music therapy clinical practice have found greater emphasis being placed on both assessment and evaluation procedures. Lathom (1982) discovered that 80 percent of her subjects reported that they evaluated every client, but only 52 percent provided documented input into initial treatment plans for new clients. Furthermore, 78 percent of therapists employed at facilities using an evaluation team for initial planning reported being members of that team. A later survey of music therapists nationwide found that the ability to establish music therapy goals based on documented assessments was viewed as a highly desirable competency for entry level therapists (Taylor, 1987).

Unquestionably, many significant changes in clinical practice have influenced the assessment process. Most therapists are routinely involved in establishing goal-directed interventions and communicating their findings through written and/or verbal avenues. In addition, the Standards of Clinical Practice published by the National Association for Music Therapy (1988) include assessment and documentation as two of the six basic procedural steps that every certified clinician follows in the delivery of services. The linkage of specific treatment goals and observed changes in behavior has allowed music therapists (and other health professionals) to document treatment effectiveness.

The objective of this chapter is to provide the reader with a synthesis of existing and potential areas for music therapy assessment in adult psychiatry based on the research literature. It is not the author's intention either to generate or recommend one specific assessment model. Additionally, this chapter will focus on assessment rather than evaluation, although the author fully recognizes the need for evaluation measures to be implemented after treatment begins. In fact, in actual clinical practice, the assessment and evaluation instruments are often identical.

THE NEED FOR ASSESSMENT

In general, the goal of any assessment is to generate information that will be helpful to the therapist in making decisions regarding a client's needs and treatment protocol. Various methods, such as the use of personality inventories and behavioral rating forms, are utilized to indicate an individual's level of and ability to function across several domains. Regardless of the method, the assessment process should assist in determining:

1. the client's current strengths and weaknesses in various performance areas (e.g., cognitive, social, and motor);
2. a differential diagnosis;
3. whether results from previous assessments are consistent with current findings;
4. if intervention is needed and what services (if any) should be provided;
5. goals and objectives of the treatment program;
6. a method for evaluating effectiveness of treatment procedures through analysis of initial and follow-up assessments.

In addition to influencing diagnosis and intervention programming, assessments are integral to securing third-party reimbursement for services as well as to meeting accreditation requirements for the agencies providing these services.

METHODS OF ASSESSMENT

Traditionally, clinicians have relied on interviewing, observing, testing, and reviewing existing data to gather necessary information about their clients.

Interviewing

The interview is a well-established method of evaluation, reflecting the widely-held belief that meeting and talking with people is the best way to get to know them. In professional surveys of occupational therapists, interviewing was reported as the most common form of assessment procedure used in psychiatric practice, with 47 percent of the respondents stating that the interview method was their *only* means of evaluation (Hemphill, 1982).

There are two basic techniques used in interviewing. Interviews can be *structured,* in which there are predetermined questions and answers allowing for comparisons with established "norms" and varying populations, or *unstructured,* in which the interviewer explores issues that are germane to a particular individual at a particular time. Interviewing may be conducted verbally or via written questionnaire. Of course, in order for the interview to be maximally informative, regardless of format, the client needs to perceive the interviewer as nonthreatening, supportive, and encouraging of self-disclosure. In addition to factual answers, the skilled interviewer also considers the client's nonverbal messages (e.g., tone of voice, gestures, body posture, physical appearance, and eye contact) before making recommendations about the individual's abilities. Music therapists often use the interview format for collecting data regarding past musical experiences, music preferences, and inducers of stress.

Observing

Observation of a client in either a natural, unstructured, or contrived structure setting generates data regarding the frequency and/or duration of specific behaviors and is not dependent on language to portray psychological assets or limitations. Behavioral assessment is often used in tandem with the entire treatment process: to define the problem, to narrow it, to provide a record of what needs to be changed, and to report progress. Documenting the occurrence of certain desirable or undesirable responses provides the clinician with baseline measurements. These measurements may be compared to findings made after treatment procedures have been implemented, in order to evaluate the effectiveness of those interventions. Several authors (Greer & Dorow, 1976; Hanser, 1980, 1987; Madsen, 1981) have provided excellent models for measuring behavior relating to a particular goal. All emphasize the importance of defining treatment objectives including specific parameters of how, when, and where the behavior occurs. In general, music therapists are well oriented toward behavioral assessment techniques and comfortable in using them in clinical practice.

Testing

Testing allows for comparison of an individual's response to the responses of others. Many psychological tests are standardized, which provides a reasonable assurance of reliability (repeated administrations of the test will yield similar results) and validity (the test measures what it purports to measure). Standardization has two basic components: standardizing the administration procedure in utilizing the test, and collecting the normative data from predictive use of the results. Psychological tests fall into three categories: psychological inventories (e.g., MMPI), projective tests (e.g., Rorschach Test, Thematic Apperception Test), and intelligence tests (e.g., WAIS, WISC). Because of the lack of available formal testing procedures grounded in a music environment, music therapists rarely use this method of assessment with adult psychiatric populations. However, the possible application of music in a projective test environment will be discussed in this chapter.

Reviewing Existing Information

Many therapists get most of the information they need from an individual client's medical chart. Hemphill (1982) believes that 80 percent of the pertinent information needed by activity therapists exists in the client's medical record. Since the client's record provides information regarding the client's medical and social history, admission summary, results of psychological and other testing, problems at admission, and initial recommendations, a music therapist must be careful not to bombard the newly admitted client with redundant and repetitive questions.

RATIONALE FOR A MUSIC THERAPY ASSESSMENT

With members of so many disciplines (e.g., psychologists, occupational therapists, social workers) conducting a variety of assessments, the need for a music therapy evaluation could be questioned. Would such an assessment make an important or different contribution to the considerable amount of evidence already available? Would such an assessment significantly contribute to the overall understanding of the client or merely provide redundant or irrelevant information? Michel and Rohrbacher (1982) have addressed these important issues:

> Music is a form of human behavior which is unique from other forms. Clients react differently within musical situations, listening to, moving to, or performing music. It is generally recognized that clients may be seen from a different perspective—sometimes radically different—when under music stimuli conditions. Thus, special assessment by music therapists or clients under music conditions is important. The assessment form itself may resemble other forms, but the unique difference is that behaviors observed will be those a client exhibits under some type of music condition. (p. iii).

Although several members of the treatment team contribute to the assessment, Lathom (1980) concurs that "redundancy in testing is important because some areas are able to elicit behavior not seen in other areas of the treatment team assessment." (p. 7). Bruscia (1988) believes that the creative arts therapies as a whole have a significant contribution to make to the overall process of clinical assessment because of their attractiveness, universal acceptance, and their symbolic and nonverbal nature. These attributes give the client the opportunity for a multisensory awareness that may not be possible in the assessments conducted by members of other disciplines.

Although the aforementioned authors were directing their comments primarily toward services provided for handicapped children, the implication for all music therapists seems obvious. Certainly music therapists involved with adult psychiatric populations should be an integral part of the assessment process because:

1. Each individual interacts with music in a unique way and the opportunity should be provided for its evaluation.

2. Assessments need not be limited to traditional visual, verbal, and kinesthetic modes of testing. A music therapy assessment offers the opportunity to observe the client's response to auditory, yet nonverbal, stimuli. In fact, certain skills are ideally suited for evaluation within a musical context. Auditory perception and memory may be tested through singing a song. Verbal and nonverbal responses to a musical selection may reveal either healthy or incongruent social and emotional patterns of behavior.

3. Assessments are a prerequisite to the establishment of goals and objectives and need to be done prior to the delivery of any music therapy services. Using the music therapy assessment, the client's diagnosis, and information from other disciplines and sources, the music therapist is able to develop a program plan that includes goals that focus on the client's needs while defining the steps necessary for achieving the goals.

4. Music therapists must be able to participate in assessment procedures required by accrediting or regulatory agencies. For example, the *Consolidated Standards Manual,* (Joint Commission on Accreditation of Health Care Organizations, 1987) requires that "an activities assessment of each patient is undertaken and includes information relating to the individual's current skills, talents, attitudes, and interests" (p. 74). However, music therapists should not restrict themselves to the "activities" section but also look at how their programming interfaces with the total facility procedures and plans (Scalenghe, 1986). As an additional benefit, the existence of a music therapy assessment may also enhance the stature and recognition of both the practitioner and profession, especially if the information obtained can be directed toward the client's nonmusical, rather than musical, areas of functioning (Isenberg-Grzeda, 1988).

MODELS OF MUSIC THERAPY ASSESSMENT

Assessment for Differential Diagnosis

Tests ranging from personality inventories to IQ measures have been utilized to assist clinicians in reaching a meaningful diagnosis for the adult client with mental disorders. One category, the projective test, has an especially rich history dating back to the teachings of Freud. The Rorschach Ink Blot Test and the Thematic Apperception Test (TAT) are landmark devices that reputedly focus on unconscious conflicts, latent fears, sexual and aggressive impulses, and hidden anxieties (Rosenhan & Seligman, 1984). Although the subjective interpretation of data inherent in these types of tests has been widely criticized, many believe that such information, when analyzed by a well qualified clinician, is crucial to understanding an individual's general personality factors, motivation, and dynamic structure.

Projective tests, although rooted in psychoanalytic theory, may also offer avenues for behavioral observation. Objective content measures, such as total number of responses, number of human responses, and number of animal responses, as well as procedural measures (total time taken, and delay in responding) may reveal important information germane to the client's pathology. In fact, Hemphill (1982) cautioned occupational therapists not to become so involved in analyzing the content of projective material that they miss the most significant symptoms of dysfunction simply because they did not carefully observe the testing process.

AUDITORY PROJECTIVE TESTS

In their innovative pilot study, Bean and Moore (1964) hypothesized that auditory stimuli could facilitate fantasy production and increase verbalizations for schizophrenics who tend to be more receptive to sound than language, pictures, or objects. Their Sound Apperception Test (SAT) was developed as an equivalent measure of sorts to the TAT. Containing six semistructured sound patterns (altered every day environmental sounds), the test was administered initially to more than 500 "normal" subjects. After norms had been established, 24 schizophrenics were presented with 16 pictures from the TAT and 16 sound patterns from the SAT. Subjects were evaluated on their total word count and amount of fantasy production under each test condition and classified as either auditory predominant (high score on SAT) or visually predominant (high score on TAT), with questionable cases being dropped. Placed in homogeneous groups, subjects were seen by a music therapist for 24 sessions and rated on attentiveness, active participation, talkativeness, and general interest. The data revealed that the auditory subjects made larger gains in mean scores overall, which suggests the tests may be appropriate for selecting clients for music therapy services.

MUSIC PROJECTIVE TESTS

The IPAT Music Preference Test of Personality, developed and researched by Cattell and his colleagues (Cattell & Anderson, 1953; Cattell & Saunders, 1954; Cattell & McMichael, 1960), attempted to determine whether different music preferences existed between normal and various pathologic, psychotic, and neurotic groups. Composed of 100 musical excerpts correlated to the 16 Personality Factor Questionnaire, the test delineated eight personality factors (e.g., introspectiveness vs. social contact, adjustment vs. frustrated emotionality) underlying musical preference. These factors "correspond with fundamental differences in the toleration of rhythm and speeds and in the liking for different kinds of emotional stimulation" (Cattell & Kline, 1977, p. 139). Although reliability and validity data were scanty, the authors concluded that the device demonstrated that normals could be distinguished from mental hospital patients on these variables and that the device held promise as a diagnostic instrument.

Healey (1973) administered the IPAT Music Preference Test of Personality to 67 normal and hospitalized subjects. Although the reliability claims made by Cattell were in general agreement with Healey's finding, Healey noted several examples of marked departure regarding validity. He concluded that musical preference may not be influenced by the onset of psychiatric illness. Further efforts at replication have failed to support the earlier claims of Cattell. Robinson (1976) constructed a musical preference inventory based on Cattell's work but found no significant distinction between pathological groups. The study lacked a normal comparison group, however, and may have suffered from insufficient subject groupings.

Instead of investigating music preference as a projective concept, Van Den Daele (1967) used music as a fantasy stimulus. As justification for this approach, the author offered convincing arguments for providing a musical projective test (listening to one-minute musical excerpts) while the subject was required to verbalize:

1. Music is apparently an excellent stimulus for fantasy production.
2. The task of verbalizing after a sound stimulus has ended often results in mere identification of sound without fantasy production.
3. Redundancy in music insures a continuity of the stimulus so that the subject is not overwhelmed by excessive change.
4. Information concerning the subject's response to ongoing variation is potentially important diagnostic information, perhaps related to the subject's adaptation to change in the real world (p. 49).

Statistical analysis of the scores of 20 state hospital patients (schizophrenics) and 20 college students revealed that the schizophrenics had longer reaction time before verbalization to music, spoke less while the music played but more between excerpts of music, made references to more animal content and less human content and visual imagery during the test. The college subjects produced stories more associated with the music stimulus (i.e., slow music-sad story) than did the hospitalized patients. Although the author concluded that the music projective test appeared to be a reliable instrument, useful in differentiating diagnostic groups, and potentially valuable as a clinical tool, no further evidence of its use was found in the research literature. Based on a similar theoretical framework, Wells (1988) developed a three-task assessment procedure targeted for emotionally impaired adolescents. According to the author, information gathered from the client's song selection, written story to background music, and instrumental improvisation can provide useful diagnostic data as well as aiding in determining suitability for music therapy services. No comparisons to other subject groups were offered.

Some researchers have examined specific parameters of music performance as a possible diagnostic device. Stein (1977) discovered consistent errors in imitating rhythms among patients previously diagnosed as schizophrenic. Using a flashing light metronome, she found generally that more errors were made in slower tempos. Several patients drew parallels between their dislike for slow music and their perception that the world around them was also intolerably slow. Seven of the 16 cases were reviewed and reclassified with a manic diagnosis. Stein hypothesized that a relationship may exist between tempo errors and mania. Based on the assumption that tempo errors may be a psychomotor feature of depressives as well as manics, Migliore (1985) investigated the possible relationship between a test of rhythmic competency and the psychomotor subtest of the Hamilton Rating Scale for Depression. Although significant negative correlations existed among the Hamilton scale and several subsets of the rhythm test for his 26 endogenously depressed inpatient adult subjects, the relationships were modest. In his conclusion, Migliore questioned whether physical imitation (patting knees, marching in place, marching across the room) was a reliable indicator of psychomotor retardation. Conversely, later research with psychotic inmates diagnosed as manic found their scores to be superior to non-manic psychotic inmates and non-psychotic controls on several tasks involving rhythmicity and tempo performance on a drum (Cohen, 1985).

Musical expression in playing an instrument has also been evaluated for possible correlation with psychopathology. As with Migliore, Steinberg, Raith, Rossinagl, and Eben (1985) found that endogenously depressed patients could be distinguished from neurotically depressed patients by the weakened motoric qualities in their playing. Schizophrenics tended to display performance difficulties in the area of musical logic and order. Improvement in psychopathologic condition (as determined by a short psychiatric rating scale administered by a psychiatrist) was significantly correlated to improvement in musical expression. Overall, controls, as well as chronic patients, showed few differences in mean musical expression over the six-week testing period.

In a somewhat related domain, psychophysical scaling of line lengths and music preferences has also been investigated (Koh & Shears, 1970). One hundred and seventy-five schizophrenics and normal subjects judged lengths of lines and preferences for musical excerpts by category rating (very, very long/pleasant to very, very short/unpleasant) and magnitude estimation (proportional ranking to first stimuli presented). Although some differences in the schizophrenic's scale range for the musical excerpts were more pronounced than for line lengths, the experimenters warn that the results may only indicate stimulus overload and not necessarily represent other personality characteristics.

Other researchers have used music to influence results of existing projective tests rather than measuring the results of a music-based test to substantiate them. Greenberg and Fischer (1971) assessed the differential effect of exciting and calming background music on two projective tests (TAT and Draw-a-Person) and two structure tests (Bass Famous Saying and Buss-Durke Hostility Scale) for 40 female subjects. With only hostility being measured, significant differences existed for the projective tests alone. Exciting music produced more female power themes and high hostility themes on the TAT and taller figures on the Draw-a-Person test. In a separate study, 60 stories written by college students about an ambiguous picture from the TAT were judged to have significantly different emotional content, depending on whether the subjects wrote while tension-producing music ("Mars" from Holst's "The Planets"), calming music ("Venus" from the same work), or no music was played (McFarland, 1984).

Assessment of Psychosocial Abilities

This area of assessment provides information regarding the client's family relationships, organizational involvement, attitudes, and level of social isolation. The linkage between social isolation and inadequate social skills with high recidivism rates for adult psychiatric clients has already been described in Chapter 7. The importance of social skills training (e.g., role playing, modeling, leisure time planning, and assertion training) and the necessity of available support systems (e.g., family relationships, community-based agencies, and recreational activities) have been widely recognized over the past decade. Still, some service programs have not been effective due to insufficient periods of treatment, lack of generalization and long-term maintenance outside of the training situation, and inappropriate placement initially. Programs that do not assess and delineate the individual's specific needs before implementation begins may predispose the client to failure. Many of the functional assessments have been found to be inadequate (especially for institutionalized adult psychiatric clients) because they either are too broad, contain too few steps to reflect progress, and/or begin above the client's current level of functioning (Anthony & Farkas, 1982).

Several examples of the potential role of music therapy in assessing levels of social functioning have begun to appear in the research literature. Braswell,

Brooks, Decuir, Humphrey, Jacobs, and Sutton (1983, 1986) developed a questionnaire, the Music/Activity Therapy Intake Assessment for Psychiatric Patients, which contained an attitude survey as one of its major components. Based largely on self-report measures, the attitude survey provided data pertinent to psychosocial functioning, self-concept, interpersonal relationships, and altruism/optimism. After administering the survey to 214 university students and 93 institutionalized psychiatric patients, the authors found that the attitude scales displayed internal consistency for both the patient and student samples, meaning that the scales measured independent attitudinal domains. A discriminate function analysis revealed that two of the three scales discriminated significantly ($p. < .05$) among the groups of university students and all three measures discriminated significantly ($p. < .01$) among the diagnostic groups of patients. Although the authors did not address specifically the feasibility of using the instrument as a diagnostic device, comparison of the mean scores of both subject groups indicate that possibly significant differences existed on at least one of the subscales. (Students had a mean score of 64.17 on the self-concept scale in which the patients' overall mean was 71.36. Mean scores on the other two measures were nearly identical).

An improvisational music therapy assessment is one model that may aid in identifying psychosocial abilities. This assessment involves engaging the client in musical improvisation, either alone, with the therapist, or within a group. Bruscia (1987) believes that through both improvised and structured musical tasks, the therapist is able to evaluate the intramusical (within the client's music), intrapersonal (within the client's personality, or between the client and his music), intermusical (between the client's music and the music of the other person or group), and interpersonal (between the client and the other person) responses of the client (p. 522). For example, how the client demonstrates awareness of his and other's music, role, and feelings when involved in a musical interaction may guide the therapist in understanding the individual's ability to engage in appropriate interpersonal relationships both in and outside of the music therapy session. In addition, the music section of the Expressive Arts Group Assessment (Pulliam, Somerville, Prebluda, & Warja-Danielsson, 1988) purports to open avenues for accessing intrapsychic material as well as interpersonal skills. Based on the client's interpretation of song themes and his individual or group improvisational responses, the therapist may make recommendations regarding the client's abilities.

The need to comply with documentation requirements of state and federal funding sources has prompted the development of many different types of client assessment forms, especially for programs servicing the chronically mentally ill. Since many standardized assessments are inappropriate for this clientele, Egeler (1986) hypothesized that the music therapy setting would provide an effective assessment environment for evaluating, as well as modifying, social behaviors of chronically mentally ill patients. Her study was an attempt to develop initial standardization data on the Day Treatment Client

Assessment (DTCA) Scale by determining the concurrent validity and reliability of the Social Skills subscale through data collected in music therapy sessions. The items assessed were eye contact, appropriate conversation, nonverbal communication, group participation/socialization, assertion, and risk-taking. Using music therapy activities that promoted desirable social skills, she found the DTCA Social Skills subscale to be reliable and valid. The author concluded that because the music therapy sessions can be structured to elicit nearly any social skill or deficiency, the sessions may be a valid setting for assessing or modifying social behavior of chronically mentally ill adults.

Assessment of Musical Abilities, Interests, and Preferences

A cursory review of several examples of assessment used in adult psychiatric settings reveals that information regarding a client's musical abilities, interests, and preferences appears to be universally evaluated by the music therapist.

Without question, this information is of benefit in identifying past patterns of leisure time planning as well as the most potentially effective music for a given client in music therapy sessions. Since evolving research strongly suggests that an individual is more responsive to music he likes than music he does not like, several methods have been developed to determine musical preferences. The methods range from the use of sophisticated measuring devices of time spent engaging in music activities to simply asking the client what type of music he enjoys. Regardless of the procedure, careful observation of the client's behavior in a music experience is still encouraged, since such data may be more reflective of client preference than a verbal report.

Cohen and Gericke (1972) devised a music therapy assessment that combined judgmental determination (based on clinical observation) with factual data (about factors directly related to musical capability) to form the basis for recommending therapeutic intervention. Although geared toward the developmentally disabled population, the questions—regarding the client's degree of musical involvement, musical interests, current music skills, prehospital leisure time activities, and prior formal musical training—are appropriate for any client, including adults with mental disorders. The previously mentioned Music/Activity Therapy Intake Assessment for Psychiatric Patients (Braswell et al. 1983, 1986) contained an Activity Preference Inventory subsection listing 19 activities that ranged from watching TV movies to reading comics. In it, the client's degree of preference (i.e., 1 = not interested to 4 = has participated a lot) and level of involvement (i.e., 1 = performs activity alone to 4 = has done activity with large groups) could be calculated. Of the 12 activities reported, scores of the four diagnostic groups (schizophrenic, adjustment reaction, substance abuse, and affective disorder) differed significantly, with the adjustment reaction subjects and younger clients responding more positively to performing music (the only music involvement option in the questionnaire).

Assessment in Relation to Treatment Philosophy

In addition to providing information relevant to a client's needs and therapeutic objectives, the assessment process can also aid in selecting the most appropriate treatment philosophy and techniques for reaching the targeted clinical objectives. Without question, music therapy programming, actual clinical intervention, may be influenced by the therapist's or agency's philosophical orientation to treatment. Because of this fact, various assessment models may include specific indices that suggest various models of therapy. For example, proponents of the behavioral orientation to therapy would regard observation and testing of overall functioning as prerequisites to the identification of target behaviors that warrant modification. Practitioners of the humanistic approach would more likely be interested in identifying incongruencies or polarities within the client in an effort to foster establishment of an internal, rather than external, locus of evaluation.

Anchored in behavior therapy, the multimodal therapy model developed by Lazarus requires assessment of, if not intervention in, each modality of the BASIC ID (behavior, affect, sensation, imagery, cognition, interpersonal, and drug) in order for the therapeutic process to be complete (Brunell, 1978; Roberts, Jackson, & Phelps, 1980). Furthermore, lasting change is viewed as a product of a *combination* of techniques, strategies, and modalities that can be representative of various therapies. For example,

> Psychoanalysis would concentrate largely in the areas of cognition and affect and their interactions, Roger's client-centered therapy would focus on those same domains, while the neo-Reichian school of bioenergetics places its emphasis on behavior (body language) and the sensory and affective areas. Also, encounter groups and Gestalt therapy are likely to neglect the cognitive area and emphasize the affective and sensory modalities. The multimodal therapist concludes that the traditional therapies (e.g., psychoanalysis, client-centered, Gestalt, etc.) do not typically cover all of the modalities in the BASIC ID. (Roberts, Jackson, & Phelps, 1980, p. 151)

Rather than referring clients indiscriminately to various therapies, each available discipline is utilized based on its particular ability to address one or more of the seven basic modalities. For example, a problem (low self-esteem) related to a specific modality (cognition) would dictate an appropriate treatment (reinforce assets such as musical ability). Once the activity or creative art therapies are subjected to a more formal multimodal analysis, it becomes apparent that music therapy is one discipline that crosses over many, if not all, of the seven modalities. Adelman (1985) explored possible assessment and treatment approaches for music therapists working within this model and was able to respond effectively to each modality.

The realities of the mental health community, however, dictate that music therapists may need to be aligned, either by choice or facility orientation, with specific models of therapy. They should be able to adjust the assessment format to be reflective of that treatment approach. The role of music assessments in relation to other than behavioral theories of psychotherapy has been increasingly reported in the professional literature. Using Erikson's psychosocial theory of personality development as a basis, Nichols (1987), developed a music therapy assessment for treatment planning and intervention with psychiatric clients. She correlated responses to such tasks as song identification, mirroring, improvisation, story/poem/artwork evoked by music, and a music preference survey with Eriksons' eight stages of man. Another psychoanalytically oriented approach to counseling, Sullivan's theory of interpersonal psychology, has been the foundation for a model of music therapy intervention. Using the six main phases of therapy (security, empathy, observation, hypothesis, contradiction, and correction) as a structure, Broucek (1987) proposed an interpersonal music therapy improvisation model that offers possible parallels between musical interactions and specified interpersonal behavior. Central to this approach is the ability of the therapist to identify and contradict musically the client's disordered assumptions with verbal, nonverbal, and musical responses that do not compliment or perpetuate the distorted expectations. Using the 16 interpersonal categories of Kiesler's 1982 Interpersonal Circle (1983) as a foundation, Broucek formulated eight pairs of contrasting musical interactions as the basis for the assessment (Figures 10-1 and 10-2). Although the model is a theoretical construct and unsubstantiated through testing, it offers the music therapist a way of relating musical responses (e.g., range of expression, timing of expression, intensity of expression, and ability to change that expression as the context changes) to characteristic interpersonal responses.

Other improvisational approaches to assessment that have also been developed are rooted in psychoanalytical theory. Priestly's model of analytical music therapy includes an assessment technique known as the "emotional spectrum" in which three core emotions (love, joy, and peace) form a triad correlated with the tonic, mediant, and dominant positions of the musical scale (Priestly, 1975). A picture of the client's emotional make-up is derived via musical improvisation, fantasies, verbalizations, body language, expressive movement, and artwork. Responses are scored and deemed positive or negative based on their frequency, intensity, and appropriateness, among other factors (Bruscia, 1987). Alvin's free improvisation therapy lacked formal assessment procedures although a synthesis of her concerns in evaluation has recently been published (Bruscia, 1987).

The realities of the health care marketplace dictate that objective data be generated in order to allow for evaluation of the efficacy of treatment. Hanser (1987) has developed a data-based model of music therapy that includes procedures for assessments of the client's needs regardless of the treatment orientation of the therapist or facility. Although behaviorist in nature, the model encourages the therapist to choose the research-based approach that seems appropriate. Even in psychotherapy environments, broad goals can be

Figure 10–1.
Musical Assessment, Showing
Complementary Responses
(Broucek, 1987)

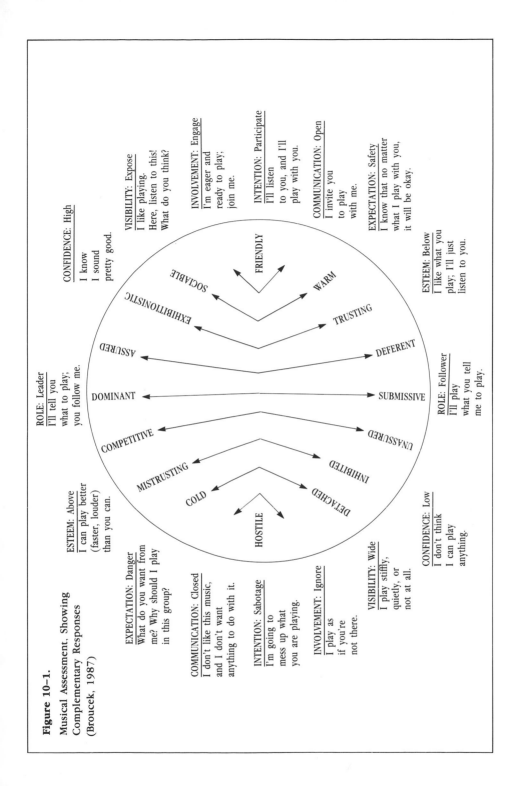

CONFIDENCE: High
I know
I sound
pretty good.

VISIBILITY: Expose
I like playing.
Here, listen to this!
What do you think?

INVOLVEMENT: Engage
I'm eager and
ready to play;
join me.

INTENTION: Participate
I'll listen
to you, and I'll
play with you.

COMMUNICATION: Open
I invite you
to play
with me.

EXPECTATION: Safety
I know that no matter
what I play with you,
it will be okay.

ROLE: Leader
I'll tell you
what to play;
you follow me.

ESTEEM: Above
I can play better
(faster, louder)
than you can.

ESTEEM: Below
I like what you
play; I'll just
listen to you.

ROLE: Follower
I'll play
what you tell
me to play.

EXPECTATION: Danger
What do you want from
me? Why should I play
in this group?

COMMUNICATION: Closed
I don't like this music,
and I don't want
anything to do with it.

INTENTION: Sabotage
I'm going to
mess up what
you are playing.

INVOLVEMENT: Ignore
I play as
if you're
not there.

VISIBILITY: Wide
I play stiffly,
quietly, or
not at all.

CONFIDENCE: Low
I don't think
I can play
anything.

FRIENDLY
SOCIABLE
EXHIBITIONISTIC
WARM
ASSURED
TRUSTING
DOMINANT
DEFERENT
SUBMISSIVE
COMPETITIVE
UNASSURED
MISTRUSTING
INHIBITED
COLD
DETACHED
HOSTILE

139

Figure 10-2.

Musical Assessment, Showing
Anti-Complementary Responses
(Broucek, 1987)

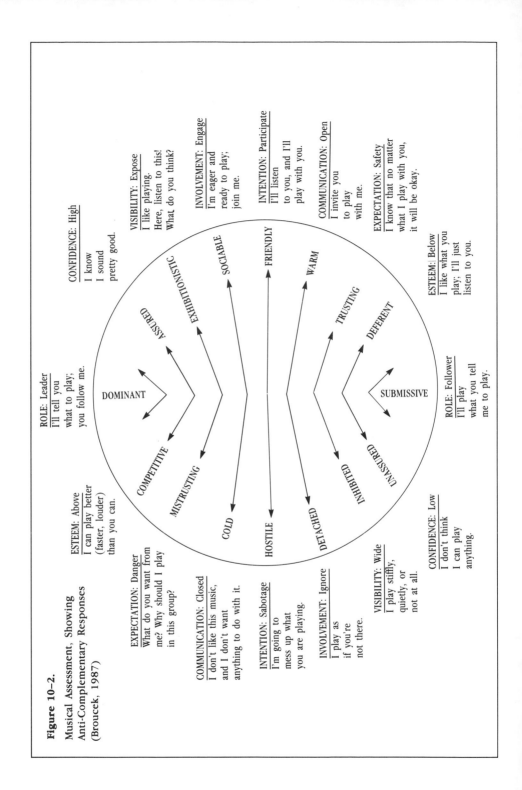

140

translated into measurable objectives and hierarchies of responses (Hanser, 1984).

CONCLUSIONS

As recently as the early 1970s, activity therapists were cautioned that their role in assessing and diagnosing a client was limited to sharing information with the primary physician (Mosey, 1973). Certainly that restrictive philosophy has changed, along with increased professional qualifications of all members of the treatment team and the recognition of the benefits achieved through diversity of programming. The role of activity and creative arts therapists in the assessment process is also evolving, with music therapists now documenting the client's *unique* response to the music environment and its implications for diagnosis, the establishment of goals and objectives, and appropriate intervention planning.

Several questions remain unanswered: Should the music therapy discipline attempt to develop a single and universal approach to assessing the adult psychiatric population? Should we concern ourselves with both musical and nonmusical behaviors? Should we justify either the inclusion or the exclusion of clients for music therapy services? Should we further determine whether a client is an appropriate candidate for a specific level of service (e.g., activity versus insight-oriented music therapy)? Should the assessment function mainly as an aid for the music therapist or should the client's responses be interpreted and incorporated to compliment other professionals' understandings of the individual's needs? The many innovative models of music therapy assessment already in existence warrant further investigation of their effectiveness in assisting the music therapist in answering these important questions.

Because the needs of adults with mental disorders are often multifaceted, so too are the evaluative tools used. Assessing a client in a music environment allows for a richer and more complete understanding of the individual.

REFERENCES

Adelman, E. J. (1985). Multimodal therapy and music therapy: Assessing and treating the whole person. *Music Therapy, 5*(1), 12–21.

Anthony, W., & Farkas, M. (1982). A client outcome planning model for assessing psychiatric rehabilitation interventions. *Schizophrenia Bulletin 8,*13–38.

Bean, K. L., & Moore, J. R. (1964). Music therapy from auditory inkblots. *Journal of Music Therapy, 1,* 143–147.

Braswell, C. (1959). The goal-directed hospital music program. In E. H. Schneider (Ed.), *Music therapy 1959.* Lawrence, KS: National Association for Music Therapy.

Braswell, C., Brooks, D., Decuir, A., Humphrey, T., Jacobs, K., & Sutton, K. (1983).

Development and implementation of a music/activity therapy intake assessment for psychiatric patients. Part I: Initial standardization procedures in data from university students. *Journal of Music Therapy, 20*(2), 88–100.

Braswell, C., Brooks, D., Decuir, A., Humphrey, T., Jacobs, K., & Sutton, K., (1986). Development and implementation of a music/activity therapy intake assessment for psychiatric patients. Part II: Standardization procedures in data from psychiatric patients. *Journal of Music Therapy, 23*(3), 126–141.

Broucek, M. (1987). *An interpersonal model of music therapy improvisation.* Unpublished master's thesis, Hahnemann University, Philadelphia.

Brunell, L. F. (1978). A multimodal treatment model for a mental hospital: Designing specific treatments for specific problems. *Professional Psychology,* November, 570–579.

Bruscia, K. E. (1987). *Improvisational Methods of Music Therapy.* Springfield, IL: Charles C. Thomas.

Bruscia, K. E. (1988). Standards for clinical assessment in the arts therapies. *Arts in Psychotherapy, 15,* 5–10.

Cattell, R. B., & Anderson, J. C. (1953). The measurement of personality and behavior disorders by the IPAT music preference test. *Journal of Applied Psychology, 37,*446–454.

Cattell, R. B., & Kline, P. (1977). *The scientific analysis of personality and maturation.* New York: Academic Press.

Cattell, R. B., & McMichael, R. E. (1960). Clinical diagnosis by the IPAT music preference test. *Journal of Consulting Psychology, 24,*333–341.

Cattell, R. B., & Saunders, D. (1954). Musical preferences and personality diagnosis: A factorization of one hundred and twenty themes. *Journal of Social Psychology, 39,*3–24.

Cohen, G., & Gericke, O. C. (1972). Music therapy assessment: Prime requisite for determining patient objectives. *Journal of Music Therapy, 9*(4), 161–189.

Cohen, J. (1985). Rhythm and tempo in mania. *Music Therapy, 6,*13–29.

Egeler, S. (1986). *A study of the reliability and validity of a social skills rating scale for use with chronically mentally ill.* Unpublished master's thesis, Western Michigan University, Kalamazoo.

Greenberg, R., & Fischer, S. (1971). Some differential effects of music in projective and structured psychological tests. *Psychological Reports, 28,*817–818.

Greer, R. D., & Dorow, L. G. (1976). *Specializing education behaviorally.* Dubuque, IA: Kendall/Hunt.

Hanser, S. B. (1980). *Music therapy practicum: A manual for behavior change through music therapy.* Oakland, CA: Pea Press.

Hanser, S. B. (1984). Music group psychotherapy: An evaluation model. *Music Therapy Perspectives, 1*(4), 14–16.

Hanser, S. B. (1987). *Music therapist's handbook.* St. Louis: Warren Green.

Healey, B. (1973). Pilot study in the applicability of the music preference test of personality. *Journal of Music Therapy, 10,*36–45.

Hemphill, B. J. (1982). The evaluation process in psychiatric occupational therapy. Thorofare, NJ: Charles B. Slack.

Isenberg-Grzeda, (1988). Music therapy assessment: A reflection of professional identity. *Journal of Music Therapy, 25*(3), 156–169.

Joint Commission on Accreditation of Health Care Organizations. (1987). Consolidated standards manual (for child, adolescent, and adult psychiatric, alcoholism, and drug share facilities). Chicago.

Keisler, D. J. (1983). The 1982 interpersonal circle: A taxonomy for complementarity in human transactions. *Psychological Review, 90*(3), 185–214.

Koh, S. D., & Shears, G. (1970). Psychophysical scaling by schizophrenics and normals. *Archives of General Psychiatry, 23.*

Lathom, W. (1980). *Role of music therapy in the education of handicapped children and youth.* Lawrence, KS: National Association for music Therapy.

Lathom, W. (1982). Survey of current functions of a music therapist. *Journal of Music Therapy, 19,*(1), 2–27.

Madsen, C. K. (1981). *Music therapy: A behavioral guide for the mentally retarded.* Lawrence, KS: National Association for Music Therapy.

McFarland, R. A. (1984). Effects of music upon emotional content of TAT stories. *Journal of Psychology, 116,*227–234.

Michel, D. E. (1965). Professional profile: That NAMT member and his clinical practices in music therapy. *Journal of Music Therapy, 2*(4), 124–129.

Michel, D. E., & Rohrbacher, M. (Eds.). (1982). *The music therapy assessment profile for severely/profoundly handicapped persons, research draft III (0-27 months level).* Denton, TX: Texas Women's University.

Migliore, M. J. (1985). *The hamilton rating scale for depression and rhythmic competency: A correlational study.* Unpublished master's thesis, Western Michigan University, Kalamazoo.

Mosey, A. C. (1973). *Activities therapy.* New York: Raven Press.

National Association for Music Therapy, (1988). Standards of clinical practice. Washington, DC.

Nichols, J. (1987). *Using Erikson's psychosocial theory for music therapy assessment, treatment planning and interventions with psychiatric clients.* Papers presented at annual conference of the National Association for Music Therapy, San Francisco.

Priestly, M. (1975). *Music therapy in action.* St. Louis: Magnamusic-Baton.

Pulliam, J. C., Somerville, P., Prebluda, J., & Warja-Danielsson, M. (1988). Three heads are better than one: The expressive arts group assessment. *Arts in Psychotherapy, 15,* 71–77.

Roberts, T. K., Jackson, L. J., & Phelps, R. (1980). Lazarus' multimodal therapy model applied in an institutional setting. *Professional Psychology, 11,* 150–156.

Robinson, W. L. (1976). The musical preferences of mental patients based on Cattell's interpretations of factors associated with certain aspects of personality. *Dissertation Abstracts International,* 149A (University Microfilms No. 77–13, 931).

Rosenhan, D. L., & Seligman, M. (1984). *Abnormal psychology.* New York: W. W. Norton.

Scalenghe, R. (1986). The accreditation process and its impact on music therapy practice. In K. Gfeller (Ed.), *Fiscal, regulatory, and legislative issues for the music therapist* (pp. 22–29). Washington, DC: National Association for Music Therapy.

Stein, J. (1977). Tempo errors and mania. *American Journal of Psychiatry, 134*(4), 454–456.

Steinberg, R., Raith, L., Rossinagl, G., & Eben, E. (1985). Music psychopathology: Musical expression and psychiatric disease. *Psychopathology, 18,*274–285.

Taylor, D. (1987). A survey of professional music therapists concerning entry level competencies. *Journal of Music Therapy, 24*(3), 114–145.

Van den Daele, L. (1967). A music projective technique. *Journal of Projective Techniques, 31*(5), 47–57.

Van de Wall, W. (1946). *Music in hospitals.* New York: Russell Sage Foundation.

Wells, N. F. (1988). An individual music therapy assessment procedure for emotionally disturbed young adolescents. *Arts in Psychotherapy, 15,* 47–54.

PART THREE

TAXONOMY OF CLINICAL MUSIC THERAPY PROGRAMS AND TECHNIQUES

LEVELS OF MUSIC THERAPY INTERVENTIONS

In a multiaxial differentiation of treatment approaches, it is suggested that psychiatric music therapy not only spells out treatment of different clinical programs and techniques but also classifies its interventions along a continuum of levels of psychotherapeutic services according to characteristics and needs of its psychiatric clientele.

Many mental health workers have stressed the fact that different clinical settings and psychopathologies require different goals and approaches in treatment and rehabilitation, and thus call for respective adaptation of current psychotherapy procedures (Pattison, Briserdeh, & Wohl, 1967; Wolberg, 1977; Yalom, 1983). Research has shown that traditional group therapy, whether long term, cathartic, or insight-oriented, might be counterproductive in acute inpatient work or with chronic schizophrenic disorders (Watson, & Lacey, 1974; Kanas, Rogers, Kreth, Patterson, & Campbell, 1980).

Clinical music therapy procedures have encompassed several classifications of clinical practice in the last 10 years. The classifications range from concepts of activity therapy to in-depth, psychodynamically oriented approaches, depending on the clientele being served and the philosophical treatment-orientation of the therapist (Gaston, 1968; Tyson, 1966; Priestley, 1975). In order to adapt these classifications systematically to standards of clinical practice in mental health, Wheeler (1983) has proposed three levels of clinical practice in music therapy, based on clinical and research data and incorporating previous classification systems in psychotherapy (Wolberg, 1977). The following levels are an adaption of Wheeler's work, and incorporate levels of inpatient group therapy suggested by Yalom (1983). Specific clinical programs and techniques in music therapy can be

145

implemented on each of these levels, depending on the client's clinical needs and the adaptability of the specific intervention technique.

Supportive, Activities-Oriented Music Therapy

On this level, clinical goals are generally achieved through active involvement in therapeutic activities rather than through insight and verbal investigation. Music therapy activities are designed to provide the experience of participation and promote the practice of healthy behavior. Insight, reflection, and verbal processing take only a small part of the session time, and they focus on the here-and-now and overt behavior during the actual activity. The activities are aimed at strengthening defenses, developing appropriate mechanisms of behavior control, supporting healthy feelings and thoughts, breaking social isolation, providing safe, reassuring reality stimulation, exposing the patient to the influence of basic group dynamics, and diverting the patient from possible neurotic concerns. Activities are tightly structured to promote the experience of success, tangible benefits, support, and reduction of anxiety to the patient. The therapist facilitates, supports, and clarifies as well as offers reassurance, advice, information, and direction to the patient. Patients who benefit from music therapy at this level can range from individuals with basically sound ego structures who have broken down temporarily under stress, to acute or chronic patient groups who are fragmented, regressed, or delusional, who suffer from severe schizophrenic, affective, or organic symptoms, or who are too phobic and anxious to participate in more demanding levels of therapy. These patients are more in need of support, integration, and "sealing over" than verbal investigation of their problems.

Reeducative, Insight and Process-Oriented Music Therapy[1]

On this level, active involvement in therapeutic activities is complemented by verbalization among patients and the therapist, which becomes an increasingly important part of the therapeutic process. Music therapy activities are designed for feelings and thoughts that are then subjected to verbal processing within the therapy session. The therapeutic emphasis is on exposition of personal thoughts, feelings, and interpersonal reactions. The focus of attention is on the here-and-now of the interactional process between therapist and patients. Defenses as well as maladaptive interpersonal behavior might be challenged. Often personal agendas and goals are set to promote new and better forms of behavior.

Therapy activities, therefore, are designed to emphasize identification of feelings, creative problem solving, and facilitation of behavioral change. On this

---

1. The terminology, "Reeducative Music Therapy" and "Reconstructive Music Therapy" has been adapted from Wheeler (1983). The authors are indebted to Dr. Wheeler for identifying these terms.

level, however, no probing for unconscious conflicts takes place. Still, the patient is required to give a greater amount of self-disclosure than on the supportive level and should be interested and able to gain insight into and understanding of his behavior. The reeducative therapy experience is aimed at helping the patient to reorganize his values and behavioral patterns, to acquire new tension- and anxiety-relieving interpersonal attitudes, and, through projection of personal thoughts and feelings in the therapy process, to learn to assume responsibility for them.

Reconstructive, Analytically and Catharsis-Oriented Music Therapy

On this level, therapeutic activities are utilized to uncover, relive, and resolve subconscious conflict situations that have negatively affected an individual's personality development. Better adaptive behavior is sought, not by concentrating on conscious thoughts and feeling material or present behavior patterns, but by eliciting unconscious materials—for instance, in areas of repression—that have come into conflict with reality during a person's life. The materials are then used to reorganize the personality by building new defenses, deeper self-understanding, better impulse control, and more mature drives and instincts. Therapeutic activities are often used to elicit images or feelings that are associated with the patient's present or past. The difference between reconstructive and reeducative therapeutic efforts lies in the degree and quality of insight required of the patient and the focus on past experiences. The objective on the reconstructive level of therapy is to elicit awareness of crucial, unconscious conflicts and to encourage change by a living through, with insight, of deepest fears and conflicts. Often, reconstructive therapy is used to influence psychosomatic dysfunctions and to break neurotic behavior systems.

Therapists working on this level usually require advanced training and supervision in applicable treatment methods. Patients who can benefit from music therapy at this level have to be able and motivated to commit themselves to usually long-term therapy that challenges existent personality structures.

REFERENCES

Gaston, E. T. (1968). *Music in therapy*. New York: Macmillan.

Henderson, S. M. (1983). Effects of a music therapy program upon awareness of mood in music, group cohesion, and self-esteem among hospitalized adolescent patients. *Journal of Music Therapy, 20,* 14–20.

Kanas, N., Rogers, M., Kreth, E., Patterson, L., & Campbell, R. (1980). The effectiveness of group psychotherapy during the first three weeks of hospitalization: A controlled study. *Journal of Nervous and Mental Disease, 168,* 483–492.

Pattison, E., Briserdeh, A., & Wohl, T. (1967). Assessing specific effects of inpatient group psychotherapy. *International Journal of Group Psychotherapy, 17,* 283–297.

Priestly, M. (1975). *Music therapy in action.* London: Constable & Co.

Ridgeway, C. L. (1976). Affective interaction as a determinant of musical involvement. *Sociological Quarterly, 17,* 414–438.

Roederer, J. (1974). The psychophysics of musical perception. *Music Educators Journal, 60,* 20–30.

Tyson, F. (1966). Music therapy in private practices: Three case histories. *Journal of Music Therapy, 3,* 8–18.

Watson, J., & Lacey, J. (1974). Therapeutic groups for psychiatric inpatients. *British Journal of Medical Psychology, 47,* 307–312.

Wheeler, B. (1983). A psychotherapeutic classification of music therapy practices: A continuum of procedures. *Music Therapy Perspectives, 1,* 8–16.

Wolberg, L. R. (1977). *The technique of psychotherapy.* New York: Grune & Stratton.

Yalom, I. D. (1983). *Inpatient group psychotherapy.* New York: Basic Books.

Taxonomy of Programs and Techniques in Music Therapy for Mental Disorders

I. *MUSIC PERFORMING*
   A. Instrumental Group Improvisation (process oriented)
   B. Instrumental Performance Ensemble (product oriented)
   C. Group Singing Therapy (process oriented)
   D. Vocal Performance Ensemble (product oriented)
   E. Individual Instrumental Instruction (product oriented)
   F. Individual Vocal Instruction (product oriented)
   G. Individual Music Improvisation/Interaction (process oriented)

II. *MUSIC PSYCHOTHERAPY*
   A. Supportive Music Group and/or Individual Therapy
   B. Interactive Music Group and/or Individual Therapy
   C. Catalytic Music Group and/or Individual Therapy

III. *MUSIC AND MOVEMENT*
   A. Movement Awareness
   B. Movement Exploration
   C. Movement Interaction
   D. Expressive Movement
   E. Dance (Folk, Square, Social, Contemporary)
   F. Music and Exercise

IV. *MUSIC COMBINED WITH OTHER EXPRESSIVE ARTS*
   A. Music and Fine Arts (Drawing, Sculpting)
   B. Music and Writing (Poetry, Prose)

V. *RECREATIONAL MUSIC*
   A. Music Games
   B. Music Appreciation Awareness
   C. Recreational Music Performance Groups
   D. Leisure-Time Skill Development

VI. *MUSIC AND RELAXATION*
   A. Music with Progressive Muscle Relaxation Training
   B. Music for Surface Relaxation
   C. Music Imagery
   D. Music-Centered Relaxation

I. Music Performing

A. INSTRUMENTAL GROUP IMPROVISATION (PROCESS ORIENTED)

A technique using musical instruments to provide experiences for socialization, communication, and expression of feelings and emotions among group participants. The group functions as a laboratory of behavior and interaction patterns using an affective medium to create a structured environment for practice of feeling expression, socially appropriate behavior, sensory and reality-ordered behavior, and task mastery leading to better self-esteem. The emphasis of this technique is on the creative process of immediate music making, which is facilitated through the use of elementary musical materials. The clients learn to use their instruments as an emotional outlet, as a bridge to social participation, and to release feelings of tension and anxiety. Limited attention is given to teaching and rehearsing formal musical skills.

The therapist provides elementary musical forms in which the group members learn to alternate between playing as a group and playing individually. The main musical elements are volume, tempo, timbre, register, texture, rhythm, and melody. Themes for improvisation can be musical (e.g., different dynamic, rhythmic, or melodic ideas) and nonmusical (e.g., emotions, dramatic scenes, images, poems, pictures). Instruments most frequently used are pitched and nonpitched percussion instruments, keyboard, and guitars.

Often, in clinical settings, clients who cannot communicate appropriately in the verbal mode interact and express themselves properly on musical instruments.

B. INSTRUMENTAL PERFORMANCE ENSEMBLE (PRODUCT ORIENTED)

A technique using client's existing musical skills, as well as newly acquired skills, to form teaching and rehearsing performance groups on various musical instruments. The emphasis of this technique is on the musical product that results from the group's cooperative effort in following directions, adhering to group procedures, and learning the musical material. The clients subordinate individual needs to group musical goals; practice focused attending behaviors; exhibit group responsibility; develop interaction patterns that facilitate accomplishment of group goals; accept guidance, leadership, and social feedback; work toward task mastery; and have the satisfaction of achieving an aesthetically pleasing experience.

150

The therapist orchestrates the instrumental ensembles with a variety of instrumental combinations. Group members function in assigned musical roles as required by the musical materials. The following types of musical ensembles are associated with this technique: jazz ensemble, rock combo, Latin-American-style ensemble, hand bell choir, Orff ensemble, rhythm band, guitar ensemble, folk band, concert band, orchestra, and chamber ensemble. Music is notated. The group meets on a regular schedule to rehearse and develop music repertoire for performance.

C. GROUP SINGING THERAPY (PROCESS ORIENTED)

A technique using singing activities to provide experiences for socialization, communication, and expression of feelings and emotions among group participants. The group functions as a laboratory of behavior and interaction patterns, using an affective medium to create a structured environment for practice of feeling expression, socially appropriate behavior, sensory and reality ordered behavior, and task mastery leading to better self-esteem. The emphasis of this technique is on the process of immediate music making through the use of vocal music materials of common experience. The clients learn to use their singing voices as an emotional outlet and a bridge to social participation and to release feelings of tension and anxiety. Limited attention is given to teaching and rehearsing formal musical skills.

The therapist plans various types of structured singing activities, ranging from informal singing to creative or improvisatory vocal groups. The group process of informal singing allows for broad participation and reality orientation for clients on all levels of functioning as well as selection of songs according to appropriate mood and feeling states. Creative and improvisatory vocal groups utilize techniques such as song writing, lyric improvisation on standard musical forms (e.g., blues, scat singing, chanting, choral speaking, sprechgesang). Themes for song writing and improvisation can be musical (e.g., different voice arrangements, textures, and dynamic, rhythmic, or melodic ideas) and nonmusical (e.g., personal experiences, emotions, story lines, images). Often, in clinical settings, vocal improvisation can be facilitated by the use of props that trigger the use of the singing voice, such as kazoos or microphones.

D. VOCAL PERFORMANCE ENSEMBLE (PRODUCT ORIENTED)

A technique using existing and newly acquired vocal music skills to provide experiences in cooperation among group participants through teaching and rehearsing. The emphasis of this technique is on the music product that results from the group's cooperative effort in following directions, accepting group procedures, and learning the music material. The participants learn to accept guidance, leadership, and social feedback; they must subordinate personal needs to group music goals and develop interaction patterns that facilitate accomplishment of group goals. Attention is given to formalized teaching and rehearsing practices to achieve an aesthetically satisfying experience from the music product.

The therapist plans and directs vocal ensembles using a variety of ensemble sizes and voice combinations. The group members function in assigned music roles as required by the music material. Examples of ensembles are: secular and/or sacred choirs, small vocal ensembles (trios, quartets), madrigal singers, motet groups, barbershop choruses, jazz choirs, and folk and pop singing ensembles. The music is notated; vocal arrangements vary from melodies sung in unison to multivoice parts. Formalized vocal warm-up exercises at the beginning of regularly scheduled rehearsals are used. Instrumental accompaniment is frequently employed. Performances are planned at times appropriate for all group members, and special consideration is given to the location of the performance and to the audience membership and size.

In clinical settings the vocal instrumental performance ensemble provides the clients with the opportunity to learn and practice the responsibilities of membership in a formal group organized for a specific purpose to reach a specific goal.

E.   INDIVIDUAL INSTRUMENTAL INSTRUCTION (PRODUCT ORIENTED)

A technique focused on the acquisition of musical skills by an individual client on any one of a variety of musical instruments. The client may seek to exercise and improve an existing musical skill or to learn and develop a new musical skill. The emphasis of this technique is on the musical product resulting from the individual's effort to learn musical material. The client accepts instruction and evaluative feedback, asks questions, solves problems, and practices the musical tasks assigned by the therapist. The experiences are intended to improve communication in a one-to-one situation, increase frustration tolerance, provide ego support through musical accomplishment, and improve useable musical and interpersonal skills for possible participation in music groups and/or as an outlet for personal expression.

The therapist instructs the client in playing techniques at an appropriate learning level, and assigns practice tasks of which the client is capable. The therapist may instruct verbally, model the proper playing skills, and/or accompany the client on another instrument. Common instruments include the following: band and orchestra instruments (brass, woodwinds, strings, percussion), keyboard instruments (piano, organ), folk instruments (acoustic guitar, banjo, autoharp, dulcimer, mandolin), and pop/rock instruments (trap drum set, electric guitar, harmonica). Notated music is used frequently.

Performances are planned and accomplished when the client can benefit. Special attention must be given to location and type and size of the audience.

In clinical settings individual instrumental instruction provides an individual with the opportunity to make constructive use of guidance from the therapist on a one-to-one level and to experience self-imposed practice.

F.   INDIVIDUAL VOCAL INSTRUCTION (PRODUCT ORIENTED)

A technique using the private voice lesson to provide the client with an opportunity to develop and improve singing skills through a series of formalized appointments for instruction and planned periods of individual practice. The emphasis of this technique is on the music product that results from formal study and practice by the individual learner under the direct guidance of the therapist who serves as the teacher. The individual learns to accept the responsibility of practice as a self-imposed task and relates his efforts to the accomplishment of an aesthetically satisfying music result.

The experiences are intended to improve communication in a one-to-one situation, increase frustration tolerance, provide ego support through musical accomplishment, and improve usable musical and interpersonal skills for possible participation in music groups and/or as an outlet for personal expression.

The therapist teaches breathing and vocal exercises and provides song materials adapted to the proper development of the client's voice. Attention is given to the teaching of note reading, singing diction, phrase line, and interpretation. Instrumental accompaniment is usually provided by the therapist in the early phases of the experience. Performances are planned and accomplished when the client can best benefit. Special attention must be given to location and type and size of the audience.

In clinical settings individual vocal instruction provides the client with the opportunity to make constructive use of guidance from the therapist on a one-to-one level and to experience self-imposed practice.

G.   INDIVIDUAL MUSIC IMPROVISATION/ INTERACTION (PROCESS ORIENTED)

A technique using musical instruments in individual therapy settings to provide a structured nonverbal mode for communication and expression of thoughts and feelings as well as for reality- and sensory-ordered behavior patterns between client and therapist. The emphasis of this technique is on the creative process of immediate music interaction between therapist and client that is facilitated through the use of elementary musical materials. The client learns to use the instrument as an emotional outlet and as bridge to social interaction, and to release feelings of tension and anxiety. Limited attention is given to teaching and rehearsing formal musical skills.

The therapist provides elementary musical forms in which the client learns to alternate among expressing himself freely, leading or following in a music interaction, initiating or responding in a succession of musical statements, e.g., question-answer forms, contrasting feeling expressions, and musical storytelling. The main music elements are dynamics, timbre, register, texture, rhythm and melody (e.g., modal scales and modal polyphony). Themes for individual improvisation/interaction can be musical (e.g., different dynamic, rhythmic, or melodic ideas) and nonmusical (e.g., emotions, dramatic scenes, images, poems, pictures). Instruments most frequently used are pitched and nonpitched percussion instruments, keyboard, and guitars.

Often, in clinical settings, clients who cannot communicate appropriately in the verbal mode interact and express themselves properly on musical instruments.

II. Music Psychotherapy

A. SUPPORTIVE MUSIC GROUP AND/OR INDIVIDUAL THERAPY

A technique using music activities as a starting point and catalyst for individual and group therapy processes. The emphasis at this level is on promoting supportive verbal interaction, social participation, and the practice of healthy behavior patterns within an environment that provides a safe, reassuring reality stimulation. For the client, the music stimulus provides an immediate affective experience and serves to evoke associative thoughts and feelings. The music listening experience is designed to trigger verbalizations that are relevant to personal experience. The music also offers an objective focal point, elicits discussion, and leads to exploration of new behaviors or rediscovery of old skills.

The therapist structures the music experience, determines procedures for interpersonal interactions, and guides the processing of individual and group reactions, being certain to allow sufficient time for verbal processing. The primary activities used in supportive music group and/or individual therapy are the various forms of guided music listening leading to discussion of music elements, lyric content, mood of the music, and personal interpretation of the music selection. Either the clients or therapist may decide on music selections; or the therapist selects music to facilitate predetermined session goals. At this level the therapist's function is to identify and clarify the client's expression of thoughts and feelings, and to support appropriate interpersonal behavior.

B. INTERACTIVE MUSIC GROUP AND/OR INDIVIDUAL THERAPY

A technique using music and/or music activities as stimuli for initiating individual and group therapy processes. The emphasis at this level is to focus on conscious conflicts and associated unhealthy defense mechanisms. The process includes the development of insight from observing and discussing the client's behaviors and motivations, followed by identification and consideration of alternative healthy responses. The music stimuli are used to evoke associative thoughts and to heighten awareness of feeling states related to the conflict situation. These thoughts and feelings become the focus of the interpersonal interaction. The ensuing verbal interchange provides opportunity to clarify behavior styles and encourages self-evaluation leading to healthy behavior choices.

The therapist structures the music experience, determines procedures for interpersonal interactions, and guides the processing of individual and group reactions, being certain to allow sufficient time for verbal processing. The primary activities used in interactive music group and/or individual therapy are the various forms of guided music listening leading to discussion of lyric content, mood of the music, and associations with past experiences that have personal relevance to the client's conscious conflicts. The therapist has the prime responsibility in the selection of music, which is governed by goals predetermined by the client's needs or goals emerging through the therapeutic process. Music selections can express and reflect themes and issues that are relevant to the group's process, and thus serve as a focal point for theme-centered interaction. Music can be selected to clarify an individual's interpersonal attitudes. Music can be selected to encourage and reflect states of individual and group development. The function of the therapist on this level is to facilitate the patient's efforts to encounter, express, and resolve conflicts, to adopt new, healthy responses, and to practice the chosen behavior changes.

C.   CATALYTIC MUSIC GROUP AND/OR INDIVIDUAL THERAPY[1]

A technique using music activities as the starting point and catalyst for individual and group therapy processes. The emphasis at this level is on eliciting awareness of subconscious conflicts and encouraging change by reliving and resolving situations of deepest fear and conflict. The music is used to stimulate images, feelings, and thoughts that are associated with the client's present and past. These musically induced experience states are used to uncover areas of personality development, such as repression, that have come into conflict with reality during the client's life. Music is able to tap deep unconscious levels of emotional processes, which in turn can be used to help challenge and reorganize existing personality structures.

The therapist structures the music experience, determines procedures for interpersonal interactions, and guides the processing of individual and group reactions being certain to allow sufficient time for verbal processing. The primary activities used in catalytic music group and/or individual therapy are the various forms of guided listening techniques that are utilized to encourage clients to become more aware of feelings, thoughts, and experiences that previously have been denied or repressed. One such technique, Guided Imagery and Music, utilizes music's potential to release unconscious material

---

1.   To use this technique, the music therapist must have thorough training and supervision to understand psychopathology, individual and group psychodynamics, and applicable verbal therapy techniques. Often the music therapist functions as a co-therapist with an experienced psychotherapist.

that can be used therapeutically. This specialized approach requires specific training in order to be used most effectively. Individual therapy is often indicated, due to the in-depth psychological material uncovered at this level. The client and therapist decide on musical selections according to predetermined treatment goals in order to trigger intrapsychic processes in the client. The selection process is determined by musical preference and experience, as well as associations and symbolic meanings that are attached to certain music. The function of the therapist on this level is to bring about awareness of unconscious feelings and material and to help build new, healthy defenses, better self-understanding, and more mature drives and instincts.

For further reference on Guided Imagery and Music, see the works cited under References.

REFERENCES

Bonny, H. (1978). *Facilitating GIM sessions.* Savage, MD: Institute for Music and Imagery.

Bonny, H. (1980). *The role of taped music programs in the GIM process.* Savage, MD: Institute for Music and Imagery.

Bonny, H. (1980). *GIM therapy: Past, present, and future implications.* Savage, MD: Institute for Music and Imagery.

Osborne, J. (1981). The mapping of thoughts, emotions, sensations, and images as responses to music. *Journal of Mental Imagery, 5,* 133–136.

Summer, L. (1985). Imagery and music. *Journal of Mental Imagery, 2,* 275–290.

III. Music and Movement

Movement Accompaniment Techniques

The following seven types of accompaniment are used with musical movement techniques. They appear in capital letters along with the designated number specified for each technique.

1. BACKGROUND ACCOMPANIMENT. Live or recorded music serves as background stimulus to encourage and facilitate movement activities. Music is chosen to express the desired mood and general tempo of the movement activity (e.g., upbeat, energizing, fast vs. solemn, slow, contemplating), and to provide psychological and physiological stimulation to bring about a movement response in the clients. The movement response does not have to be rhythmically synchronized to the music.

2. TIMING CUE. Usually live music serves as an acoustic signal or timing cue to provide temporal structure in movement activities. For example: (a) a staccato chord on the piano introduces a fast motion that turns into a slow motion when a legato chord is sounded; (b) during a certain chord progression clients will gradually move from one still position into another still position; (c) a cymbal sound indicates change in solo movement sections. Music may lead or follow the movement.

3. CATALYTIC STIMULUS. Live or recorded music serves initially for listening experiences that in turn provide a theme for movement interaction and expression. For example: (a) clients listen to a recording of "Pictures at an Exhibition" (by Moussorgsky) and try to imagine movement activities that express the musical program, with the eventual goal of performing movement along with the music; (b) patients listen to the song "I Am a Rock" (by Simon and Garfunkel) and assume a "human rock" position to express and experience the message of the lyrics. This experience can be followed by a song that focuses on building relationships with others. Clients may be encouraged to change from a withdrawn still position to moving into a group or partner situation. The music experience precedes the movement experience.

4. REPRESENTATIONAL ACCOMPANIMENT. Usually live music serves to reflect the character, style, flow, tempo, and other external characteristics of the movement. For example: (a) music tempo relates to the tempo of the movement; (b) chord texture relates to "light" vs. "heavy" movements, e.g., through change in muscle tone; (c) high or low register relates to space levels of movement; (d) melodic lines vs. block chords relate to change in style of locomotion; (e) sharp vs. sustained attack on the music instrument relates to sharp vs. sustained motions. Music may lead or follow the movement.

5. CONTENT ACCOMPANIMENT. Live or recorded music serves to enhance the internal aspects of the movement action. The music will

only focus on external movement characteristics as part of the internal content of the movement. Music may lead or follow the movement.

6. DESIGNATIVE ACCOMPANIMENT. Usually live music will be used as direct and predetermined translation of movement elements into music elements to guide or accompany movement activities. Each movement component is synchronized to the music events and vice versa. For example: (a) interval leaps relate to jumping and hopping; (b) trills and melodic turns relate to turning, spinning, and rotating; (c) single chords vs. melodic motion relate to still position vs. locomotion; (d) ascending/descending melodic lines relate to upward/ downward motion. Music may lead or follow the movement.

7. DANCE ACCOMPANIMENT. Live or recorded music serves to accompany a formalized set of movements, constituting a dance or dance form in tempo, rhythm, and expression. Movements are synchronized to the music in rhythm and tempo. Music leads the movement.

A. MOVEMENT AWARENESS

A technique using music and movement activities to encourage clients to interact and express themselves on an introductory level through body movement in a group setting. The emphasis on this level is to provide a comfortable movement experience in which the group participants can focus on the task at hand and eliminate self-conscious behaviors that inhibit movement and the expression of feelings. The clients may move alone or with partners. The goal of these beginning music and movement activities is to provide a safe and comfortable environment in which to move with music in a less self-conscious manner, with the ultimate aim of developing the ability to explore other types of movement activities. This encourages creativity within music and movement to achieve a better understanding of feelings, thoughts, and emotions through expressive movement individually or in groups.

The therapist structures music and movement exercises in which the clients move to music or provide music accompaniment on instruments. The therapist may guide the client's movement by demonstrating a movement that the client may model, which makes the activity less inhibiting. Music selections are used at this level as a (1) BACKGROUND ACCOMPANIMENT to the movement. The rhythm and texture as well as other music elements serve to draw the participants into feeling less self-conscious, and free them to move their bodies with the music. The therapist chooses the movement activity and music selection in an effort to elicit movement responses. Themes for movement should be short, concrete, age-appropriate, and enjoyable, and encourage interaction and self-expression. The function of the therapist on this level is to bring about an elementary awareness of the client's ability to move in a less restricted fashion. Such awareness may in turn help the client to develop the ability to express feelings and emotions through movement.

Often in clinical settings, clients who have difficulty communicating verbally find that they can learn to express their feelings through bodily movement.

B. MOVEMENT EXPLORATION

A technique using music stimuli and the elements of movement to explore and improve the client's body image and feelings of competence in moving effectively and comfortably. The emphasis on this level is to develop a repertoire of body movements that can be used expressively and functionally, and to learn of the client's own movement potential in a state of reality contact and conscious control. Clients may move alone or with partners in activities and exercises where the focus is on their own bodies.

The therapist designs music and movement experiences in which the patients participate by moving to music or providing music accompaniment on instruments. The therapist guides and demonstrates movements to facilitate learning through encouragement and modeling. Movement exercises focus on the exploration of the five basic elements of movement, i.e., locomotion, elevation, rotation, gesture, and position, within the three movement dimensions of time, space, and dynamics. Tasks for exercises on this level include experimentation with concepts such as fast vs. slow motion, sharp vs. smooth motion; moving through space on different levels, directions, and pathways; and moving with different degrees of force/muscle tone.

Movement exercises are designed to aid clients in developing good posture, and in moving from position to gesture to locomotion in order to develop awareness and control of body movements. Clients are encouraged to experiment with various movements within a structured music environment. In movement exploration, music can function as a (2) TIMING CUE, (4) REPRESENTATIONAL ACCOMPANIMENT, and/or (6) DESIGNATIVE ACCOMPANIMENT for the movement activity.

The function of the therapist on this level is to assist and support the clients in developing awareness, control, competence, and confidence in their body movements in order to improve their body image, self-esteem, and abilities to use their bodies expressively and functionally.

Basic characteristics of movement (e.g., slow, deliberate, flowing) are emphasized within the clients' abilities. The combination of music and movement, utilizing the auditory and kinesthetic experience, enhances the emotional, social, physical, and aesthetic experience for the clients.

C. MOVEMENT INTERACTION

A technique using music and movement activities to provide the opportunity to experience social and emotional concepts in an affective, essentially non-

verbal modality. The emphasis on this level is movement in conjunction with other clients, with the music providing cohesive elements and giving meaning and feedback to the situation. The focus is on self, on self in relation to others, and on the task as expressed or accompanied by the music and/or lyrics.

The therapist initiates music and movement experiences in which clients participate by either moving to music or providing music accompaniment on instruments. The therapist selects themes for activities structured so as to provide a secure base for interactive movement leading to meaningful expression and nonverbal interaction. Materials and themes that lend themselves to group interaction are drawn from stories, poems, sketches, dramatic expressions, visual designs, musical sounds, and social concepts. The music serves as a starting point, leading the movement experience, or it serves as an accompaniment, following the movement. In movement interaction, music can function as a (1) BACKGROUND ACCOMPANIMENT, (2) TIMING CUE, (3) CATALYTIC STIMULUS, and/or (4) REPRESENTATIONAL ACCOMPANIMENT for the movement activity.

The function of the therapist on this level is to assess whether the client's movements are reflective of the client's development of social awareness, as indicated by improved levels of cooperation and communication, and self-esteem by evidence of improved self-confidence and appropriate self-assertion. The therapist also serves to identify behavioral cues related to feeling states such as happiness, sadness, fearfulness, boredom, and apathy.

Basic movement characteristics (e.g., slow, deliberate, flowing) are emphasized within the clients' abilities, with attention to movement planning and levels of coordination. The combination of music and movement, utilizing the auditory and kinesthetic experience, enhances the emotional, social, physical, and aesthetic experience for the clients.

D. EXPRESSIVE MOVEMENT

A technique using music and movement activities to assist clients in becoming aware of feelings and emotions that are relevant to their personal functioning and coping abilities in daily life. Expressive movement activities function as a testing ground to experience and express emotions in an affective, essentially nonverbal modality. Subconscious conflicts, or images and feelings that are related to significant personal experiences, might be elicited in the client. The clients learn to use music and movement techniques as a vehicle for emotional self-expression and to relieve feelings of tension and anxiety.

The therapist designs music and movement exercises in which the clients participate by either moving to music or providing music accompaniment on instruments. Music themes are selected to encourage the experience and expression of feeling concepts such as love, loss and grief, depression, social isolation and withdrawal, interpersonal conflict, hope, and joy. Significant interaction experiences such as help, rejection, and acceptance are also used on this level. Pertinent music and lyrics that express emotional themes can serve as a catalyst for the emotional experience, which is then expressed through movement; the experience may be expanded by original music accompaniment. In addition to being a (1) BACKGROUND ACCOMPANIMENT, (2) TIMING CUE, and/or (3) CATALYTIC STIMULUS, the music also serves to amplify and support the emotional content of the movement experience when the therapist is using the techniques of (4) REPRESENTATIONAL ACCOMPANIMENT and (5) CONTENT ACCOMPANIMENT.

Due to the process nature of expressive movement activities, improvised music is often used on this level. Basic movement characteristics, such as slow, deliberate, and flowing, are emphasized within the clients' abilities with regard to their potential for expressing feelings. The combination of music and movement, utilizing the auditory and kinesthetic experience, enhances the emotional, social, physical, and aesthetic experience for the clients.

E. DANCE

A technique using established and prestructured dance forms, steps, and styles with music to encourage social interaction, self-confidence, and recreational skills. Concomitant benefits include improved reality orientation, motor coordination, perceptual processing, memory, attention, and physical exercise. The emphasis is on learning and performing structured dance movements that occur in patterned sequences in rhythm with the music. The focus is on the cognitive and perceptual/motor tasks performed in coordination and cooperation with others.

The therapist plans and organizes the dance activity, taking into account the requirements of particular dance forms, such as predetermined gender roles, necessary numbers of participants, technical difficulty in the execution of dance steps, and appropriate music selections. These decisions are made according to the capabilities and needs of the group participants while considering their interests and cultural backgrounds. Typical dances in this category include: folk dance (ethnic and national origins), square dance, social/ballroom dance (waltz, fox trot, polka, and tango), and social/contemporary dance (rock, disco, etc.). The (7) DANCE ACCOMPANIMENT provides the rhythmic structure for the dance steps, dictates and/or complements the dance form, and sometimes directly relates to associated cultural rituals.

The therapist may, in conjunction with the group participants, use traditional dance forms or stylized dance steps in a creative manner to construct original structured dances. This approach may serve either as a creative, cooperative task for the client group, or as a necessary adaption of materials to better meet the clients' abilities and needs.

F. MUSIC AND EXERCISE

A technique using music to provide the temporal framework for adaptive physical exercise. The emphasis is on the use of music at selected tempi to encourage physical exercise for individual or group participants to attain, maintain, or regain predetermined physical objectives. Attention is given to adapting music to support or accompany exercises for strength, endurance, muscle tone, flexibility, agility, body control, vital capacity, and cardiovascular efficiency. Music with strong rhythms can activate the motor system, help regulate motor coordination, and increase physical endurance.

The therapist selects participants in consultation with the client's physician and other team members (physical therapy staff) and identifies contraindications or precautions. The choice of exercises is based on predetermined objectives and the client's abilities. Exercises are presented in a progressive manner (regarding the number of repetitions, level of rigor, and endurance required). The function of the therapist on this level is to choose music that is rhythmically compatible with the designated movements in the specific exercise. Variable-speed music reproduction equipment or live performance allow for flexibility in accompaniment. The therapist will demonstrate and lead the exercise program, focusing on the beat of the music that fits the exercise movement. The therapist will document physical gains by objectively assessing various physiological responses such as measurements of strength (i.e., number of repetitions), flexibility, vital capacity, and pulse rate.

It should be noted that appropriate exercise to music can be matched to any age group or to any level of movement ability, and vary from limited movement in a prone position to very vigorous exercise. Carefully selected music serves to regulate and encourage exact exercise participation.

IV. Music Combined with Other Expressive Arts

A. MUSIC AND FINE ARTS (DRAWING, SCULPTING)

A technique focused on combining music and fine arts (drawing, drama, and sculpting) to provide for expression of feelings and emotions among group participants or on a one-to-one basis. The emphasis of this technique is on increasing the individual's awareness of self through a nonthreatening multifaceted medium. The individual will be required to integrate both visual and aural stimuli while reflecting emotional content. An individual should demonstrate the ability to reflect changes in feelings and emotions in conjunction with changes in musical stimuli.

The therapist serves as a facilitator to implement the multisensory experiences. Background music is played to set a mood or to heighten the group or individual experience while the secondary medium is used. The music can also provide thematic material for the art experience. The therapist has a choice of providing the group or individual with either a structured (e.g., sculpt a picture of someone important to you in your childhood) or unstructured (e.g., draw feelings) task-oriented activity.

In clinical settings, a multisensory approach will provide an additional modality for the individual who is nonspeaking or withdrawn to express feelings without words.

B. MUSIC AND WRITING (POETRY, PROSE)

A technique focused on combining music and writing (i.e., poetry, prose) to provide experiences for expressions of feelings and cognitive responses among group participants on a one-to-one basis. The emphasis of this technique is on increasing the individual's awareness of self through a nonthreatening multifaceted medium. The individual will be required to integrate auditory/visual perception and discriminatory thinking while reflecting emotional content. The individual may be asked either to listen and interpret existing written material (i.e., stories, plays, poetry) or to write imaginatively and creatively to encourage self-disclosure and expression of feelings.

The therapist serves as a facilitator to implement the multisensory experiences. Music is provided by the therapist as an accompaniment to existing material (i.e., stories, plays, poetry) to inspire creative expression of feelings, and to encourage discussion.

In clinical settings this multisensory approach will provide a language modality for the individual who is nonspeaking and/or withdrawn to organize thinking and encourage language expression.

164

V. Recreational Music

A. MUSIC GAMES

A technique using music games to provide experiences in which human behavior can be acted out in play form, which provides participants with an opportunity for emotional and social learning in a safe and predictable environment. The emphasis of this technique is on the cooperative process necessary for successful group participation and on the development of adaptive social skills. The participants will be encouraged to demonstrate attending behaviors, exhibit group responsibility, develop interaction patterns that facilitate the accomplishment of group goals, and work toward mastery of a task. This technique will provide a vehicle for spontaneity and the freedom of play skills.

The therapist serves as a facilitator for the development and playing of the music games and ensures that the activity is designed to foster successful participation of all group members. Games may fall into four categories of play (Piaget, 1962):

1. exercise play—sensory-motor repetitive action;
2. symbolic play—a self-expressive language;
3. games with rules—social interaction;
4. games of construction—adaptations or solutions to problems and intelligent creations.

Music games such as music bingo, name that tune, lummi sticks, concentration, and music charades provide opportunities to experience competition and enjoyment while encouraging less verbal group members to participate more fully. Games with rules can produce significant changes in peer relationships; winning or losing experiences can provide objective reality testing as well as healthy development of self-confidence leading to better self-concept.

In clinical settings, music games can provide a beginning step to resocialization, promote leisure-time skills, and serve as a prerequisite for more in-depth music group participation.

B. MUSIC APPRECIATION AWARENESS

A technique using a variety of music stimuli to provide the experience of listening, and at times creating and performing music in a group or on a one-to-one basis. The emphasis of this technique is analogous to the empha-

165

sis of music education, where opportunities are provided for an aesthetic experience that is common to all people. The participants will be exposed to many and differing music experiences in an attempt to broaden their music understanding and awareness. The individuals will be encouraged to develop group cooperation and tolerance for varying music styles, and to take risks in sharing music preferences.

The therapist provides an environment for sharing and discussing a variety of music selections (e.g., listening to records of various periods and styles, and arranging for live music performances) in a supportive, nonthreatening atmosphere.

In clinical settings, music appreciation helps provide confidence in asserting individual opinions while it encourages concentration, on-task behavior, and independent thinking.

C.   RECREATIONAL MUSIC PERFORMANCE GROUPS

A technique providing diversional and success-oriented music experiences using instrumental and/or vocal media. The group setting serves as an initial nonthreatening, enjoyable opportunity for the client to gain orientation to easily acquired music skills. The emphasis is on experimentation and enjoyment rather than a perfected product. The clients are expected to participate in a beginning music group process in order to reinforce self-confidence, risk taking, and discussion of potential leisure-time activities.

The therapist provides a variety of socio-recreational music experiences that will ensure that each client's contribution will be fundamental to the group's performance. The following types of music media are associated with this technique: omnichord, ukelele, recorder, autoharp, guitar, electronic keyboard, pitched and non-pitched percussion, and voice.

The music may or may not be notated, depending upon the existing music skills of the participants.

D.   LEISURE-TIME SKILL DEVELOPMENT

A technique to emphasize music's role in a client's discharge planning and community follow-up. The client is given the opportunity to experience and then focus on appropriate enjoyable musical activities available in the community. Leisure-time planning can be accomplished by either individual or group counseling. The emphasis of this technique is on heightening the client's awareness of the need for appropriate leisure-time skills and then on providing suitable musical options. The client is responsible for making decisions and following through with selected activities, with the therapist's assistance.

The therapist sets the occasion for relevant discussion of post-discharge leisure-time needs and guides the client in creating and developing a leisure-time plan. The therapist also assists by sharing information about available community resources (e.g., church choirs, square dance groups, community bands) and by facilitating the client's involvement in such activities when necessary.

REFERENCE

Piaget, J. (1962). *Play, dreams, and imitation in childhood* (C. Gattengo & F. M. Hodgson, Trans.). New York: W. W. Norton. (Original work published 1945). See chap. IV, "The beginnings of play."

VI. Music and Relaxation

A. MUSIC WITH PROGRESSIVE MUSCLE RELAXATION TRAINING

A technique using music in conjunction with progressive muscle relaxation training. A client will learn to select and use appropriate recorded music that has been found to be effective in eliciting a state of relaxation for that individual. The emphasis of this technique is twofold: to pair relaxation training with appropriate selected music, and to condition the client to use music as the overall focus for relaxation.

Appropriately selected music serves as a stimulus to block negative associations and elicit positive mood and feeling responses that facilitate relaxation. The client will learn to discriminate between relaxation and tension responses and to substitute acquired relaxation responses for anxiety/stress responses.

The therapist will assist the client in learning the technique of relaxation training, and in selecting music that heightens the relaxation response. The therapist may also develop relaxation tapes as well as written materials to be memorized for relaxation training for use pre- and post-discharge.

Relaxation training can occur in individual or group settings.

B. MUSIC FOR SURFACE RELAXATION

A technique using music as a medium for temporary respite from anxiety/ stress conditions. The individual will learn to use music's potential to facilitate relaxation based on individual preferences regarding style, tempo, volume, and timbre, and to locate appropriate resources (e.g., records, tapes, radio). The emphasis of this technique is to provide concrete resources for a client in a short-term setting. Unlike other relaxation techniques, surface relaxation requires no long-term training by the client.

The therapist will provide a variety of musical stimuli for the client to experience as possible resources for relaxation. Additionally, the therapist helps the client understand how the elements of music influence mood, behavior, and physical responses.

Relaxation training can occur in individual or group settings.

C. MUSIC IMAGERY[1]

A technique that involves listening to music in a relaxed state to facilitate increased self-awareness, which in turn may facilitate psychological and physical relaxation. The emphasis of this technique is to encourage the client to

---

1. This technique is not intended to reach deep intrapsychic material, as would Guided Imagery and Music. GIM is a specialized technique that requires specific training and more appropriately fits into Category II, MUSIC PSYCHOTHERAPY, C. Catalytic Music Group and/or Individual Therapy.

reach and explore altered states of consciousness for the purpose of allowing imagery, symbols, and latent feelings to surface from the inner self. Carefully selected music programs allow the client to recall memories initiate fantasies, and stimulate creative thinking. As part of the music imagery training, the client will learn how to use music to aid in concentration and relaxation.

The therapist exposes group members to different styles of music and initiates open-ended scenarios that promote imagination and fantasy production. In addition, the therapist facilitates a discussion of material among the clients at the conclusion of the imagery.

D. MUSIC-CENTERED RELAXATION

A technique using music as a perceptual focus and stimulus for relaxation training. The music stimulus diverts the client's attention from states of psychological and physical tension that cannot be dissolved by techniques based on conscious mental and physical efforts, which focus on the particular tension. This relaxation technique utilizes the potential of music as a pleasant stimulus to block out sensations of anxiety, fear, and tension, and to divert attention from unpleasant thoughts. Through this positive perceptual experience a reassuring experience of self will occur. The therapist teaches the client initially to focus away from self, and then gradually return attention to self in the perceptual process.

The therapist will provide music selections according to the clients' preferences, and will instruct them to follow the music without anticipatory attitude or deliberate intellectual or emotional efforts that would influence the listening experience. Clients are encouraged to follow different elements or events in the music as they attract their immediate attention, without abandoning the attitude of passive concentration. On a second level, once the clients feel comfortable and safe in their listening experience, they are encouraged to let their attention gradually expand to wandering freely back and forth among the music, their bodies, and their thoughts and feelings. Through focusing on the music the clients will gain a safe and pleasant perceptual experience that may break pathological attachment and anticipation of, for example, psychosomatic or anxiety experiences.

Any body position the client finds comfortable, whether sitting or lying down, is acceptable in the beginning. Body positions will usually develop into more relaxed positions during the training process.

PART FOUR

CLINICAL INTERVENTIONS IN ADULT PSYCHIATRIC DISORDERS

The last section of this book is presented in tabular form for quick, ready reference. The music therapist will find listed patient symptoms and needs, and appropriate music therapy interventions, programs, and techniques for specific diagnostic categories.

The tables were developed by the primary authors, whose clinical experiences are lengthy and broad based in various psychiatric treatment agencies. The diagnostic categories were selected from the *Diagnostic and Statistical Manual of Mental Disorders,* Third Edition, and later modified with the changes in terminology in the Third Edition, Revised. The illnesses described are those found most frequently in patients in the kinds of units where music therapists are employed. Included are: (1) schizophrenic disorders, (2) mood disorders, and (3) generalized anxiety disorders. The bipolar mood disorder is separated into two parts: (a) depressive episode, (b) manic episode. Personality disorders are not included in this volume, nor is there a section for the major depression as separate from the bipolar disorder, depressed episode.

USE OF THE TABLES

The tables are set under seven headings. The materials under the first heading, "Diagnostic Symptoms," and the second, "Clinical Features," are adapted from DSM III-R. Under the third heading, "Characteristic Behaviors," there is a brief description of behavior associated with the particular clinical feature. The entries under the remaining headings identify the patients' "Needs," "Music Therapy Interventions" recommended, music therapy "Programs," and music therapy "Techniques." Roman numerals under "Programs" and capital letters under "Techniques" refer to the appropriate section of Part Three, "Taxonomy of Clinical Music Therapy Programs and Techniques."

It should be made clear that these tables are intended as a guide to be used by professionally trained music therapists who can make appropriate treatment judgments. For example, when several techniques for relief of a symptom are recommended, the therapist chooses the one most appropriate for a particular patient. The settings may determine individual versus group choices. Only primary techniques are suggested; others are potentially useful for certain patients. All programs and techniques can be used on a variety of levels. Improvisation technique, for example, can be precisely structured or highly creative and free; progressive muscle relaxation can be guided and structured, or it can be practiced under complete control of the individual client.

Effective treatment is a consequence of good timing in the selection and use of interventions to stimulate in the patient the development of improved behaviors and improved health.

Tables start on page 174.

I. Schizophrenic Disorders

DIAGNOSTIC SYMPTOMS	CLINICAL FEATURES	CHARACTERISTIC BEHAVIORS	NEEDS
Disturbed affect	Blunting and flattening	Voice is usually monotonous, face is immobile	Stimulation of feeling responses
			Means for affective self-expression
	Inappropriate affect	Discordant with content of the individual's speech or ideation	Appropriate identification and expression of feelings and emotions

MUSIC THERAPY INTERVENTIONS	PROGRAMS	TECHNIQUES
Guided music listening techniques to evoke feeling responses	Music Psychotherapy (II)	Supportive Music Group and/ or Individual Therapy (A) *Interactive Music Group and/ or Individual Therapy (B)
Structured music and movement techniques to evoke feeling responses	Music and Movement (III)	Movement Awareness (A) Dance (E)
Expressive music and movement techniques using feeling concepts as performance themes	Music Performing (I)	Instrumental Group Improvisation (A) Group Singing Therapy (C) Individual Music Improvisation/Interaction (G)
	Music and Movement (III)	Movement Interaction (C)
Guided music listening techniques to evoke feeling responses	Music Psychotherapy (II)	Supportive Music Group and/ or Individual Therapy (A) *Interactive Music Group and/ or Individual Therapy (B)
Expressive music and movement techniques using feeling concepts as performance themes	Music Performing (I)	Instrumental Group Improvisation (A) Group Singing Therapy (C) Individual Music Improvisation/Interaction (G)
	Music and Movement (III)	Movement Interaction (C)

(*continued*)

* Post acute phase.

DIAGNOSTIC SYMPTOMS	CLINICAL FEATURES	CHARACTERISTIC BEHAVIORS	NEEDS
	Dysphoric mood	Anger, depression, and/or anxiety	Mood lifting stimulation and outlet for negative feeling processes

MUSIC THERAPY INTERVENTIONS	PROGRAMS	TECHNIQUES
Supportive verbal interaction to identify feelings and emotions	Music Psychotherapy (II)	Supportive Music Group and/or Individual Therapy (A) Interactive Music Group and/or Individual Therapy (B)
Guided music listening techniques to alter feeling states	Music Psychotherapy (II)	Supportive Music Group and/or Individual Therapy (A) Interactive Music Group and/or Individual Therapy (B)
	Music and Relaxation (VI)	Music with Progressive Muscle Relaxation Training (A) Music for Surface Relaxation (B)
Expressive music and movement techniques using feeling concepts as performance themes	Music Performing (I)	Instrumental Group Improvisation Group Singing Therapy (C) Individual Music Improvisation/Interaction (G)
	Music and Movement (III)	Movement Awareness (A) Movement Interaction (C)
Supportive verbal interaction to express and process feelings and emotions	Music Psychotherapy (II)	Supportive Music Group and/or Individual Therapy (A) Interactive Music Group and/or Individual Therapy (B)

DIAGNOSTIC SYMPTOMS	CLINICAL FEATURES	CHARACTERISTIC BEHAVIORS	NEEDS
Disturbed content and form of thought	Delusional thinking	Expression of simple persecutory delusions (i.e., being spied on, others planning harm)	Opportunities for reality testing on verbal and non-verbal levels
	Delusions of reference	Events, objects, and people are given unusual significance (i.e., TV commentator is mocking the patient)	
	Loosening of associations	Talk shifts from one subject to another	Reality focus and task structure for verbal interaction
	Poverty in speech content	Speech may be vague, repetitious, stereotyped, overly concrete or overly abstract	
	Impaired cognitive functioning	Impaired auditory discrimination and memory function	Supportive techniques to retrain auditory and perceptual skills and memory function

MUSIC THERAPY INTERVENTIONS	PROGRAMS	TECHNIQUES
Pleasant, nonthreatening reality orientation through musical tasks on verbal and nonverbal levels	Music Performing (I)	Instrumental Group Improvisation (A) Group Singing Therapy (C) Individual Music Improvisation/Interaction (G)
	Music Psychotherapy (II)	Supportive Music Group and/ or Individual Therapy (A) Interactive Music Group and/ or Individual Therapy (B)
	Recreational Music (V)	Music Games (A) Music Appreciation Awareness (B) Recreational Music Performance Groups (C)
Use of music activities to provide theme-centered verbal interaction	Music Psychotherapy (II)	Supportive Music Group and/ or Individual Therapy (A) Interactive Music and/or Individual Therapy (B)
	Music Performing (I)	Group Singing Therapy (C)
Use of music as mnemonic device to aid in memory and sequencing tasks, and as sensory stimulation to retrain auditory-perceptual skills	Music Performing (I)	Instrumental Performance Ensemble (B) Vocal Performance Ensemble (D) Individual Instrumental Instruction (E) Individual Vocal Instruction (F)
	Recreational Music (V)	Music Games (A)
	Music and Movement (III)	Movement Exploration (B)

DIAGNOSTIC SYMPTOMS	CLINICAL FEATURES	CHARACTERISTIC BEHAVIORS	NEEDS
Disturbance in volition	Ambivalence with regard to action	Frequent fluctuation from one activity to another, constant uncertainty and indecision in problem solving	Safe and structured opportunities to practice problem solving and decision making
	Lack of goal-directed initiative	Inability to engage in routine goal-directed activities (i.e., socialization, work, self-care), immobilization except for ritualistic, automatic, or compulsive actions	Stimulation of adequate interest and drive to pursue appropriate activities
	Lack of perseverance	Disinterest in or cessation of an activity before its completion	Support and encouragement to follow a course of action to its logical conclusion

MUSIC THERAPY INTERVENTIONS	PROGRAMS	TECHNIQUES
Use of sensory and social feedback in process of performance activities to practice problem solving and decision making	Music Performing (I)	Instrumental Group Improvisation (A)
		Group Singing Therapy (C)
		Individual Music Improvisation/Interaction (G)
	Music and Movement (III)	Movement Exploration (B)
		Movement Interaction (C)
		Expressive Movement
Use of music as a pleasant and attractive medium to stimulate motivation and promote involvement in goal-directed activities	Music Performing (I)	Instrumental Performance Ensemble (B)
		Vocal Performance Ensemble (D)
		Individual Instrumental Instruction (E)
		Individual Vocal Instruction (F)
	Music and Movement (III)	Movement Awareness (A)
		Dance (E)
		Music and Exercise (F)
	Music Combined with Other Expressive Arts (IV)	Music and Fine Arts (A)
		Music and Writing (B)
	Recreational Music (V)	Music Appreciation Awareness (B)
		Recreational Music Performance Groups (C)
		Leisure Time Skill Development (D)
Performance techniques that ensure immediate and long-term musical success as reinforcement and supportive feedback in pursuit of activities	Music Performing (I)	Instrumental Performance Ensemble (B)
		Vocal Performance Ensemble (D)
		Individual Instrumental Instruction (E)
		Individual Vocal Instruction (F)
	Music and Movement (III)	Movement Awareness (A)
	Recreational Music (V)	Recreational Music Performance Groups (C)

DIAGNOSTIC SYMPTOMS	CLINICAL FEATURES	CHARACTERISTIC BEHAVIORS	NEEDS
Disturbed sense of self	Distorted self image	Disturbed perception of individuality and uniqueness	Opportunities to develop appropriate self-worth
	Lack of ego boundaries and self-direction	Extreme perplexity and confusion about one's own identity and meaning of existence, delusions involving control by an outside force	Structure and nonthreatening interaction with environment
			Sense of autonomy through pleasant and safe role experiences in goal-oriented activities

MUSIC THERAPY INTERVENTIONS	PROGRAMS	TECHNIQUES
Use of sensory and social feedback from performance techniques that ensure immediate and long-term musical success	Music Performing (I)	Instrumental Group Improvisation (A)
		Group Singing Therapy (C)
		Individual Music Improvisation/Interaction (G)
	Music and Movement (III)	Movement Interaction (C)
		Expressive Movement (D)
Use of rhythm, form, dynamics, melody, and harmony in music performance, and structure of interaction of self with environment	Music Performing (I)	Instrumental Group Improvisation (A)
		Instrumental Performance Ensemble (B)
		Group Singing Therapy (C)
		Vocal Performance Ensemble (D)
		Individual Instrumental Instruction (E)
		Individual Vocal Instruction (F)
		Individual Music Improvisation/Interaction (G)
	Music and Movement (III)	Movement Awareness (A)
		Body Exploration (B)
Goal-oriented performance of composed and improvised music and movement materials	Music Performing (I)	Instrumental Performance Ensemble (B)
		Vocal Performance Ensemble (D)
	Music and Movement (III)	Movement Interaction (C)
		Dance (E)
	Recreational Music (V)	Recreational Music Performance Groups (C)

DIAGNOSTIC SYMPTOMS	CLINICAL FEATURES	CHARACTERISTIC BEHAVIORS	NEEDS
Disturbed relationship to external world	Social isolation	Withdrawal from involvement with external world	Activities that stimulate social participation
	Response to internal stimulation	Preoccupation with expressed ideas and fantasies, emotional detachment	Pleasant and motivating reality stimulation

MUSIC THERAPY INTERVENTIONS	PROGRAMS	TECHNIQUES
Participation in music activities stimulating theme-centered group interaction	Music Performing (I)	Instrumental Group Improvisation (A)
		Instrumental Performance Ensemble (B)
		Group Singing Therapy (C)
		Vocal Performance Ensemble (D)
	Music Psychotherapy (II)	Supportive Music Group and/or Individual Therapy (A)
	Music and Movement (III)	Movement Awareness (A)
		Movement Interaction (C)
	Recreational Music (V)	Music Games (A)
		Music Appreciation Awareness (B)
		Recreational Music Performance Groups (C)
		Leisure Time Skill Development (D)
Use of music as multisensory external stimulus to support reality perception	Music Performing (I)	Instrumental Group Improvisation (A)
		Instrumental Performance Ensemble (B)
		Group Singing Therapy (C)
		Vocal Performance Ensemble (D)
	Music Psychotherapy (II)	Supportive Music Group and/or Individual Therapy (A)
	Music and Movement (III)	Movement Awareness (A)
		Movement Interaction (C)
	Recreational Music (V)	Music Games (A)
		Music Appreciation Awareness (B)
		Recreational Music Performance Groups (C)
		Leisure Time Skill Development (D)

DIAGNOSTIC SYMPTOMS	CLINICAL FEATURES	CHARACTERISTIC BEHAVIORS	NEEDS
Disturbed psychomotor behavior	Reduced spontaneous movements and activity	Motor retardation, immobility	Stimulation of movement responses
	Stiffness, rigidity	Shuffling gait	Practice of relaxed, smooth movements
	Poor body awareness	Poor discernment of body parts and their use	Safe and pleasant movement activities to develop positive body image
	Stereotyped and/or ritualistic movements	Purposeless mannerisms, grimmacing, pacing, rocking, and posturing	Distraction from movement mannerisms and practice of relaxed, smooth movement
Disturbed Perception	*Hallucinations	A response to false sensory perception without external stimulation	

* Hallucinations: Relief of this clincial feature is generally achieved through psychotropic medication. Music activities, however, may be used to refocus the patient to reality-based stimuli.

MUSIC THERAPY INTERVENTIONS	PROGRAMS	TECHNIQUES
Use of introductory music and movement techniques to elicit movement responses	Music and Movement (III)	Movement Awareness (A) Dance (E) Music and Exercise (F)
Structured movement techniques, dance, and physical exercise with supportive music accompaniment to promote body awareness and functional movement	Music and Movement (III)	Movement Awareness (A) Movement Exploration (B) Dance (E) Music and Exercise (F)
Movement control and relaxation exercises using music as feedback and support stimulus	Music and Movement (III)	Movement Awareness (A) Movement Interaction (C)
	Music and Relaxation (VI)	Music with Progressive Muscle Relaxation Training (A) Music for Surface Relaxation (B)

II. Bipolar Disorder, Depressed Episode

DIAGNOSTIC SYMPTOMS	CLINICAL FEATURES	CHARACTERISTIC BEHAVIORS	NEEDS
Disturbed affect and mood	Anhedonia	Lack of interest and pleasure in usual activities and pas-times	Participation in success-oriented activities
	Depressed appearance	Sad face, tearful, brooding, slumped posture	Appropriate identification and expression of feelings and emotions
Disturbed sense of self	Feelings of worthless-ness or guilt	Exaggerated self-criticism and sense of responsibility for some untoward or tragic event	Mood-lifting stimulation

MUSIC THERAPY INTERVENTIONS	PROGRAMS*	TECHNIQUES*
Performance techniques that promote immediate and long-term musical success	Music Performing (I)	Instrumental Group Improvisation (A) Group Singing Therapy (C) Individual Music Improvisation/Interaction (G)
Supportive verbal interaction to identify feelings and emotions	Music Psychotherapy (II)	Supportive Music Group and/or Individual Therapy (A) Interactive Music Group and/or Individual Therapy (B)
Expressive music and movement techniques using feeling concepts as performance themes	Music Performing (I)	Instrumental Group Improvisation (A) Group Singing Therapy (C) Individual Music Improvisation/Interaction (G)
	Music and Movement (III)	Movement Awareness (A) Movement Exploration (B)
Guided music listening techniques to alter feeling states	Music Psychotherapy (II)	Supportive Music Group and/or Individual Therapy (A) Interactive Music Group and/or Individual Therapy (B)

(continued)

* During the acute phase of the depression, the patient's participation in the selected program may need to be mandatory rather than voluntary.

DIAGNOSTIC SYMPTOMS	CLINICAL FEATURES	CHARACTERISTIC BEHAVIORS	NEEDS
			Positive feedback through success experiences

MUSIC THERAPY INTERVENTIONS	PROGRAMS	TECHNIQUES
Performance techniques that encourage immediate and long-term musical success	Music Performing (I)	Instrumental Group Improvisation (A)
		Group Singing (C)
		Individual Music Improvisation/Interaction (G)
Use of sensory and social feedback in musical and movement interaction to promote appropriate self-evaluation	Music Performing (I)	Instrumental Group Improvisation (A)
		Group Singing Therapy (C)
		Individual Music Improvisation/Interaction (G)
	Music and Movement (III)	Movement Awareness (A)
		Movement Exploration (B)
		Movement Interaction (C)
		Dance (E)
	Recreational Music (V)	Recreational Music Performance Groups (C)

(*continued*)

DIAGNOSTIC SYMPTOMS	CLINICAL FEATURES	CHARACTERISTIC BEHAVIORS	NEEDS
	Interpersonal withdrawal	Withdrawal from friends and family	Activities that stimulate social participation
	Preoccupation with death	Thoughts of death or suicide, suicide attempts	Outlet for expression of negative feelings

MUSIC THERAPY INTERVENTIONS	PROGRAMS	TECHNIQUES
Participation in music activities stimulating theme-centered group interaction	Music Performing (I)	Instrumental Group Improvisation (A)
		Group Singing Therapy (C)
		Individual Music Improvisation/Interaction (G)
	Music Psychotherapy (II)	Supportive Music Group and/or Individual Therapy (A)
		Interactive Music Group and/or Individual Therapy (B)
	Music and Movement (III)	Movement Awareness (A)
		Dance (E)
	Recreational Music (V)	Music Games (A)
		Music Appreciation Awareness (B)
		Recreational Music Performance Groups (C)
Expressive music and movement techniques to encourage appropriate feeling concepts as performance themes	Music Performing (I)	Instrumental Group Improvisation (A)
		Group Singing Therapy (C)
		Individual Music Improvisation/Interaction (G)
	Music and Movement (III)	Movement Interaction (C)
Supportive verbal interaction to express and process feelings and emotions	Music Psychotherapy (II)	Supportive Music Group and/or Individual Therapy (A)
		Interactive Music Group and/or Individual Therapy (B)

(*continued*)

DIAGNOSTIC SYMPTOMS	CLINICAL FEATURES	CHARACTERISTIC BEHAVIORS	NEEDS
	Hypochon-driacal pre-occupation	Excessive concern over physical health	Activities that promote responsibility for self and diversion from hypochondriacal concerns
Psychomotor agitation or retardation	Sleep disturbance	Insomnia or hypersomnia	Activities that provide physical exercise and relaxation
	Decreased energy	Sustained fatigue, slow moving	Activities that provide motivating sensory stimuli

MUSIC THERAPY INTERVENTIONS	PROGRAMS	TECHNIQUES
Expressive performance techniques to build self-confidence, motivation, and positive focus for attention	Music Performing (I)	Instrumental Group Improvisation (A)
		Instrumental Performance Ensemble (B)
		Group Singing Therapy (C)
		Vocal Performance Ensemble (D)
		Individual Instrumental Instruction (E)
		Individual Vocal Instruction (F)
		Individual Music Improvisation/Interaction (G)
	Music and Movement (III)	Movement Awareness (A)
		Movement Exploration (B)
		Movement Interaction (C)
		Dance (E)
Use of music as auditory stimulus to facilitate physical exercise	Music and Movement (III)	Music and Exercise (F)
Relaxation techniques combined with music listening techniques	Music and Relaxation (VI)	Music with Progressive Muscle Relaxation Training (A)
		Music for Surface Relaxation (B)
Use of music as multisensory external stimulus to provide pleasant and motivating reality experiences	Music Performing (I)	Instrumental Group Improvisation (A)
		Group Singing Therapy (C)
		Individual Music Improvisation/Interaction (G)
	Music and Movement (III)	Movement Awareness (A)
		Dance (E)
	Music Combined with Other Expressive Arts (IV)	Music and Fine Arts (A)
		Music and Writing (B)

(*continued*)

DIAGNOSTIC SYMPTOMS	CLINICAL FEATURES	CHARACTERISTIC BEHAVIORS	NEEDS
	Difficulty concentrating or thinking	Distractible, poor memory, indecisive, uncertain	Involvement in attention-focusing activities in a structured and calming environment

MUSIC THERAPY INTERVENTIONS	PROGRAMS	TECHNIQUES
Goal-oriented performance of composed and improvised music and movement to focus attention	Music Performing (I)	Instrumental Performance Ensemble (B) Vocal Performance Ensemble (D) Individual Instrumental Instruction (E) Individual Vocal Instruction (F)
	Music and Movement (III)	Movement Exploration (B) Movement Interaction (C) Dance (E)
Guided music listening techniques to focus attention and provide theme-centered structure for verbal interaction	Music Psychotherapy (II)	Supportive Music Group and/or Individual Therapy (A)
Relaxation techniques combined with music listening techniques	Music and Relaxation (VI)	Music with Progressive Muscle Relaxation Training (A) Music for Surface Relaxation (B)

III. Bipolar Disorder, Manic Episode

DIAGNOSTIC SYMPTOMS	CLINICAL FEATURES	CHARACTERISTIC BEHAVIORS	NEEDS
Disturbed affect and mood	Elevated mood, euphoria	Excessively cheerful, unceasingly and un-selectively enthusias-tic	Outlet for feeling expression in a calming environment
			Appropriate identification and expression of feelings and emotions
			Involvement in task-oriented activities to encourage reality awareness
	Lability of mood	Rapid shifts to anger or depression	Stabilization of mood, and control over rapid mood swings

198

MUSIC THERAPY INTERVENTIONS	PROGRAMS	TECHNIQUES
Expressive music and movement techniques using appropriate feeling concepts as performance themes	Music Performing (I)	Instrumental Group Improvisation (A) Group Singing Therapy (C) Individual Music Improvisation/Interaction (G)
	Music and Movement (III)	Movement Exploration (B)
Supportive verbal interaction to identify feelings and emotions	Music Psychotherapy (II)	Supportive Music Group and/or Individual Therapy (A) Interactive Music Group and/or Individual Therapy (B)
Use of music activities to provide reality stimulation, structure, and limits for feeling processes	Music Performing (I)	Instrumental Performance Ensemble (B) Vocal Performance Ensemble (D) Individual Instrumental Instruction (E) Individual Vocal Instruction (F)
	Music Psychotherapy (II)	Supportive Music Group and/or Individual Therapy (A) Interactive Music Group and/or Individual Therapy (B)
	Recreational Music (V)	Music Games (A) Music Appreciation Awareness (B) Recreational Music Performance Groups (C)
Supportive verbal interaction to identify and express feelings and emotions appropriately	Music Psychotherapy (II)	Supportive Music Group and/or Individual Therapy (A) Interactive Music Group and/or Individual Therapy (B)

(continued)

DIAGNOSTIC SYMPTOMS	CLINICAL FEATURES	CHARACTERISTIC BEHAVIORS	NEEDS
	Irritability	Low frustration tolerance	Supportive and structured environment to increase frustration tolerance, and to promote coping skills and psychological relaxation

MUSIC THERAPY INTERVENTIONS	PROGRAMS	TECHNIQUES
Guided music listening, movement, and performance techniques to provide mood-lifting stimulation	Music Performing (I)	Instrumental Group Improvisation (A) Group Singing Therapy (C) Individual Music Improvisation/Interaction (G)
	Music Psychotherapy (II)	Supportive Music Group and/ or Individual Therapy (A) Interactive Music Group and/ or Individual Therapy (B)
	Music and Movement (III)	Movement Awareness (A) Dance (E)
	Recreational Music (V)	Music Appreciation Awareness (B) Recreational Music Performance Groups (C)
Supportive verbal interaction to identify and express feelings and emotions appropriately	Music Psychotherapy (II)	Supportive Music Group and/ or Individual Therapy (A) Interactive Music Group and/ or Individual Therapy (B)
Relaxation techniques combined with music listening techniques	Music and Relaxation (VI)	Music with Progressive Muscle Relaxation Training (A) Music for Surface Relaxation (B)

DIAGNOSTIC SYMPTOMS	CLINICAL FEATURES	CHARACTERISTIC BEHAVIORS	NEEDS
Psychomotor agitation	Hyperactivity and physical restlessness	More energy than usual, decreased need for sleep, pressured speech	Structured outlet for appropriate physical expression
			Relaxation and calming of physical restlessness
	Distractibility, flight of ideas	Nearly continuous flow of accelerated speech with abrupt changes of topic	Involvement in attention-focusing activities in structured and calming environment

MUSIC THERAPY INTERVENTIONS	PROGRAMS	TECHNIQUES
Guided music and/or movement techniques to provide constructive outlet for physical energy	Music Performing (I)	Instrumental Group Improvisation (A) Group Singing Therapy (C) Individual Music Improvisation/Interaction (G)
	Music and Movement (III)	Movement Awareness (A) Movement Exploration (B) Music and Exercise (F)
Relaxation techniques combined with music listening techniques	Music and Relaxation (VI)	Music with Progressive Muscle Relaxation Training (A) Music for Surface Relaxation (B)
Goal-oriented performance of composed and improvised music and/or movement to focus attention	Music Performing (I)	Instrumental Performance Ensemble (B) Vocal Performance Ensemble (D) Individual Instrumental Instruction (E) Individual Vocal Instruction (F)
	Music and Movement (III)	Movement Exploration (B) Movement Interaction (C) Dance (E)
Guided music listening activities to focus attention and provide theme-centered structure for verbal interaction	Music Psychotherapy (II)	Supportive Music Group and/or Individual Therapy (A)
Relaxation techniques combined with music listening techniques	Music and Relaxation (VI)	Music with Progressive Muscle Relaxation Training (A) Music for Surface Relaxation (B)

DIAGNOSTIC SYMPTOMS	CLINICAL FEATURES	CHARACTERISTIC BEHAVIORS	NEEDS
Disturbed sense of self and social awareness	Inflated self-esteem, grandiosity	Uncritical self-confidence	Supportive environment to encourage accurate self-assessment

MUSIC THERAPY INTERVENTIONS	PROGRAMS	TECHNIQUES
Use of sensory and social feedback in music and/or movement interaction to promote appropriate interpersonal behavior and self-esteem	Music Performing (I)	Instrumental Group Improvisation (A) Instrumental Performance Ensemble (B) Group Singing Therapy (C) Vocal Performance Ensemble (D)
	Music and Movement (III)	Movement Awareness (A) Movement Exploration (B) Movement Interaction (C)
	Recreational Music (V)	Recreational Music Performance Groups (C)
Supportive verbal interaction to provide reality orientation and nonthreatening structure for self-evaluation	Music Psychotherapy (II)	Supportive Music Group and/or Individual Therapy (A) Interactive Music Group and/or Individual Therapy (B)

(*continued*)

DIAGNOSTIC SYMPTOMS	CLINICAL FEATURES	CHARACTERISTIC BEHAVIORS	NEEDS
	Lack of judgment	Excessive involvement in pleasure activities with lack of concern for consequences (i.e., buying sprees, sexual indiscretions)	Practice of impulse control, appropriate decision making, and social behavior in safe and structured environment

MUSIC THERAPY INTERVENTIONS	PROGRAMS	TECHNIQUES
Use of sensory and social feedback in music and/or movement interaction to promote appropriate interpersonal skills and social judgment	Music Performing (I)	Instrumental Group Improvisation (A) Instrumental Performance Ensemble (B) Group Singing Therapy (C) Vocal Performance Ensemble (D)
	Music and Movement (III)	Movement Awareness (A) Movement Exploration (B) Dance (E)
Performance activities that require observation of rules, awareness of others, and cooperation, and provide role experience of leading and following in group settings	Music Performing (I)	Instrumental Group Improvisation (A) Instrumental Performance Ensemble (B) Group Singing Therapy (C) Vocal Performance Ensemble (D)
	Music and Movement (III)	Movement Awareness (A) Movement Exploration (B) Movement Interaction (C) Dance (E)
	Recreational Music (V)	Music Games (A) Recreational Music Performance Groups (C)

DIAGNOSTIC SYMPTOMS	CLINICAL FEATURES	CHARACTERISTIC BEHAVIORS	NEEDS
Disturbed content and form of thought	Delusional thinking	Expression of simple persecutory delusions (i.e., being spied on, others planning harm)	Opportunities for reality testing on verbal and nonverbal levels
	Delusions of reference	Events, objects, people are given unusual significance (i.e., TV commentator is mocking the patient)	
	Loosening of associations	Talk shifts from one subject to another	Reality focus and task structure for verbal and nonverbal interaction
	Poverty in speech content	Speech may be vague, repetitive, stereotyped, overly concrete, or overly abstract	
	Impaired cognitive functioning	Impaired auditory discrimination and memory function	Supportive techniques to retrain auditory and perceptual skills and memory function

MUSIC THERAPY INTERVENTIONS	PROGRAMS	TECHNIQUES
Nonthreatening reality orientation through musical tasks on verbal and nonverbal levels	Music performing (I)	Instrumental Group Improvisation (A)
		Group Singing Therapy (C)
		Individual Music Improvisation/Interaction (G)
	Music Psychotherapy (II)	Supportive Music Group and/or Individual Therapy (A)
		Interactive Music Group and/or Individual Therapy (B)
	Recreational Music (V)	Music Games (A)
		Music Appreciation Awareness (B)
		Recreational Music Performance Groups (C)
Use of music activities to provide theme-centered verbal and nonverbal interaction and an alternative mode of communication	Music Psychotherapy (II)	Supportive Music Group and/or Individual Therapy (A)
		Interactive Music Group and/or Individual Therapy (B)
	Recreational Music (V)	Music Games (A)
		Music Appreciation Awareness (B)
		Recreational Music Performance Groups (C)
Use of music as a mnemonic device to aid in memory and sequencing tasks, and as sensory stimulation to retrain auditory-perceptual skills.	Music Performing (I)	Instrumental Performance Ensemble (B)
		Vocal Performance Ensemble (D)
		Individual Instrumental Instruction (E)
	Recreational Music (V)	Music Games (A)
	Music and Movement (III)	Movement Exploration (B)
		Movement Interaction (C)

IV. Generalized Anxiety Disorder

DIAGNOSTIC SYMPTOMS	CLINICAL FEATURES	CHARACTERISTIC BEHAVIORS	NEEDS
States of chronic anxiety, or acute anxiety attacks	Motor tension	Trembling, twitching shakiness, muscle tension, aches or soreness, restlessness, easy fatiguability	Physical outlet for motor energy and relief of state of muscular tension
	Autonomic hyperactivity	Sweating, pounding or racing heart, upset stomach	Control over physiological stress symptoms and relaxation of physical and physiological tension
	Apprehensive expectation	Anxious, worried, anticipates a crisis	Reassuring experiences in trusting oneself, and diversion of attention from internal apprehension and fear

MUSIC THERAPY INTERVENTIONS	PROGRAMS	TECHNIQUES
Expressive music and movement techniques to provide constructive outlet for physical energy	Music Performing (I)	Instrumental Group Improvisation (A) Group Singing Therapy (C) Individual Music Improvisation/Interaction (G)
	Music and Movement (III)	Dance (E) Music and Exercise (F)
Relaxation techniques combined with music listening activities	Music and Relaxation (VI)	Music with Progressive Muscle Relaxation Training (A) Music for Surface Relaxation (B) Music Imagery (C) Music Centered Relaxation (D)
Relaxation techniques combined with music listening activities	Music and Relaxation (VI)	Music with Progressive Muscle Relaxation Training (A) Music for Surface Relaxation (B) Music Imagery (C) Music Centered Relaxation (D)
Expressive music and/or movement techniques to build self-confidence and motivation, and provide positive focus for attention	Music Performing (I)	Instrumental Performance Ensemble (B) Vocal Performance Ensemble (D) Individual Instrumental Instruction (E) Individual Vocal Instruction (F)
	Music and Movement (III)	Movement Awareness (A) Movement Interaction (C)
	Recreational Music (V)	Music Games (A) Recreational Music Performance Groups (C)

(*continued*)

DIAGNOSTIC SYMPTOMS	CLINICAL FEATURES	CHARACTERISTIC BEHAVIORS	NEEDS
	Vigilance/ scanning	Hyperattentiveness resulting in distracti- bility and irritability	Involvement in pleasant, rewarding, attention- focusing, and relaxing ac- tivities

MUSIC THERAPY INTERVENTIONS	PROGRAMS	TECHNIQUES
Performance techniques that promote immediate and long-term success	Music Performing (I)	Instrumental Group Improvisation (A)
		Instrumental Performance Ensemble (B)
		Group Singing Therapy (C)
		Vocal Performance Ensemble (D)
		Individual Instrumental Instruction (E)
		Individual Vocal Instruction (F)
		Individual Music Improvisation/Interaction (G)
	Music and Movement (III)	Movement Awareness (A)
		Movement Exploration (B)
		Movement Interaction (C)
	Recreational Music (V)	Music Games (A)
		Music Appreciation Awareness (B)
		Recreational Music Performance Groups (C)
		Leisure Time Skill Development (D)
Goal-oriented performance of composed and improvised music and movement material to focus attention	Music Performing (I)	Instrumental Performance Ensemble (B)
		Vocal Performance Ensemble (D)
		Individual Instrumental Instruction (E)
		Individual Vocal Instruction (F)
	Music and Movement (III)	Movement Interaction (C)
		Dance (E)
	Recreational Music (V)	Recreational Music Performance Groups (C)
Relaxation techniques combined with music listening activities	Music and Relaxation (VI)	Music with Progressive Muscle Relaxation Training (A)
		Music for Surface Relaxation (B)
		Music Imagery (C)
		Music Centered Relaxation (D) *(continued)*

DIAGNOSTIC SYMPTOMS	CLINICAL FEATURES	CHARACTERISTIC BEHAVIORS	NEEDS
	Mildly to moderately depressed moood	Sad, tearful, lack of energy	Mood lifting stimulation

MUSIC THERAPY INTERVENTIONS	PROGRAMS	TECHNIQUES
Guided music listening techniques to alter feeling states	Music Psychotherapy (II)	Supportive Music Group and/or Individual Therapy (A)
		Interactive Music Group and/or Individual Therapy (B)
		Catalytic Music Group and/or Individual Therapy (C)
Structured music and movement techniques to evoke feeling responses	Music and Movement (III)	Movement Awareness (A)
		Movement Exploration (B)
		Dance (E)

NAME INDEX

SUBJECT INDEX

A

Accompaniment, 158–159; background, 158, 159, 161, 162; catalytic stimulus, 158, 161, 162, content, 158–159, 162; dance, 159, 162; designative, 159, 160; representational, 158, 160, 161, 162; timing cue, 158, 160, 161, 162
Activity therapy, music therapy as, 91
Adult psychiatric patients, 92
Advertising, music and, 57
Aesthetic distance, 79–80
Aesthetic objects, special properties, 79–80
Affect and arousal in music, 3–11
Affect modification and behavioral change and music, 19–22
Affect, music and, 75–76
Anxiety/relaxation states, effect of music on, 9
Applications in clinical settings, practical, 42–45; auditory rhythm, 44; auditory stimulus, 44; chanting, 42; concurrent rhythmic chant, 44; high-low pitches, use of, 45; rehearsal strategies, 44; speech synchronization, 44; stationary gross muscle response, 44
Appreciation awareness, music, 165–166, 179, 181, 185, 193, 199, 201, 209, 213
Arousal, affect and reward, 9–10
Arousal influencing properties of music, 10
Assessment, 126–141; Day Treatment Client Assessment Scale, 135; Expressive Arts Group Assessment, 136; interviewing, 128; methods, 127; Music/Activity Therapy Intake Assessment, 135, 136; musical abilities, interests, preferences, 135–136; observing, 128; psychological abilities, 134–135; rationale, 129–130; reviewing existing information, 129; structured, 128; testing, 128–129; treatment philosophy, 137–141; unstructured, 128

Autism, 13
Automatization of movement patterns, 39–40
Autonomic Nervous System (ANS), 5, 33–35, 112, 113, 120
Auditory feedback, 40, 42

B

BASIC ID, 137
Behavior modification, music in, 9
Behavioral philosophy, 137
Behavioral rating form, 127
Behaviorally based research, 20–21
Biologically adaptive value of emotional reactions, 5
Bipolar disorder, 110; depressive episode, 171, 188–197; manic episode, 198–209
Brain: autism, 13; Broca's aphasia, 13; diffuse brain damage, 45; forebrain dopamin pathways, 12; hypothalamus, 12; imaging techniques, 16; left brain, 13–15, 56; left brain damage, 13; lesions to left hemisphere, 13; limbic brain structures, 16–19; limbic forebrain, 12; limbic system and brain reward, 15–19; music stimuli and hemispheric processing, 13–15; reward system, 17–19; right brain, 13–15, 56; right brain damage, 13; processing, sequential mode, 13; processing, simultaneous mode, 13
Broca's aphasia, 13

C

Catalytic music group therapy, 156–157, 215
Central Nervous System (CNS), 3, 6, 10, 11, 19, 23, 33–35, 112, 113, 120; processing, music stimuli and, 11–19
Cerebellum, 39
Cerebral palsy, 37, 45
Chang form, 41
Chinese culture, music in, 63
Clinical interventions, 171–215